PURPLE HEARTS
and
GOLDEN MEMORIES
35 Years With The Minnesota Vikings

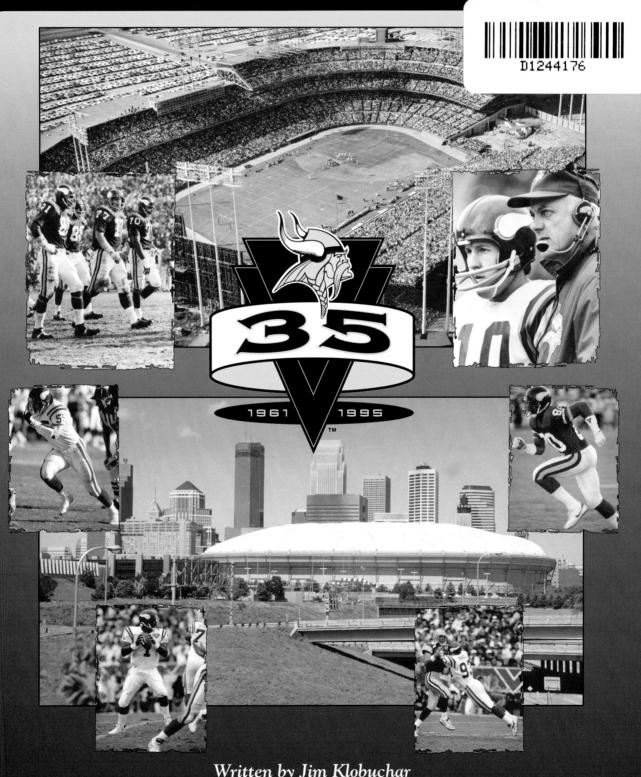

35
1961 1995

Written by Jim Klobuchar
Foreword by Bud Grant

*In memory of Jimmy Eason,
and all of the decent guys
who have passed through his
equipment room*

Cover designed by
Mick McCay

All photographs compliments of:
Minnesota Vikings Archives
NFL Photos
Rick Kolodziej
Scott Irwig
Star Tribune

For information write:

Quality Sports Publications
#24 Buysse Drive
Coal Valley, IL 61240
(309) 234-5016
(800) 464-1116

Duane Brown, Project Director
Melinda Brown, Designer
Susan Smith, Editor

Printed in the U.S.A. by
Richardson Printing, Inc.
Kansas City, Missouri

ISBN 1-885758-15-4

Table of Contents

Acknowledgments

The publisher and author wish to thank the Minnesota Vikings for making available historical files that were valuable in the research for this book. Special thanks to Sammy Casalenda for lending his personal collection of Vikings memorabilia for use in this book. They also wish to thank the Vikings and particularly Bob Hagan, Assistant Director of Public Relations and Kernal Buhler, Director of Marketing, for giving access to the organization's large photo file, the source of many of the pictures used in this book. The author wishes to note that the format and concept of the book are essentially that of an illustrated journal of the team's history and its personalities. It makes some judgments and looks into some of the controversies. It is not within this book's scope to make a full investigation of some of those controversies, much as that would delight the author and perhaps the reader. That is another book. This is intended to be a broad scan of 35 years in the life of a football team, one that has had more than the normal pro football allotment of triumph and bafflement, comedy and genuine drama. While the Vikings have fully cooperated in the book's publication, they have exerted no editorial control over its content.

The author expresses appreciation for the well wishes of Steve Anderson of the Ross and Haines Company, publishers of the author's earlier biography of the Vikings "True Hearts and Purple Heads," which in expanded form contained a few of the anecdotes related here.

Finally, the author wishes to thank some of his former sparring mates of Vikings teams past, whose memories (and occasional apologies) for those times contributed to this book. That number includes, but isn't confined to, Paul Flatley, Darrin Nelson, Greg Coleman, Bud Grant, Alan Page, Mike Lynn, Paul Dickson, Chuck Foreman, Mick Tingelhoff, Ron Yary, Wally Hilgenberg, Francis Tarkenton, Rip Hawkins, Fred Cox, Jim Marshall, Bobby Reed and more. Dennis Green and Roger Headrick made time available. The conversational hours with some of those old warhorses were rewarding, as much reunion as they were interview.

Maybe there ought to be a Hall of Fame for people who almost won the Super Bowl.

Jim Klobuchar
August 1995

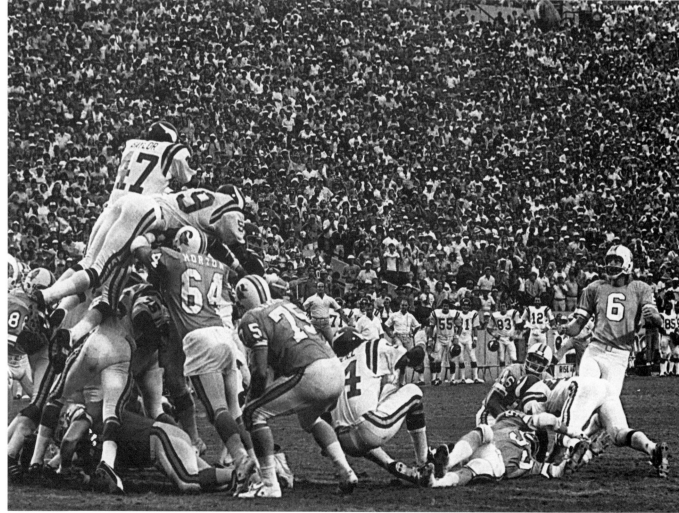

Foreword

By Bud Grant
NFL Hall of Fame 1994
Head Coach 1967-83 and 1985

Football has been a part of my life since I was a kid growing up in Superior, Wisconsin. Every year the New York Giants would come to town for their training camp. I got hooked on NFL football at age 12. Bronko Nagurski, Red Grange, Johnny "Blood" McNally and Don Hudson were some of the NFL players I followed.

I have watched the evolution of NFL football for 55 years, and the Vikings since their beginning 35 years ago. Today I have gone full circle and am following the NFL and the Vikings as a fan again rather than as a player or coach.

I have many wonderful memories of the people in football, not only of the players, coaches, and managers, but also the fans. Playing and coaching in cities around the country, I discovered that Vikings fans are more knowledgeable and supportive than most. Our fans came from throughout the Upper Midwest, and they expected a competitive team. But they also showed compassion and support in times of disappointment. That made my experience with the Vikings one that I would never exchange.

As a coach I remember feeling the team being lifted by the energy coming from the fans, and how the fans would respond to the triumphs and heart-breaks played out on the field. That excitement, drama and emotions is why football will always be a great sport. And with each year the athleticism and execution becomes even better, as players continue to be stronger, bigger, faster and more talented.

This book is a collection of memories about the Vikings organization's first 35 years. Jim Klobuchar was there covering the team on a daily basis as a reporter in the beginning, and then as an observer and a columnist in its later years. There are great moments to remember, and many more ahead for the Vikings.

I'm grateful that I had the opportunity to be a part of the Viking's history as a coach, and you can look forward to reliving some of the Vikings' history incorporated in this book.

Bud Grant

Introduction

At about midnight before the Vikings-Lions game in Detroit in the early 1960s, the head coach of the Vikings, Norm Van Brocklin, stuck his head through the beaded curtains of the hotel lounge and angrily motioned to a newspaper writer at the nearby table. He wanted the writer to come out into the lobby to talk. Since I was the writer, and I'm normally congenial around midnight, I joined him in the lobby.

Van Brocklin was furious. This was a relatively normal condition for the Dutchman. He was also slightly paranoid, another mood that often overtook him during the football season. The Dutchman wanted to know what I was doing talking to the Viking general manager, Bert Rose. I said we were talking about the declining quality of the steaks at the chophouse down the block, which was the truth. The Dutchman was angry because he wanted all Viking information to come from the Dutchman, despite the general manager's rather conspicuous role as the chief administrative officer. I made this point briefly. The Dutchman went nuts. He wanted to know if we should duke it out right there in the lobby or if we should go to his room and fight like rational people. The Dutchman was 6 feet 2 inches tall and weighed 220 pounds. This gave him a big spot in reach and weight to go with a deeper red neck. I told him to forget it. He said I was a typical gutless reporter. I said, all right, let's go to your room and duke it out. We went to his room. I asked him if he wanted to turn on the TV to drown out the screams and fracturing teeth. He started to swing a right. I came inside at close quarters and clinched. We fell on the bed and rolled into the TV, which smashed onto the floor. The fight was over. The Dutchman said he was going to dummy up anytime I asked a question after a ballgame. The Dutchman called at 3 a.m., two hours later. He said we should talk it over. He said he would order breakfast from room service, a platter of scrambled eggs and six-pack of beer. The Dutchman was not seized with a sudden impulse to join the Quakers. He was worried that I was going to file a story about the incident. I said, "Dutchman, we're two hours past my deadline. You're safe." He said what about tomorrow. I said there would be something crazier to write tomorrow. There was. The Vikings almost beat the Lions, the best defense in football.

That was a snippet of Viking football in the early years, but it was more. It was something definitive. It reflected the loopy, off-the-wall, play-for-today, jungle-law romance of that time in pro football, when it was almost literally a private world despite the growing embrace of television. A reporter, trying his best to objectively write the game and its characters, could nonetheless fight and swear with them. And still, in ways that did not disrupt the reporter's contract with the reader, he could consider some of them friends. Not close friends. But people with whom a kind of trust was available, even if at arm's length.

The game, of course, is a super visible industry today. The money is enormous. The best players are millionaires. It does not mean they play less intensely. It simply means they are rich, and they are mobile, and they may be playing for the Bears next year and the Giants the year after that. It is still an immensely fascinating game despite the yammering and jeering most of the commentators dump on it today. It deserves a lot of that. Pro football is probably overorganized, and its pace and performers may not achieve the intimacy with public and press that a game like baseball or even a game like pro basketball might. But it is successful because the public likes it, the tempo, the collisions, the crazy hype, the Monday night and the ad nauseam replays. The Vikings' role in all of this is simply to have been one of the more successful organizations of them all, despite that missing Super Bowl ring. And I know its public has found the procession of players, coaches and events as absorbing as the writer has; a Bud Grant, Fran Tarkenton, Alan Page, Carl Eller, Jim Marshall, Hugh McElhenny, Jerry Burns, Mick Tingelhoff, Bill Brown, Chuck Foreman, Cris Carter, hundreds of them. They have given entertainment and sometimes trauma, because that's what they're paid to do. But they have also created a kind of fraternity among the fans, a collage of memories and faces and moments of electricity. It makes those 35 years worth remembering, and remembering warmly.

Jim Klobuchar

A Road to Canton

He was by legend the man with a granite face and eyes that cut like a diamond drill. But he was blubbering for millions to see.

His lips trembled and moisture rolled down his cheek. He was giving a testament about his life and football, sharing it with the world, and he was almost out of control, all of his old shields of reserve and privacy peeled away.

In the years Bud Grant played and coached football, nobody had any reason to foresee that a moment like this would be believable.

Yet it was. For the longtime Grant-watchers in Minnesota, it revealed a more intimate side of the glacial personality with which they'd lived for years. It also seemed to recapitulate the times and struggles of a football team that had taken them to the gates of glory and to the pits of grief, sometimes on the same play. That is the destiny of all football fans, but the day Bud Grant was inducted into the Hall of Fame in the summer of 1994 was the time when he was finally embraced by his constituency. It was not so much because he was now a Hall of Fame football coach but for those simple and enduring reasons that make humans come a little closer to other humans when they are remembering a shared experience.

The shared experience was professional football in Minnesota, of which Grant was the centerpiece for nearly two decades. It evoked faces and memories, images that had generated apoplexy, pride, anguish, sighs over the might-have-beens, pandemonium and gut-splitting laughs. They also produced an occasional burst of love as well as the depression of a suburban businessman who disappeared for four days because he didn't trust himself to be in civilized society after the Vikings lost their fourth Super Bowl.

The bitterness and depression were forgiven, of course, on the day Bud Grant accepted the tribute of his peers and his audience.

The warm and good parts clung. Grant spoke loyally of his players and coaches. They should be standing where he was, he said, sharing the honor. He talked about the ambitions of his childhood, when pro football teams trained in his hometown of Superior, Wisconsin. He told his father he would play on a team like those one day, and he did.

He couldn't have foreseen the faces that came later. The names he recited on July 30, 1994 in Canton, Ohio, were the rubric of his years as

Photo Credit: Paul Spinelli/NFL Photos

CANTON. OHIO

PRO FOOTBALL HALL OF FAME
CANTON, OHIO
FESTIVAL

the Minnesota Viking coach. And to those, the Viking watchers in his TV audience must have added their own, the players who came before and after the Grant seasons, so that Bud Grant's emotional sifting of the years turned the hour into a joyous and sentimental mural of Minnesota Viking football.

You could have stretched those images from the frozen grass of Metropolitan Stadium, now extinct, to the landlocked balloon of the Metrodome. Some of the scenes are sure and truly dramatic. A lot of them are nutty. You get choices: Francis Tarkenton's

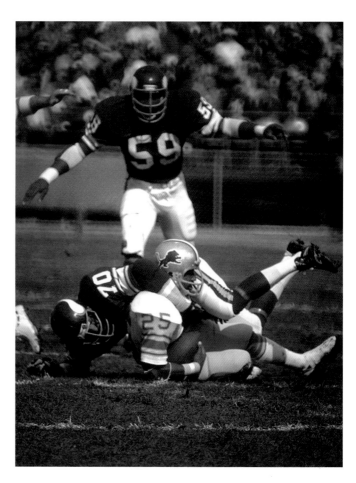

Bud Grant's judgment of two of his greatest players was terse. But it conveyed one football man's respect for another. No one, he said, gave more on each play and in each game than Jim Marshall (making a tackle against the Lions, above). And no quarterback he coached matched the command, mind and ingenuity, he said, of Fran Tarkenton.

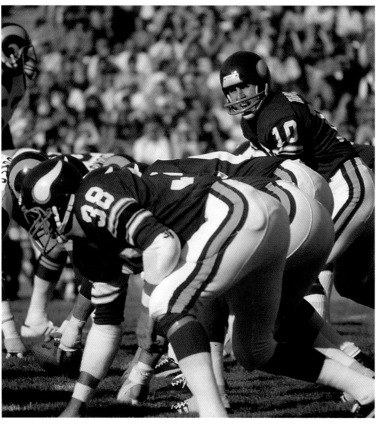

coast-to-coast scrambles to escape decapitation; another quarterback, Joe Kapp, declining to duck linebackers but instead assaulting them like a tavern bouncer; Jim Marshall playing football exuberantly for a whole generation; Chuck Foreman's open-field gyrations; Alan Page fuming at bonehead officials who didn't think there was a defensive tackle alive who could bolt into the backfield as fast as Page did without being offsides (Page knew better); "Boom Boom" Brown barging recklessly into targets ranging from carnivorous linemen to stationary goal posts; Hugh McElhenny's last symphonic runs as a great halfback; Paul Krause peeling off interceptions like a happy grape-plucker in a vineyard; Hub Meeds, the Viking horned warrior on the sidelines, brandishing his sword to summon Thor or another blocked kick by Matt Blair; Ahmad Rashad winning a championship with an end zone grab of a ball that ricocheted off everybody but the peanut vendor; Karl Kassulke being brought onto the field in his wheelchair, waving his arm, smiling indomitably; the frowning elf, Jerry Burns, prowling the sidelines; A.C. Carter lancing through the secondary; Joey Browner's concussive tackles; Tommy Kramer's theatrics in the last two minutes of a dozen games; the galleries imploring Carl Eller with a chant, voiced partly in fondness and partly in desperation, "Kill, Carl, kill."

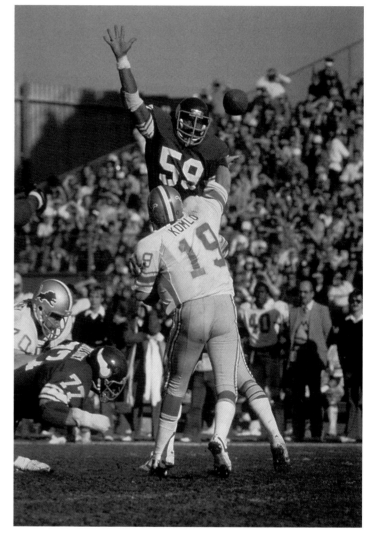

Lower right: Matt Blair (leaping to block a pass against the Lions) wowed the Minnesota fans and his peers with his acrobatic linebacking.

Lower left: Jerry Burns, on the other hand, wowed his players with his wacky superstitions, his hairy language and his double talk from the coaching booth. But they liked him, and they played for him.

It stretches the mind to realize that so much in football and so much diversity in the people who played it could be packed into just 35 years. The package is more than players, of course. Wrapped in it are the coaches, the creative ones and the buffoons, the millionaires in the board rooms (the creative ones and the buffoons), and the howling and moaning fans in the stadium and the living rooms. In the beginning, building a public – a community of people genuinely attracted to pro football in a state that once dominated the college game – was the critical hurdle. Pro football in Minnesota until 1960 belonged to the era of the Sunday rotogravures and Rudolph Valentino. The Duluth Eskimos had played in the National Football League but fell slightly short of immortality. In the 1960s the football public in Minnesota knew the pro game by the George Halases and Vince Lombardis and Paul Hornungs, but wasn't sure Minnesota was ready for it.

It's doubtful Minnesota was ready for Norman Van Brocklin, the tumultuous first coach.

But more than three decades later, the

Joey Browner terrorized opposing runners and receivers with the force of his tackles (like the one shown above) and his owly playing disposition.

On the other hand, Moose Eller (making a tackle, right) didn't spend a lot of time and energy trying to intimidate the other side. What he did best was to flatten people. He did it often.

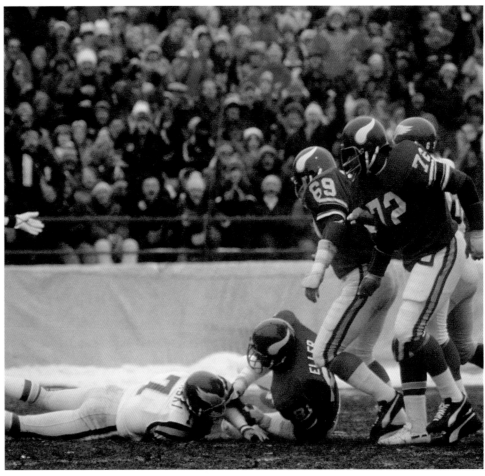

Vikings had accumulated a body of history and a gallery of heroes and knaves and the assorted in-betweens that were intriguing enough to create albums of memories. The faces in that Viking album eventually reached from the Hall of Fame in Canton to high finance, to Dogpatch cartoons and folklore. The calendar said only 35 years. But in the way pro football's culture is measured, it was an eon between Norman Van Brocklin and Denny Green. The first was tyrannical, boisterous and smart. The latter was a drum-playing offspring of the modern game in every way, chatty but hard-boiled, comfortable with the public, but also smart, private and just as obsessive about winning as the ones who came before.

Van Brocklin was obsessive about winning but didn't have the resources to do it often; Grant had them and did it often. But Grant would have won often whether he coached at Metropolitan Stadium or on Mars; Les Steckel had resources but the misfortune to follow Grant for a year, and he also had a dilemma. His players were never sure whether Les was propelling them toward the Detroit Lions or an invasion beach in the Pacific. Jerry Burns, profane and waspish but still a decent spirit, nearly made it to the Super Bowl and Denny Green has the look of a man who is almost sure to get there.

But you're not likely to see the name of Palmer Pyle in Canton, disregarding the fact that for a couple of years he was an offensive lineman of passing grade. Palmer is the kind of improbable creature the long-term Viking fans remember hungrily, probably because the era can't be duplicated. It would have made beautiful soap opera. Palmer was a man of unpredictable movements and a great ingenuity in avoiding normal behavior. He never played for Bud Grant. Both men should consider that a gift. Palmer did occasionally play for Van Brocklin, whenever they could locate him. Pyle's tendencies to roam made his life a constant source of suspense and often got him into the deep muck with his wife at the time, a beautiful woman from Chicago named Marie. The second half of her maiden name happened to be Accardo, which also happened to be the name of Anthony (Tough Tony) Accardo, who for years was linked with the hierarchy of the Chicago Mafia. Tough Tony was Marie's father. From Tony, she might have inherited both her temper and her urges for bold action. Both of these qualities turned out to be useful on a Sunday night after one of the home games

The Vikings' coach of the early 1960s was Norm VanBrocklin. The coach who came in the early 1990s was Denny Green (below). Thirty years isn't much in the solar system. But 30 years in the NFL took the Vikings from a coach who was snarling, abrasive and a gut-fighting competitor to a coach who played drums in his spare time, wired his office for rock music – and was a gut-fighting competitor. Maybe 30 years isn't that long in pro football.

when the Viking players and their wives or girlfriends were invited to a social in the Bloomington apartment suite of one of the players.

Palmer began the rites earlier than most of the others. By the time the couples began arriving for the party, he was progressing unevenly toward his date with his wife by way of his teammates' apartments. He was still several apartments removed from his home. Marie, in the meantime, had dressed gorgeously and awaited the arrival of her purple knight to take her to the party. The appointed hour of 7 o'clock rolled on without word from the knight. Another half hour went by, then another, and another. At approximately 9:30 p.m., the knight lurched into their apartment with an apology. He said he was sorry, honey, the time got away from him and he was weary from all his exertions on the football field and from consoling his teammates. He wandered into the bedroom, removed his clothes, collapsed undraped on the bed and then remembered that he was hungry. Honey, do you mind fixing a pizza, he called. Silence.

"Honey."

She said it would take 10 minutes.

What a wonderful human being, he mumbled.

In ten minutes his wife swept into the bedroom where the large undraped knight lay sprawled in deep sleep. "Here's your pizza," she said.

It was delivered swiftly and with unerring aim. It went splat in the middle of Palmer's hairy chest, steaming with hot cheese and The Works – pepperoni, sausage, green pepper and flying anchovies.

When he woke up later, Palmer said, he thought he was in a crematorium.

No Palmer Pyle surfaced on Viking rosters of the later years. That was a pity but it was a favor to the team's lawyers and to its truancy officers. Throw in its burn doctors. Pro ball eventually outgrew the Palmer Pyles. This may be a sign of progress but it is also grounds for quiet tears of regret. In the genealogy of pro football, the Vikings came on as a kind of bridge between pro ball's clanking Middle Ages and the swank and showtime of today. When the Vikings played their first game they were in the era of Bobby Layne, the snarling quarterback for Detroit and Pittsburgh who chewed out his stumbling linemen in the huddle and nearly asphyxiated them with the aromas of his nightclubbing sprees of the night before. It was the time when the Pittsburgh Steelers kept a little ceremonial cannon at the back of their end zone and fired it with a belch of smoke and loud roar whenever the Steelers scored a touchdown. On one play, the Steelers' Buddy Dial caught a pass deep in the end zone and turned toward the end line at the precise moment the cannon went off three feet in front of him. Dial nearly passed out on the spot, convinced he was gut-shot.

Pro football in those years often gave the appearance of a game played by nature's rowdy children, banging and crunching for the raw joy of it as much as for the money. The impression wasn't wide of the mark. The Viking contributions to that culture were substantial. Dale Hackbart was a defensive back who played the position like a man on a jailbreak. Lonnie Warwick was a linebacker with a massive jaw and fierce eyebrows. He played football so primitively that you got the feeling he wanted to discard his helmet because it felt so good when he drove his head into the fullback's gut. It was no coincidence that one of the memorable off-the-field fights in the Vikings' history matched Warwick against another mad bomber in shoulder pads: Joe Kapp, the quarterback. It happened at a team party where the players were supposed to deepen their camaraderie and their

Lonnie Warwick (left) was a brick-jawed linebacker from the southern hills. Joe Kapp (below) was a two-fisted Hispanic from California who never walked away from a brawl and occasionally threw forward passes that spiraled. It was inevitable that each would admire the other's gusto, and just as inevitable that they would get into a fight some day. They did at a team party. They had the good sense to go outside, where nobody could see their awful pugilism. Many punches were thrown. Few struck skin. They made up the next day, at the flinty suggestion of Bud Grant. Grant said he would be so disappointed if it happened again that it would cost them hundreds of bucks each. Peace suddenly reigned.

undying love for one another. Halfway through it the horseplay between Warwick and Kapp graduated into some serious umbrage. Under the moonlight and the falling leaves of autumn, they jabbed and jostled and snorted and head-butted. Few blows were landed although at least a dozen were sincerely aimed. The next morning Grant summoned the inept pugilists into his office. They both appeared in sunglasses, to camouflage their bloodshot eyes more than their wounds. Both apologized profusely and the incident was forgotten by Warwick and Kapp, but not necessarily by Grant. It was nice and handy leverage to prevent any further uproars. It did, convincingly.

The fan sifting 35 years of Minnesota Viking football treasures some of those funky snapshots but looks more inquisitively for some way to identify this team and separate it from the others, a distinctive signature. And the identity most fans find in the Minnesota Vikings is that dogged hunt for a Super Bowl championship, the grail of professional football teams and the particular penance of the Minnesota Vikings.

Denver and Buffalo arrived in later years to join the Vikings in the circle of NFL teams so often invited to the dance but so often dumped at the

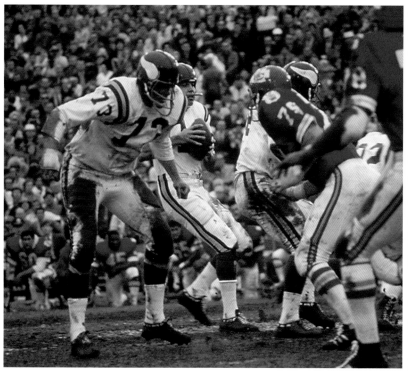

door. Until then, it looked as though some heavy-handed destiny had picked Minnesota to wear the Super Bowl's horns of futility.

Denver and Buffalo, thank God, proved that it can happen to anybody.

But from January of 1970 to January of 1977, it happened to the Minnesota Vikings four times. Four times they played in it, four times they lost. They lost with Joe Kapp at quarterback once and Tarkenton at quarterback three times. They lost when their offense was loaded and they lost when their defense was filled with Purple People Eaters.

Theories abounded. They filled the letters columns and the talk shows on radio, those squirrel cages of public opinion, whenever the Vikings lost. A gravel pit worker from LeSueur, Minnesota, theorized that the Vikings failed miserably in the Super Bowl because of the unnatural behavior of their cholesterol. He said he had volunteered for cholesterol studies at the University of Minnesota. There he discovered that the Super Bowl losses had something to do with the Vikings playing in cold weather in Minnesota in December and early January and then being transported to such alien lands as New Orleans, Houston and Pasadena for the Super Bowl. "Because of hard winters," he said, "we build up more fat than people do in warmer parts of the country. Toward springtime this fat begins to dissipate and our blood thins. Before that, there's an interim period when the chemical changes

The Chiefs made it unanimous in the Super Bowl of January 1970. They mauled Joe Kapp's Viking offense (above) and stonewalled the Purple People Eaters (below), Carl Eller, Gary Larsen, Alan Page and Jim Marshall.

PURPLE HEARTS AND GOLDEN MEMORIES

bring about a light-headedness and a muscular sluggishness. We call that spring fever. Now if you're suddenly transferred to a warm climate in the middle of winter, the same phenomenon occurs."

What made it even more ruinous was the people the Vikings met in the warm climates: Larry Csonka, Art Shell, Mean Joe Greene and a few dozen more.

The gravel pit worker's theory was outpointed by the popular one at the time, that Minnesota couldn't win the big one. There was supposed to be some kind of runner-up syndrome hounding Minnesota athletes, politicians and corporate executives. Psychology professors got into it. One of them said Minnesota was a place where orderly folk lived, that its residents weren't conditioned to claw and scratch and go for broke. And maybe this explained why Hubert Humphrey lost for president and Minnesota had pretty cities but not sensational cities, and why Minnesota used to get turned down in the bidding for big spectacles. Maybe all of that, the professor said, rubbed off on the mercenaries who represented Minnesota in the Super Bowl. And it explained why the Vikings lost to Kansas City, lost to Miami, lost to Pittsburgh and then, to demonstrate that none of these was a fluke, lost to the Oakland Raiders.

In the middle of the mass demoralization that always accompanied a Viking loss in the Super Bowl, the words of Bud Grant – still standing there imperturbably in a snowstorm in his Sorrel boots and his fur parka – usually quelled the fan rebellion. Yet his explanation for why the Vikings lost those games was never quite accepted as the revealed truth. The real reason they lost, the fans grumbled, had to be more complicated than Grant's theory.

Grant said this: Consider the outside chance that the other guys had a better team.

This notion usually produced a thunderclap of silence. Nobody bought it. Maybe, somebody said, the cholesterol guy had it right. Or maybe the team needed to play with more emotion. Maybe Grant should have coached with more emotion. Maybe Fred Cox should have kicked field goals with more emotion.

Bill Brown turns it up in the Vikings' first Super Bowl game, against Kansas City in New Orleans. Favored by 13 points, the Vikings lost 23-7. Brown played hard and lost hard. It took him weeks to recover. It took the Viking fans longer.

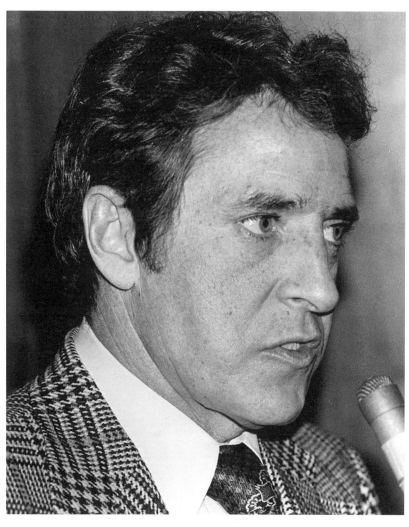

In his 10-year partnership with Bud Grant, Vikings' General Manager Jim Finks produced or set the foundation for four Super Bowl teams. He was a man whose integrity, insight and personality commanded great respect both in football and baseball. After leaving the Vikings, he became the general manager of the Chicago Bears and New Orleans Saints and also directed the Chicago Cubs baseball team for a time. He died in 1994. Jim Finks was inducted into the Hall of Fame in 1995.

No acceptable answer has ever surfaced. Eventually the misery dissolved. Life went on. Yet the Super Bowl pratfalls obscured what the record showed with simple clarity: The Minnesota Vikings have had abnormal success on the field and financially in their 35 years in the NFL. That success has been a common cord uniting such radically contrasting personalities as Joe Kapp and Warren Moon on the field, Jim Finks and Mike Lynn as the general managers, Bud Grant, Jerry Burns and Denny Green as its prime coaches since 1967, and its administrators from the H.P. Skoglunds, Bernie Ridders, Bill Boyers and Max Winters through Lynn and now Roger Headrick and his associates. In the 27 seasons from 1968 through 1994 the Vikings won 14 division titles. Nobody else in the NFL won more. In the same span the Vikings made 18 playoff appearances, a figure exceeded only by Dallas' 20. Their record of 272 regular season victories, 221 defeats and eight ties makes them one of the most productive teams in the NFL, ranking with Dallas, the Raiders, the 49ers, the Pittsburgh Steelers, Buffalo, Denver and the Giants.

Why? In the middle years, Grant and Finks accounted for much of that productivity. Great players like Fran Tarkenton, Alan Page, Jim Marshall, Carl Eller, Paul Krause, Mick Tingelhoff, Steve Jordan, Tommy Kramer, Randall McDaniel and Henry Thomas did. But there's a large and hard-to-measure element that belongs in there. This was the insistence by the club's ownership that the coach ought to be allowed to coach and the general manager should make a manager's decisions. That somewhat radical idea took hold in the Vikings' first years and survived the turmoil of a stock fight and a takeover maneuver in the 1980s.

The other component hard to put a number on has been Minnesota itself. Coaches preach stability, continuity. In some football climates, that stability is almost impossible to achieve. The fans and the commentators are mean and divisive. Turmoil and hair-tearing are part of the landscape. With the Minnesota Vikings, at least through the early 1990s, the atmospherics of pro ball were different. While those legendary Minnesota tolerance levels by now have been talked to bits, it is true that no football mobs in Minnesota build bear traps and piranha pools to waylay struggling coaches. The hysteria levels tend to be lower. Lynch law is a little less acceptable. Bud Grant argues that this has been very much a part of the Minnesota Viking picture, and at this stage, who's going to argue very strenuously with Bud Grant?

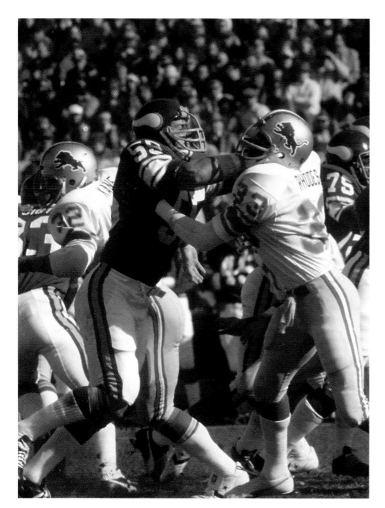

Mick Tingelhoff (left) emerged from the Nebraska cornfields to star for years as the hub of the Viking offensive line. When he was at his peak, nobody played better center in the NFL.

Henry Thomas (making a tackle against the 49ers, below) changed the rules of line play in the NFL. Henry lined up against the offensive lineman at a cockeyed angle, close and menacing. His face mask was inches away from the other's helmet. After a couple of years of that, the NFL decided to widen the space between offense and defense on the line of scrimmage. It made life a little more bearable for the offensive linemen's next of kin.

Tommy Kramer (left) made his living throwing touchdown passes in pro football. But like most veterans he knew that the first rule for quarterbacks was to avoid losing the game. His mechanics of handing off the ball were practically flawless.

A Dutchman
and
36 Stiffs

Standing in the shade of the nearest available maple tree on the sidelines in Bemidji, Minnesota, the King of the Halfbacks, Hugh McElhenny, looked tanned and vaguely appalled.

No one yet had been able to identify what kink of destiny had put him on the roster of the newly-fabricated Minnesota Vikings after nine years in San Francisco. He had freshly arrived in Bemidji on his way to eventual immortality. He wore a stylish black polo shirt and the obligatory California shades. Spectators who were clumped around the Viking practice field failed to recognize him, a dereliction that didn't wound The King's vanity. At the moment he preferred concealment to adoration.

With resourceful planning, The King had arrived in the early afternoon, in time to miss the day's second two-hour, full-pads scrimmage under the late July sun. That was another thing that mystified him in this abrupt career change that uprooted him from the Pacific surf, where he was loved and pampered, to the jackpine wilderness of northern Minnesota, where in 1961 they knew walleyes better than National Football League running backs. A letter in McElhenny's mail from the Minnesota Vikings' general manager, Bert Rose, designated the start of practice as the third week of July. Hugh McElhenny was one of those venerable running backs who liked football in sensible doses. What was the big rush to get yourself killed, starting practice a few weeks after Memorial Day?

He stood watching 80 armored nonentities sweat and pound on each other trying to look like a football team. No progress seemed imminent. The scruffy ensemble was redeemed by a few faces McElhenny recognized or knew by reputation. He couldn't possibly overlook Don Joyce, the old defensive end from the Baltimore Colts, looking very squat and globular at 300 pounds. He recognized Bill Bishop, an exile from the Chicago Bears, one of the most ornery defensive tackles ever created. Doc Middleton, the former Lions' receiver, was familiar. He knew George Shaw, the quarterback who had been smothered by injuries and a glum future playing first behind John Unitas in Baltimore and then Charley Conerly in New York. Alternating snaps with Shaw he recognized the saucy rookie from Georgia, Francis Tarkenton. Clancy Osborne and Karl Rubke he'd played with in San Francisco.

And he couldn't mistake the figure advancing toward him out of the melange of crunching bodies. The whistle was new. The coach's cap was new. The conspiratorial giggle was familiar. It was something Norm Van Brocklin always did when he was sharing a private joke or having a hell of a time. The Dutchman walked up to McElhenny with the exuberance of an island outcast greeting the first mate of a rescue ship. He draped an arm around the polo shirt, playfully removed the shades to be sure he had the right man, and welcomed Hugh McElhenny to the Minnesota Vikings.

"King," he said, "you're a beautiful sight. Come on out on the field. I want to introduce you to your new teammates. You're a start for us. We've got a start on a football team. You're going to be an inspiration to these guys."

McElhenny smiled warily. It had been several years since he'd been compared with Moses. Maybe he'd better get used to it. The Vikings were going to pay him $21,500 the first year. Everybody else on the team, including its high draft choices, got hamburger money alongside that. The Dutchman was positively eloquent. "Before we can be a football team we've got to look like a football team. With you in there, Mac, that'll start tomorrow."

The King mentally fumbled through a calendar.

"Tomorrow?"

"Right," the Dutchman said.

"Isn't tomorrow Sunday?"

"Right. We work out full go with pads."

McElhenny looked to the trees for solace. He rolled his eyes prayerfully.

"Jesus," he said.

Van Brocklin always defended the Vikings' choice of Bemidji as their first training outpost. Critics clamored for a site closer than the 250 miles separating Minneapolis and St. Paul from the scene of the team's post-incubation crawls and pratfalls. They wailed about the drive time from the Twin Cities, five hours. The Dutchman thought that was wonderful. The Dutchman had a minimal admiration for what he always called "the 36 stiffs" the NFL bestowed on

the Vikings in the first-year player pool. Practicing in sight of wild rice bogs on the fringe of the wilderness gave his team exactly what it needed, he contended: obscurity.

For the next six years, the imprint of the Dutchman's wooden shoes covered the shaky Minnesota Vikings' longboat (and a lot of the faces in it) from end to end. For the better part of 12 years in the NFL he had been a great and creative quarterback who could stand lesser minds but couldn't stand football administrators and most football writers and broadcasters. He couldn't stand people he called showboats, people who challenged his bigotries, and he couldn't stand people who didn't appease his rages. But he was a football man. He

The Dutchman, Norm Van Brocklin, was never very bashful with his verdicts. A few weeks after he left the Philadelphia Eagles to coach the first Viking team, Van Brocklin said this of the Eagles: "They were nothing when I got there, and they'll be nothing when I'm gone." He may have been unkind, but he was largely right. In his last year as the Eagle quarterback, they won the NFL title. They haven't won one since. After one look at the roster of players the Vikings culled from the rest of the league, he had a name for them: "36 stiffs." This was nasty, and not totally correct. The expatriates included Hugh McElhenny, still a great runner, and Grady Alderman, who became an all-pro lineman. No. 53 on Van Brocklin's right (above) is Mick Tingelhoff, who arrived the next year and was definitely not a stiff. (right photo, credit: David Boss/NFL Photos)

had brains, but beyond that a will as strong as the tide. He actually believed the force of his will could drive the comical collection of outcasts and novices he coached in his first years, push them to levels that were intrinsically beyond them if left to their own devices.

He had it right. They played competitively and brashly in almost every game until, in 1964, in just their fourth year, they reached a winning record and at the end of the season were actually one of the best teams in football.

In retrospect, it was a

pretty stunning performance. It was recalled years later by Tarkenton. Along with dozens of others, Francis by then found himself frozen out of Van Brocklin's private pantheon of people who he decided deserved his friendship.

"He was a hundred things good and bad but first of all he was smart. He had little wrinkles he put in. He knew the people he was trying to beat. In those few years, taking a team from nothing to a level able to compete with the Green Bay Packers of Lombardi, that was a coaching job."

His single-minded drives and his gales of wrath first lifted him and then ostracized him. They had helped to thrust Van Brocklin to the highest echelons of pro football quarterbacking and then turned his garage sale collection of misfits and kids into a hard-knuckled swat team in four years. But those same fires ultimately turned in on him. His tantrums and his Captain Bligh bullying eventually reached a critical mass. He found a game in the middle of the 1965 season that he thought stood next to Armageddon in its impact on heaven and earth. Baltimore came to Metropolitan Stadium. This game, the Dutchman decided privately, would be a test of his coaching, his team's manhood and the condition of life in Minnesota. As God was his witness.

To make it better, the Colts didn't have John Unitas, who was ailing. Gary Cuozzo quarterbacked Baltimore. And the Colts undressed Van Brocklin's football team, 41-21.

The Dutchman was mortified. His depression was not shared by the players and the owners. The fans didn't feel it and

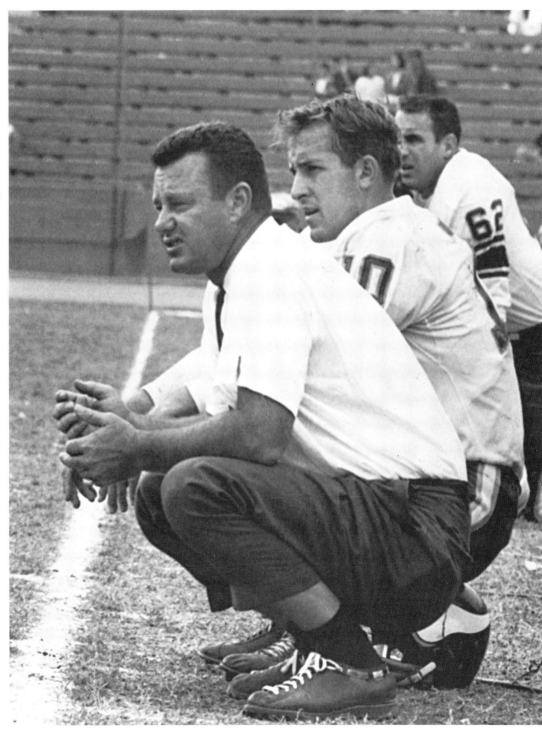

Van Brocklin handed Tarkenton the quarterbacking job a few minutes into the Vikings' opening game against Chicago. They formed a mutual admiration duet for the first season. Five years later, they couldn't stand each other. Their egos, wills and personalities collided too many times, too publicly. But both wound up in the Hall of Fame. (Photo credit: David Boss/NFL Photos)

When in 1961 the Viking management began scouring the coaching landscape for a man to organize their collection of rookies and football orphans into a football team, one of their calls went to Bud Grant. The call came from Max Winter, a friend of Grant's. It wasn't exactly an offer. Max wanted to know if Bud was interested. But Bud's Winnipeg team in Canada was winning. He looked on the Viking job as a romanticized form of professional suicide rather than a new coaching adventure. He said thanks, maybe another time. That time came six years later.

certainly nobody in heaven seemed to mind. The Colts, after all, were a better football team. If Unitas had played it would have been worse.

But Van Brocklin quit the next day in a dark spasm of self-abasement.

He said he obviously couldn't get the team over the top. It was a gloomy assessment that looked like a sign of humility but had a familiar Van Brocklin stamp – a sour judgment of the unworthies around him. His statement seemed to reflect more on the athletes than on the coach.

A couple of days later, Jim Finks, the general manager, and Bernie Ridder, the most influential of the Viking owners, talked him out of his voluntary exile. But the old Van Brocklin ferocities were no longer credible to the players. The team finished the season indifferently. It played the 1966 season the same way and in 1967, the Dutchman resigned again and Harry P. Grant arrived. He brought with him his silences, his laser eyes and his beltful of Grey Cup championships from Canada.

He could have come earlier. Before they hired Van Brocklin, before they brought in Northwestern's (and later Notre Dame's) Ara Parseghian for a quiet feeling-out encounter that quickly turned into a one-act burlesque, the Vikings nearly offered their first head coaching job to Bud Grant.

Grant later went to four Super Bowls years and the Hall of Fame. He didn't do it by being a dummy. In Winnipeg he was respected, if not exactly loved, and he was a winner. With a bunch of football orphans in

DALE HACKBART
MINNESOTA VIKINGS DEF. BACK

Minnesota, he was going to lose for years. Minnesota was where he had played his college football and basketball and where he spent a couple of seasons with the professional basketball Lakers in Minneapolis. But Grant always made his major commercial decisions with the unsentimental attitude of a lion scanning his options for dinner. The Minnesota Vikings, he decided, could come later, after the first coach or two disappeared into the woods.

The reasons for the Vikings' early interest in Grant involved both his success at Winnipeg and the Laker connection between Grant and Max Winter. Winter was one of the Vikings' owners and, before that, the Lakers' first mastermind. Winter later became the Vikings' president and prime decision-maker, although for years he steamed privately as a kind of corporate outcast on the board.

Max was one of the team's founders. Without the intervention of the Chicago Bears' George Halas, the team might have played its football in the American Football League rather than in the pedigreed NFL. And if it did, it might have been extinct before the ultimate NFL-AFL merger. In fact, Winter and his two associates, Bill Boyer and H.P. Skoglund, actually made the $25,000 deposit that was all they needed in 1959 to put Minnesota in the American Football League. To make it easier, the AFL held its organizational meeting in Minneapolis. It even held its first draft, at which the Minnesota team decided that Dale Hackbart of Wisconsin, a quarterback then, was one of the best football players in the land and drafted him in the first round.

Hackbart's subsequent career in the NFL never quite vindicated that bold judgment. But in the late '60s as a defensive back, Hackie muscled his way onto the Viking roster with sharp knuckles and generally reckless behavior. He stayed for several years.

Minnesota didn't last that long in the AFL. It

Max Winter (below) entered pro football against the backdrop of success as the general manager of the Minneapolis (later Los Angeles) Lakers basketball team. He was a longtime sports promoter, auto show director and restaurateur with roots in north Minneapolis. He, H.P. Skoglund, Bill Boyer, Bernie Ridder and Ole Haugsrud, formed the first Viking board and bought the franchise for $1 million in 1960, a figure that today would barely pay for a second string quarterback holding the clipboard. Max later served as the team's president.

rented an office and began looking for a coach but Halas butted in without much delay. He examined the consequences of a successful football rival a few hundred miles away. He considered the welfare of the NFL, but not quite as ardently as he considered the welfare of the Chicago Bears. As a member of the NFL expansion committee, he advised Winter, Boyer and Skoglund that they were blessed. They were being seriously studied as new members of the NFL. The allures of the new league tended to fade quickly for the Minnesota group. As a sports impresario, Winter was canny and opportunistic. Boyer was a silver-haired car dealer and Skoglund was a corporate plunger, a man of great girth and cordiality whose primary cash came from insurance.

But to get into the NFL, they needed more than Boyer, Winter and Skoglund. They needed, for one, a bald, benign little man from Duluth named Ole Haugsrud. Ole was a tobacco dealer who started out in business delivering newspapers to a Superior, Wisconsin, brothel. Way back into the 1920s he had made a lateral career movement and organized a pro football team called the Duluth Eskimos, which to nobody's shock was accepted into the NFL. In those years the NFL was generous with its entrance requirements. Eleven people and a ball usually got you in.

The Eskimos quickly disappeared into the polar mists of Lake Superior. But Ole's contract with the National Football League gave him prior claim on any new NFL franchise granted in Minnesota. To get into the NFL, you had to go through Ole. This sounded like a downright unkind act. Better than going through Ole was to go in with Ole. So the Twin Cities group embraced Ole as a 10 percent stockholder and then brought in Bernie Ridder, the chief executive of the St. Paul newspapers. That decision acknowledged a reality of Twin Cities culture and commerce. If this enterprise was going to be successful, it had to bury the fondly held blood oaths that divided Minneapolis and St. Paul, even if it did that superficially. No Twin Cities or Minnesota football team was going to succeed without the active partnership of St. Paul.

Ridder, his family and his resources met the specifications. Among other things, this meant 30 percent of the stock. More importantly it meant Ridder's stabilizing effect on the early years of the Viking management. He was a big and amiable guy with the relaxed carriage of a man of money and refinement. But he was no stranger to earthy talk and humor. In the few early disputes on the Viking board, he was a reconcilor and a broker for the clashing egos.

This diverse clan of prairie financiers showed up in Florida for the National Football League meeting in early 1960 and asked for a franchise.

With them were the Murchisons, et al, from Dallas, with the same request.

Done, said the league. Dallas starts in 1960. Minnesota starts in 1961. And the bill?

"A deposit of $600,000," said the newly installed NFL commissioner, a bright young fellow from California named Pete Rozelle. "After that,

$400,000."

That was the price for Minnesota. One million dollars for a National Football League franchise that today is worth anywhere from $150 to $200 million.

The Vikings hired a football handyman named Joe Thomas to be their scout and, on Rozelle's recommendation, a onetime colleague in the Rams' front office, Bert Rose, to be the general manager. Rose's limited career with the Vikings produced three achievements that were never fully recognized by his detractors. This was a sizable group that was largely incited by Van Brocklin and a couple of the Viking owners and drove Rose out of town after three seasons. Rose tapped into an existing cadre of town boosters to produce an early season ticket sale of 25,000. That provided the bedrock of a home attendance and quickly made the Vikings a commercial success. Rose hired Van Brocklin, who gave the Vikings instant credibility. And he supervised the initial talent collection that included the infamous "36 stiffs" and the team's first college draft, plus a vital first-year deal with

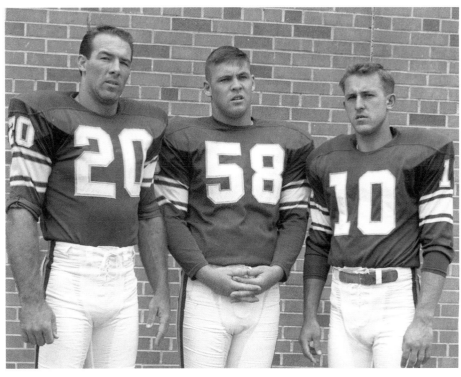

Cleveland's Paul Brown. Despite the Dutchman's carping, all of that activity gave the Vikings an eventual first-year harvest that included Tarkenton, running back Tommy Mason, McElhenny, defensive linemen Jim Marshall and Paul Dickson in the Browns' deal, rookie linebacker Rip Hawkins, rookie defensive back Ed Sharockman and offensive lineman Grady Alderman. With the exception of McElhenny, all of those people played for years. Tarkenton and McElhenny eventually were voted into the Hall of Fame. Marshall should be. Tarkenton, Alderman, Sharockman and Dickson all played in Super Bowls for future Viking teams.

At the time, though, none of them sowed much terror around the NFL. Parseghian might have

In 1960, when the Vikings held their first draft of college football players, there weren't hordes of "draftniks" watching the show on TV, tout sheets in hand. That was a pity. The Vikings' first draft rang the gong. Tommy Mason of Tulane (no. 20), the No. 1 pick, became a Pro Bowl halfback. Linebacker Rip Hawkins of North Carolina (58), the No. 2, became the team's defensive captain and Georgia's Francis Tarkenton, the No. 3, eventually set every significant passing record in pro football. Mason's first year salary was $15,000. Today, that kind of money would pay for a No. 1 pick's first night on the town. The draft included as the No. 5 choice a spiky defensive back from Pittsburgh, Ed Sharockman (left), who starred for years.

been their coach. Rose invited him from Northwestern to talk about the job. Parseghian thought it would be a discreet meeting at a Minneapolis country club. Discretion has been served better by an anvil chorus. The story was in the Minneapolis newspaper and when Parseghian got back to Northwestern, every sports reporter in Chicago had the same question.

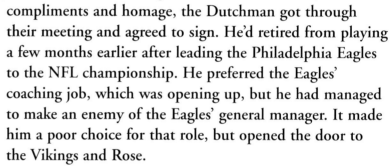

"What gives?"

Ara reorganized hastily.

He said he was at Northwestern heart and soul, and he had no interest in the Viking job.

Van Brocklin, though, did. Although he had to struggle to stay awake while the Viking owners lathered him with compliments and homage, the Dutchman got through their meeting and agreed to sign. He'd retired from playing a few months earlier after leading the Philadelphia Eagles to the NFL championship. He preferred the Eagles' coaching job, which was opening up, but he had managed to make an enemy of the Eagles' general manager. It made him a poor choice for that role, but opened the door to the Vikings and Rose.

It wasn't easy to unnerve the Dutchman. Life as a quarterback in pro football in the 1950s, when it was still splattered with athletic gypsies and headhunters, was usually shock-proof. But he shook a little when he assessed his first company of ragged mercenaries in Bemidji. He screened feverishly but also smartly. What he eventually put together was presentable. To do it he had to wade through a menagerie of strange fish and dodo birds. At the first training camp, the Vikings accepted walk-ons, soldiers of fortune and deluded volunteers. This was done under the sensible theory that no amount of bodies were enough. One of the enlistees was a truck driver who was temporarily out of work. After three of Van Brocklin's two-a-days, his resume expanded. He was not only an unemployed truck driver but an unemployed linebacker. A free agent who accepted a $1,000 bonus vanished in the dead of night after one workout, leaving a fully explanatory note for his roommate:

"My chances of surviving the Death March would be

It took Jim Marshall a few years to get entrenched in the NFL. He came to the Vikings in 1961 after playing briefly for the Cleveland Browns. He played sick in 1961 and accidentally shot himself the next year. But when he got healthy and added weight to complement his speed, he hit stride in an extraordinary career that would encompass 270 consecutive games as a starter for the Vikings.

better than they're going to be here."

Yet Van Brocklin's first offering to the inquisitive customers at Metropolitan Stadium may have been slandered by the legends that followed it. The Dutchman actually put some respectable ballplayers on the field when the Vikings materialized on a September afternoon in 1961, facing the Chicago Bears and George Halas to launch the great adventure. Shaw was the quarterback, a likable and intelligent fellow but one carrying too much baggage to be destined for any long-term employment under Van Brocklin. He had been intimidated both by injuries and Van Brocklin's snarling critiques on the practice field. Like offensive tackle Frank Youso, another target of Van Brocklin's daily diatribes, Shaw was a veteran. The Dutchman announced a few hundred times a week that he expected performance and no mistakes from NFL veterans. This overlooked the somewhat widespread evidence that veterans make mistakes all the time, in pro football, baseball, the U.S. Army, General Electric, in rain and shine, behind the wheel of a car and under the nuptial sheets.

The standards to which Van Brocklin held his retreaded football migrants were impossible. But they did serve a purpose. Nobody got bored from complacency on a Van Brocklin team. With Shaw in Van Brocklin's first backfield were McElhenny and fullback Mel Triplett, an affable plugger who some time later was driven to tears of anger for the racial slurs he detected from the head coach, not necessarily directed at Mel Triplett but at other black players on the team. He probably read those slurs correctly. This was 1961. Racist attitudes and language in pro

It took a few years for the Vikings to start winning. Until then, if they couldn't be successful they could be very belligerent. The other team's trainer and physician were usually on the field as much as the offense. Established teams hated playing the Vikings in the early years. They usually beat Minnesota, but they were a mess the following week.

He was one of those anonymous grunts who came to the Vikings in the rummage sale of the NFL player pool that stocked the first Viking team in 1961. But Grady Alderman stayed for 14 years as an offensive tackle, one of the most valued of his era.

football had barely graduated from the Jim Crow ages. You didn't see much of it among the players. The coaches were older and less influenced by the new interracial understandings that were slowly changing the mind and face of pro football. Like most of his contemporaries, Van Brocklin admired and got along with the majority of the good black players, especially the compliant ones. The marginal black players or the free spirits walked a tougher road. It came through sometimes when a coach would question a player's heart or his brains if the player blundered. If that player happened to be black, his guts and color both were brought up in those crude judgments some of the coaches made privately.

They didn't all talk that way or feel that way. But this was part of the social poison of the mid-1960s. It flowed in the football camp as well as anyplace else in the country, and it's what drove the Mel Tripletts into their private outbursts, whether tearful or profane. They were muzzled by the conventions of the time and you didn't talk out publicly against "the man."

But Mel was there against the Bears. So were willing non-heroes like Gary Huth and Erroll Linden, Bob Denton, Mike Rabold and Bill Lapham, a center whose dossier included the fascinating information that he once got hit in the head by a bullet in a hunting accident and suffered no apparent ill effects. The retrospectives of that odd football team get more intriguing with the years. The workhorse flanker was Jerry Reichow, a lanky football belligerent whom God might have intended for a number of roles in life but certainly not that of a flanker. He wasn't fast or nimble. But he was a resourceful player with a hammerhead field behavior that often obscured a first-rate mind. He was the best receiver on the squad its first three years and later became the Vikings' personnel director for decades. Not far from Reichow on the offensive line was Grady Alderman, young and articulate and a steal from the talent-crowded Detroit Lions. He, too, became a football administrator, first with the Vikings and later as the general manager of the Denver Broncos. Bob Schnelker, the Vikings' first tight end and the man who caught the first touchdown pass ever thrown by Francis Tarkenton, re-emerged years later as the Vikings' offensive coordinator.

The defensive team was not as favored but did include a slowly-maturing Jim Marshall. He was a young athlete of gymnastic quickness, although he also the victim in his first year of a illness that left him underweight and in no condition to handle the blubbery offensive tackles of his time.

"You know, in light of what he became," Tarkenton said later, "nobody who played with him in his first seasons would have said they were surprised. Marshall was an absolute panther when he was healthy and right. The offense would just stand there at the Viking bench and be amazed. He was a show. He had incredibly quick shifts in direction. And instincts for beating a block at the line of scrimmage."

At the other end was Don Joyce, a man of chivalry off the field but an alley fighter in his days in Baltimore. He was memorable in Minnesota, though, mostly for his Henry the Eighth waistline and appetite, which included a marathon thirst-quenching performance on an off-day in Bemidji. There, to compensate for the northern Minnesota heat – which meteorologists don't usually consider life-threatening – Joyce reputedly guzzled three cases of beer while he and selected teammates were recovering from one of the Dutchman's workouts. Not far from him on the

defensive line was Bill Bishop, a growling, brooding Texan who contributed significantly to the legend by getting into a fight with Van Brocklin on the team plane.

Years later, when the Vikings acquired titles, stars and the other garnishments of success, their names were either forgotten or politely buried. But they formed a kind of romantic honor roll for the hard-core Viking fans who were there at the beginning: Ed Culpepper, a bulbous defensive tackle with a red face and baggy football pants, tackle Jim Prestel, who played in shoes that might have been designed for the last brontosaurus; Jack Morris, a bald-headed defensive back who was invariably matched against the elite of the National Football League

In a game in San Francisco in 1964, Jim Marshall (left) picked up a bouncing football in the middle of a screwball play involving a fumble and chaos. He ran the ball more than 60 yards into the end zone and turned for the expected embraces of his teammates. He got hugged by a 49er lineman, who congratulated him for running the wrong way and scoring a safety for San Francisco. His career might have been destroyed by the ridicule. But Marshall's resilience got him past the trauma, and he went on to two decades as one of the game's great ironman players.

DEFENSIVE END **DON JOYCE**
MINNESOTA VIKINGS

They became the Viking co-captains, Rip Hawkins (left) and Fran Tarkenton, in an era when being captain meant more than calling the coin toss. Tarkenton's other duty during the early years was trying to avoid dismemberment when the pass rush came against his inexperienced offensive line. His scrambling style won a few games, exhausted everybody on the field, friend and foe, electrified the crowd and left Van Brocklin's game plan in shreds.

TOMMY MASON
MINNESOTA VIKINGS
HALFBACK

receivers, a Boyd Dowler or Raymond Berry. Because the Vikings lacked a pass rush, it was never quite a fair fight. Morris might have been the only pro football player who deserved a spray of lilies along with the team meal the night before the games. Morris' associates in the secondary, Rich Mostardi, Charley Sumner and Dick Pesonen, were available as the scapegoats of the coaching staffs harangues whenever Morris got a reprieve. Mostardi once bit on a fake hand-off by Green Bay's Bart Starr and ignored Dowler so gullibly that when the ball eventually arrived in the receiver's vicinity 50 yards downfield, Dowler had time to shade his eyes, adjust his helmet and give the thumbs-up sign to Max McGee on the opposite sideline before strolling into the end zone.

But also there were Tarkenton, Mason and Hawkins, the high-choice rookies with the stamp of potential stardom. Hawkins was a thick-drawling Tennessean who had the middle linebacker's dual requisites of being mean and smart. Mason was a swift and gutty runner from Tulane, the Vikings' No. 1 draft choice. And Tarkenton arrived in the Vikings first camp with gusto, brains, nerve and the clear intention of becoming the next great football quarterback.

None of that struck any of the players, including George Shaw, as being arrogant. Arrogance was a quality Francis didn't acquire until his numbers deserved it. He came in conversational and chummy, an obvious quick learner and a good mixer. Van Brocklin made him his instant favorite, partly because Tarkenton's yeasty confidence and impulsiveness made George Shaw's methodical, good soldier's struggles look inadequate. Nonetheless, Shaw started the Vikings' first game against Halas' Bears. Before the first quarter was finished, Shaw was gone, evicted by the impetuous

The first goal of the rookie stars in the Vikings' first seasons was self-preservation. There weren't many all-stars in the huddle. Players came and went weekly. But Tommy Mason and Rip Hawkins were quality players from the beginning, the forerunners of the Super Bowl all-pros who followed. Both, coincidentally, later acquired law degrees.

Dutchman for no particular error or incompetence. The Dutchman actually believed he could uproot natural law and beat the Chicago Bears with a team gathered from the rummage sales of pro football. He thought Tarkenton was the young man to ignite his schemes. It was a fantasy nobody could possibly buy except (a) Van Brocklin and (b) Tarkenton.

A couple of hours later Tarkenton had thrown for 250 yards and four touchdowns. The Vikings won 37-13 and an apoplectic Halas refused to speak to his disgraced warriors until the moment he got on the team bus for the airport. He spoke two words. One of them should be edited in courtesy to the grandchildren of the Bears who were present. "You (bleeps)," Halas said.

Hearing this later that night, Van Brocklin giggled and swore he could never mistreat any team of his with language that unkind. It was a well intentioned vow that lasted a month.

He had nothing to cry about until then. Tarkenton was the quarterback in the second game against Dallas, which the Cowboys won, but in no landslide. Because Shaw had played for the Colts and was fondly remembered by the Baltimore crowd, Van Brocklin switched to the veteran for the third game, in Baltimore. Although the Vikings lost, it may have been a spectacle even more extraordinary than the one against the Bears. They were playing against one of the quality teams in football,

Van Brocklin and Tarkenton. What do you call on 3rd and 28? Although they traded accusations in later years, Van Brocklin calling Tarkenton selfish and Tarkenton calling Van Brocklin abusive and arrogant, they created a hotwire Viking offense that rolled up scores into the 40s and by 1964 gave the Vikings their first winning season. (Photo credit: David Boss/NFL Photos)

quarterbacked by Unitas, with Raymond Berry, Lenny Moore, Ordell Braase, Art Donovan, Jim Parker, Gino Marchetti, Big Daddy Lipscomb and a half dozen other all-pros in the cast. They were playing in Baltimore. But with Shaw passing, an overweight rookie fullback named Raymond Hayes running and a moody football vagabond named Mike (Moko) Mercer kicking field goals, the Vikings led in a scoring brawl with less than a minute to play. Unitas came upfield with a couple of sideline passes. The Colts didn't have to advance much beyond midfield in those years because the goalposts were on the goal line, not 10 yards deeper on the end line as they are today.

And with time running out, Steve Myhra kicked a 52-yard field goal to win for the Colts.

Surely Van Brocklin had to observe all of the required gallantries here. He had to recognize that his grubby football team had come within seconds of defeating a great organization on its home field.

Most of these chivalries the Dutchman had no trouble ignoring.

"Myhra," he said. "That fat ass."

Gallantries were in short supply the rest of the year. Tarkenton was restored at quarterback and Mason divided the running with McElhenny and Hayes. It was a disjointed team that was nonetheless whipped up by Van Brocklin's bluster and made competitive by his ingenuity. The Vikings played belligerently but not very well. They lost, in fact, seven in a row until they did an encore with the Colts and Unitas at Metropolitan Stadium. Two days before the game, Van Brocklin decided to relieve whatever tensions were gripping his reeling players. No curfew for the weekend, he said. Do what you want but come to the ballpark with a clear head and good breath. Be ready to kick butt.

They followed instructions and beat the Colts 28-20.

The coach decided these people were now mature young men and could accept the normal weekend discipline and still win.

George Shaw was a thoughtful guy and a gifted passer. But he was also brittle. The Vikings gave the Giants a first-round draft choice for him in their first season, convinced he would be their quarterback of the future. The future lasted one quarter into the first game. Fran Tarkenton moved in to win the Vikings' opening game against the Bears and stayed in pro ball for 18 years. George became a stock broker.

They may have been mature. They may have accepted discipline. But they didn't win the next week, or the week after that, but they did beat the Rams in Minnesota before the season ended. With three victories behind them, Van Brocklin's roustabouts were able to go into Chicago respectably to listen to a brief salute and presentation to McElhenny before the game.

Although he later played a couple of nondescript seasons, one with the Vikings and then with the New York Giants, McElhenny's admirers in the Chicago press corps suspected he was playing his valedictory in the National Football League when the Vikings and Bears met in December at Wrigley Field. The occasion seemed to demand some tribute in the

minds of the Chicago writers because McElhenny was one of those rare athletes who becomes a kind of communal resource of the fans and professionals involved in the game, a little like a politician everybody loves regardless of party. It was a thrill to see him run. He ran with speed and an intuitive sense of when to shift, slide, decoy, stop-and-go or accelerate. He ran with grace and (something he was willing to admit without prodding) well developed urges for survival. But if taking a blow meant important extra yards, he took the blow. About the time he finished playing, there was a wacky Hollywood movie at large about an international car race before World War I. One of the scenes involved a massive pie fight in which all of the participants except one got royally plastered with flying gunk. The exception was actor Tony Curtis, who moved serenely through the mess in his unsullied white suit, his teeth gleaming, immune to the chaos around him.

That was pretty much the way Hugh McElhenny ran with the football. He was a Nureyev exercising his art in a crowd of angry and sweating longshoremen. If they hit him, he gave them a minimal target zone. If they wanted to nail him to the grass, he gave them a slack leg and a disappearing shoulder and was gone. Other backs before and afterward came with stylized moves to augment their speed and power – spins, high steps and pivots – but McElhenny's seemed to spring from pure instinct. His moves were invoked sparingly but sometimes they were plain astonishing. In midseason of 1961, playing at Met Stadium against the San Francisco team where he acquired most of his celebrity, McElhenny launched a sweep to the left from the

Old Metropolitan Stadium was built for baseball. Football was an afterthought. But the Twins and Vikings both moved in in 1961, and the tailgating culture promptly turned the Met into an institution. It was practically born obsolete. But the fans – at least in their spasms of nostalgia in later years – prized its homely creakiness, its open air and its sociable parking lots. The Vikings played at the Met from 1961 through 1981, when its limited 47,000 seat capacity put it into exile. Eventually it vanished but some of those creaking seats still reside in the basements of Met sentimentalists.

San Francisco 32. It became more than a play. It became a summary of The King's entire career. He escaped a half dozen times. He was dead at the line of scrimmage and again in the secondary on one side of the field and then the other. Mathematicians who saw the play on film later counted seven times that he forced tacklers to miss when they had him ready for burial. When he crossed the goal line he lifted his knees just slightly, not enough to be grandstanding but just enough to tell the audience and the man who ended his career in San Francisco, Coach Red Hickey, that this was Hugh McElhenny.

In Chicago, they gave him a plaque before the game. It was a disagreeable day with melancholy sky and squalling snow. McElhenny might have preferred the fireplace. He was a man with a pragmatic mind, and he appreciated the comforts of life. But he stood at midfield, genuinely grateful when they handed him the plaque and read the inscription. "Wouldn't football be a beautiful game if everyone played it the way Hugh McElhenny does?"

It would. And a few minutes later McElhenny ran back a punt 80 yards into the end zone. That was the way the day started. Early in the first half the Vikings had acquired a 21-0 lead. The Dutchman wasn't there to enjoy it. He was en route from Philadelphia through a snowstorm after trying to sign a draft choice over the weekend. By the time the Dutchman arrived, the Vikings were leading 21-7. By the time the game was over the Bears were in front 52-35. It was no reflection on Van Brocklin's coaching, but the coach's natural tendencies toward paranoia were even more acute on the flight back to Minnesota. He thought he heard snickering in the players' seats.

"He had that habit," Paul Flatley, one of his players, said later. "He'd have a couple of drinks back in the coaches' seats and if we lost, which was usually, he'd come forward and stop at each seat and grind on the players. Look, I thought he was a first-rate coach but at times like those he was just brutal. Some players talked back to him, but they were risking getting cut if they did. I'm surprised they didn't mug him."

It was that night out of Chicago when Bill Bishop threatened first to deck Van Brocklin and then threatened to throw him off the plane. He never explained how this sort of a hijacking could be accomplished. The scene was not isolated. In terms of dignity and quiet reflection, Viking flights after losing football games on the more placid nights compared with John Belushi's *Animal House*. On livelier nights they compared with a Caribbean election.

They won only two games in 1962, their second year. They'd lost their first draft choice for George Shaw, who was released after one season, and their second choice to Cleveland for the Marshall, Dickson, Jim Prestel collection. But a bumptious character arrived that season in what at the time seemed to be an insignificant draft choice trade with the Chicago Bears. Bill Brown looked and acted like a drill sergeant inherited from the old Prussian Army. He had a crew cut, a guttural voice and the disposition to run through walls. For such a man, the name "Bill" seemed inadequate. So they called him Boom Boom. In his 12 years as a fullback with the Vikings, he never actually broke through a wall. He made several attempts, in Bloomington, LA and Chicago, where at Wrigley Field the grandstand wall was practically part of the playing field. It was so close, in fact, that in 1962 a Viking receiver, Charley Ferguson, caught a touchdown pass from Tarkenton in full stride, leaped the short wall and ran eight rows into the stands, destroying a citizen's band that played for the Bears home games. While Brown never managed to take out a wall, he was instrumental in the league's decision to move the goal posts back 10 yards.

Younger fans are unaware that years ago the goal posts stood on the goal line to enhance field goal accuracy. For a long time, the uprights were planted exactly

Above: They came with banners and thermoses of dubious contents. On wintry days they came with arctic boots and snowmobile suits and even larger and more dubious thermoses. For this generation of fans, football at the Met was a game, a kegger and a revival meeting wrapped into a Sunday afternoon. It didn't do any good to leave early. You couldn't get out of the parking lot until nightfall.

Left: Fans loved Bill Brown. When he ran into the line he came guts-and-all. His football reached back to the game's primeval origins. He played with blood on his white pants and shirttail flying when he charged downfield. It didn't matter much who or what was in the way, linebacker or goalposts. He hit them impartially.

on the goal line. In later years they were supported by a single post dug in three yards behind the goal line, but still in the end zone. In deference to various skulls that threatened to make contact, the upright support was wrapped in padding. It was supposed to prevent broken legs and outright skull fractures. Concussions, of course, were something else. Brown acquired at least three in the 1960s. Eventually the posts were moved to the end zone line, but Boom Boom never regarded his role in that process with any air of heroism.

"Pro ball was getting big time," he said. "The goal posts were messing up the passing game. The quarterbacks were bellyaching and so were the TV producers. My concussions had nothing to do with it."

But they might have at that. The equipment custodians swore that every time Brown hit the goal posts he moved them a foot.

If Brown's introduction to pro football was traumatic – he apprenticed under George Halas in Chicago and with a teammate named Mike Ditka – Mick Tingelhoff's is mercifully blacked out. Tingelhoff joined the Vikings in 1962, destined to become an all-pro center and one of the battlewagons of Viking line play for 16 years. He came out of the Nebraska corn tassels, several of which appeared to hanging from his collar when he encountered the Viking defensive line coach, Stan

Brown and Tingelhoff both arrived in Minnesota in 1962 with cropped hair, small salaries and intentions of staying awhile. They did, for more than a decade. Brown ran recklessly but he had surprising bursts of speed in the open field and receptive hands that made him one of the game's better pass catchers. Tingelhoff played a game both savvy and bruising. He was an all-pro, but he never stopped being amazed by Dick Butkus' bad language across the line.

West, in a hotel lobby when Nebraska's 1961 season was over. Tingelhoff had been ignored by practically all scouts, probably because of an injury that made him suspect as a pro. The Vikings were in no position to suspect anybody. If the prospect passed the mirror test, he usually got an offer. In approaching Tingelhoff, the Vikings did have some nuisance competition from the young American Football League.

Tingelhoff later became known as a man of gentle and agreeable manners off the field and, by the pro

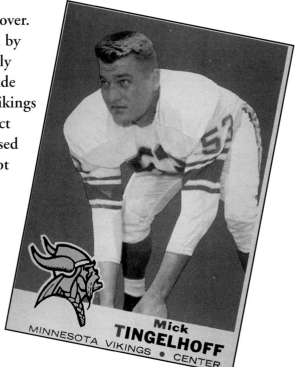

Mick **TINGELHOFF**
MINNESOTA VIKINGS • CENTER

standards of that day, temperate drinking habits. But here he was, in the O'Hare airport lounge after the Viking-Bear game, being courted by the entire coaching staff of a professional football team headed by the renowned Van Brocklin. They convinced him that much glory and wealth lay ahead of Mick Tingelhoff in Minnesota. He looked and sounded too intelligent, they insisted, to ignore this chance of a lifetime.

"It wasn't exactly Lexington, Nebraska," Tingelhoff conceded later. Because of a labor dispute, the Vikings' charter plane didn't get off the ground until 10 p.m. Van Brocklin had invited Tingelhoff to join the team on the return flight. "We stayed in that lounge for four hours celebrating the end of the Viking season," he said. "As the night got longer they had me convinced I was going to be the greatest offensive lineman of all time. They invited me to some socials the next few days in Minnesota and I finally got back to Nebraska on a Wednesday. I told myself, 'in this league, the games last four days. What am I getting into?'"

But he signed.

The money he got for a bonus probably would get you four tickets to a ball game plus two trays of nacho chips in today's dollars. In terms of what he cost them and his obscurity, Tingelhoff may have been one the bargains of the half-century.

But the man in 1962, and the year before, and most of the years that followed until he finished his extraordinary career, was Francis Asbury Tarkenton from Athens, Georgia.

In the earlier years he played with a sandlot exuberance that sometimes masked a hardnails toughness he never lost. He never lost the zest, either. Even in his final years, when he projected the crusty persona of the bloodied old warrior, in his deepest glands Tarkenton still played the game with a sort of Katzenjammer gusto. It was one reason his personality dominated most of the games in which he played. From start to finish he brought to his football and to his team an unspoken creed: "There are a lot of ways to win. There isn't any one way. If it doesn't happen, we'll make it happen."

After his retirement, stories were heard about alleged resentments against

Nobody in pro football was any shrewder than Tarkenton in switching plays at the line of scrimmage, calling the audible. After he'd learned the game in all its nuances, he loved it when the defense came with blitzing pass rushers. It left him free to send his receivers one on one, and free to improvise. That was Tarkenton's edge. Here he checks off, awaiting Tingelhoff's snap from center.

Tarkenton by his teammates. When you play 18 years and reach the visibility of a Tarkenton, you'd have to be a saint not to earn some resentments. But the truth is that there weren't many.

"I played with him for four years." Paul Flatley said, "and I've known him and the rest of the Vikings after I retired. I can tell you that the respect most of the players had for him was enormous. In his younger years he didn't knock around with many guys because he didn't drink then and he was still strongly influenced by his religious upbringing. In later years he partied with the best and naturally he made big money as he matured in pro ball, not only from football but from his other businesses. A few players thought he was selfish. Well, he did like piling up money. I don't know many who don't. But especially in his younger years he had one of those infectious personalities. With him in there, you had the idea that anything was possible. He got this big reputation as a scrambling quarterback early in his career, but if he started out playing for an established team rather than a new franchise, he could have been a classic, pocket quarterback.

"Well, I'll reconsider that a little. He played for a great team in the 1970s, the Vikings, but he wasn't exactly classic. In those years he didn't have to scramble. But he did improvise. That was Tarkenton from beginning to the end. He played the game with his feet and arm and his brains and his instincts. He was also a pretty good politician."

Most of the players in the so-called skilled positions of pro football tend to be prima donnas. They are the runners and receivers and, of course, the quarterbacks. All of them have had public attention for years by the time they get to pro ball, and they get more there. Their money partly depends on statistics, and the quarterbacks' choices affect statistics of the players around them. Political quarterbacks manage to get along with the other prima donnas by being generous and democratic in distributing the ball. They let everybody have a whack at the pass-catching stats, for example. They try to do that despite the doleful fact, enunciated later by Harry P. Grant, that "there's only one ball."

The later Viking mythology also spoke of endless bickering between Tarkenton and Van Brocklin. It was pictured as mutual dislike. There was that, but it wasn't constant and it didn't become a serious split until four or five years into Tarkenton's career. Then, it erupted into a soap opera climax in which they got rid of each other by the simple strategy of walking into the sunset in opposite directions. They retired independently, supposedly for all time, only to reappear not long afterward in new environments (Tarkenton in New York, Van Brocklin in Atlanta) where they planned to be loved and respected.

The strategy wasn't altogether successful for either.

Tarkenton came into pro football more advanced than most rookie quarterbacks of the time. He'd played in a pressure atmosphere at Georgia. He'd played confidently and intelligently, and he saw no reason why he couldn't do the same in the pros. Van Brocklin loved that self-assurance. He had it himself as a young player. He liked Tarkenton's obvious sense for the game and his ability to make quick and sound decisions. His arm was adequate. He was coachable and he was clearly going to be a pro football quarterback for years. Van Brocklin's method of showing esteem was to needle the players he liked. He called Tarkenton The Georgia Peach and P.K. (for Preacher's Kid) and in no time he installed him as the No. 1 quarterback. By the third or fourth game, Tarkenton already had built the scrambling reputation. Pro football had a kind of code for quarterbacks, perpetuated by the Van Brocklins and dozens of other coaches. The quarterback was supposed to glue himself inside the protective pocket of blockers. He was to hold the ball until the last possible moment for release. If he couldn't throw the pass with any hope of reaching friendly fingers, he was supposed to fall on his sword. They said: Take the sack. They didn't call it sack in those days. They

called it eating the ball.

"Actually, Van Brocklin and I never had any real arguments about scrambling," Tarkenton said. "Sometimes he'd chew on me in team meetings. But he didn't in public, except for that great line he used to have: 'I've told Tarkenton a hundred times, 3rd and 18 is no time to be creative.'

"I laughed every time I heard that. And, of course, he was exactly wrong. Third and 18 *is* the time to be creative. But he didn't really yell and scream when I tried to rescue a broken play. He made the obvious point that sometimes I caused it by leaving the pocket too early. How could I argue with that? What happened is that we had a young team. It was tough for the offensive linemen to hold out great pass rushers like Marchetti and Alex Karras and Roger Brown, Deacon Jones and people like that. The idea in football is to win. You'd like to do it with the artistic, orderly plays drawn up in your playbook. But if it turns into a mess, it doesn't mean you have to throw up your hands and die. Quarterbacks of today, with the rare exceptions of the Steve Youngs, won't do it the way I did. They're getting so much money the owners and coaches just won't let them risk their bodies by running with the ball or by doing all those crazy loops behind the line looking for a receiver. What was money in those days? I started at $12,000 a year.

"All I was doing by scrambling was trying to figure out a way to win on that play, buying some time or trying to save my skin. It wasn't planned. I didn't daydream ways to beat the rush while I was driving to work. I did it more than most quarterbacks of the time because we weren't competitive with a lot of the teams, and I had better reactions and quicker feet than most of the quarterbacks."

He became an almost instant legend. Opposing players and coaches

Critics blasted the quality of the Viking offensive line in the early years, but Tarkenton understood it needed time – and a little tolerance. So he stayed in the protective pocket when he could, and usually connected when he did.

By the mid 60s, the Vikings had acquired some quality linemen, including Larry Bowie of Purdue (61) at offensive guard, Mick Tingelhoff (53) at center, and Carl Eller of the University of Minnesota at defensive end.

CARL ELLER
VIKINGS
DEFENSIVE END

seriously believed many of the scramble plays were planned and diagrammed by Tarkenton and the Viking coaches. After a light scrimmage in advance of one of the Pro Bowl games, Don Shula came up to Tarkenton and said, "OK, Francis, we've got time to work on a few of your scramble plays if you'll show us how you want them blocked."

Tarkenton nearly melted into the grass laughing. He remembered an incident from a game against the Lions. The night before, network TV had shown a film that was a forerunner to the celebrated blooper series that came later. One of them showed another NFL quarterback frantically running around miles behind the line of scrimmage and then sitting down in exhaustion, still 30 yards behind the line. The next day Tarkenton scrambled against the Lions. He was approximately 30 yards behind the line, looping and reversing directions in utter panic, with the 300 pound Roger Brown closing the angle. "I was in huge trouble," Tarkenton said. "I mean the situation was grave. It was hysterical. But I actually remembered that film as I was running. It was an instant flashback. I said, this is nuts and all of a sudden, down I go, and Roger Brown is sitting on me and he's saying, 'Francis, don't you ever watch TV?'"

By 1963 and 1964, McElhenny was gone, most of the well vilified stiffs of the expansion pool were gone, and the Vikings were beginning to acquire the look of respectability. Tarkenton was averaging 20 touchdown passes a year and Mason and Brown formed one of the strongest young running back teams in pro football. The addition of Flatley with his resourcefulness and his skills at mind-reading ("you figured out where Francis was going and then ran to where he could see you") upgraded the receiving. From the Minnesota Gophers, the Vikings drafted Carl Eller. That gave them in their formative years half of what ultimately became the Purple People Eaters of the Super Bowl years. Eller and Marshall were followed a few years later by Alan Page and Gary Larsen.

Tingelhoff, Alderman and Purdue's Larry Bowie liberated the Vikings' offensive line from its disaster status of the first two years. The Vikings drafted a temperamental receiver from Southern Cal, Hal Bedsole – one of the few players capable of rendering Van Brocklin speechless, however briefly. Their other draft choices included a defensive back from Auburn, George Rose and a linebacker from Nebraska, John Kirby, who was even more liberally sprinkled with the cockleburs of the country than

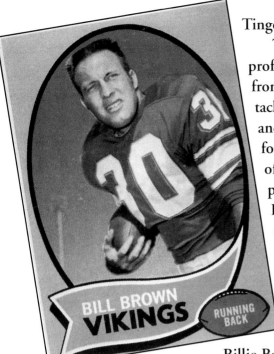

BILL BROWN
VIKINGS
RUNNING BACK

Tingelhoff.

The young veterans were acquiring professional crust. Dickson moved from the offensive line to defensive tackle, where his normal emotionalism and belligerence had a more sensible forum. Sharockman had become one of the league's better and more pugnacious defensive backs.

From the league's catalogues of expendable running backs, Van Brocklin added Phil King, "The Chief," who had run for the New York Giants for years. He also took in another ebbing old-timer, the Philadelphia Eagles' Billie Barnes. Freddie Cox kicked field goals as well as anybody. The punter, Bobby Walden, escaped the punters' stereotype. Most punters and kickers are a caste apart, derided as non-jocks by their more muscular teammates. They are also hounded by insecurity. No punter or kicker is more than two or three bad games removed from the slag pile. Walden was a noisy, extroverted rascal from the Deep South, a fast talker and an even better punter.

By 1964, Bert Rose had been cashiered as the general manager. His ouster was partly spurred by one of the most bizarre surveillance forces in NFL history, the Swedish Underground. The Swedish Underground was the creation of the late H.P. Skoglund, one of the Viking directors, who was annoyed by Bert's administrative style. Skoglund was also

Coaches cherish the so-called "gang" tackle. It builds team solidarity and acts to rattle the bridgework of enemy backs. Doug Sutherland (69) and Carl Eller show how the process works.

PAUL FLATLEY
END
MINNESOTA VIKINGS

Although he wasn't gifted with much speed, Paul Flatley became one of Tarkenton's favorite pass receivers of the mid 1960s because he had the eyes and brains to find the open spaces. He also wasn't afraid of getting conked when he caught the ball. Then there was Flatley's Law: "When Francis scrambled, I knew the first thing to do was to let him see me. So I ran to the side of the field where Francis was. That sounds simple. A lot of guys never learned it."

Soccer kickers were beginning to replace the old-style, face the goalposts field goal kickers when Fred Cox joined the Vikings in 1963. By the time he finished in 1977, his breed was almost extinct. But he led the Vikings in scoring for 12 years, played in 210 games and won dozens of them with his field goals. His leg was strong, but his greatest virtues were his self-possession and his ability to absorb a bad game without plowing himself into depression. He also was a football player, not simply a kicker, with the player's instincts. All of that made him one of the game's dependable kickers.

goaded by Van Brocklin, who wanted Rose removed. To apply pressure, they assigned a former FBI agent and security worker in Skoglund's business, Ray Johnson, to shadow Bert in the off-hours when the general manager usually stopped at the suburban watering parlors. Johnson was a likable fellow whose best sleuthing days might have been behind him. He uncovered no damning evidence, but Rose was fired nonetheless and replaced by the man as responsible as anybody for putting the Vikings into four Super Bowls in the next 13 years.

Jim Finks had played quarterback in the National Football League, had played, and administered, pro football in Canada and was widely admired at all levels. In a business where cut-throat behavior is acceptable, Finks succeeded despite what might have been a fundamental character flaw, an ingrained sense of decency. He was also a competent businessman and a conciliator in the inevitable personality clashes of a football operation. Beyond this, he had one large advantage over some of the general managers of the time: He knew football talent when he saw it. His appraisal was as sound as any of the coaches'.

The 1964 Viking team was Van Brocklin's, but with unspoken credits that also belonged to the departed Bert Rose. By the end of the season they were scoring points in box car numbers. The team had acquired a rollicking, buoyant character that was more a reflection of Tarkenton than Van Brocklin. But on defense it played most of its football with a ferocity that was pure Van Brocklin. Vince Lombardi detested playing the Vikings. Lombardi was convinced that his stars were going to be the targets of an attempted mugging. In fact, Lombardi's Packers did suffer a couple of fractures in the early games against the Vikings, although nobody on the squad can recall any Van Brocklin directives to wreck the Packers if they couldn't beat them.

VIKINGS K
FRED COX

What he did teach was blast-their-cans, black-and-blue football. Whale them every play. Well, nobody can whale them on every play. But Van Brocklin paid no attention to mathematics. He also ignored the fact that there were some very hostile people on the other side of the line of scrimmage. They played one game against the Colts that actually began with assault and battery. The Colts'

Jimmy Orr had burned the Vikings with a half dozen pass catches the previous game. In Baltimore, the Dutchman took one of his defensive backs, Earsell Mackbee, aside in the locker room and gave him the game plan: "Give Orr a shot to the mouth the first play. It'll slow him down." It didn't. But it did start a riot on the field.

They finished the season with an outpouring of 34, 30 and 41 points to beat the Rams, Giants and Bears, the last two on the road, and they were already panting for the arrival of 1965. The ledger read 8-5-1 in their fourth season. Tarkenton threw to Mason, Brown, Flatley, Gordie Smith and anybody else who was nimble enough to read the secondary on the run and to read Francis' mind. While most of the offense was structured, Tarkenton actually called a scramble play in the huddle in Green Bay. It was the first and only time in 18 years that he did. The Vikings trailed by two points with less than a minute to play. They were stuck in their own territory with 4th down and acres to go. Their only prayer was to throw deep, get out of bounds and ask Fred Cox to kick a field goal. In the huddle, Tarkenton laid it out: Everybody go down 30 yards and get open. That was it. Nothing more. The line blocked. Tarkenton ran pell mell to give the receivers time. He looked downfield and saw Tom Hall breaking open.

He threw. Hall reached for the ball. So did Gordie Smith, the tight end, who didn't see Hall. Bodies flew. The ball stuck in Smith's hands. He stepped out of bounds, Cox kicked the field goal, the Vikings won 24-23

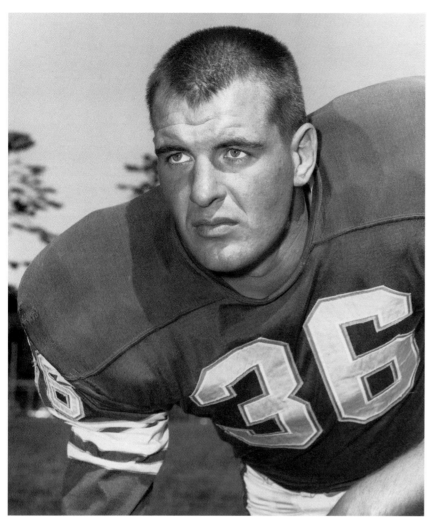

and Lombardi almost keeled over.

Van Brocklin had them steaming for the 1965 season. They mauled everything in sight in the exhibitions. But they lost their first two seasonal games to Baltimore and Detroit, beat the Rams on Cox's last-minute field goal, pounded the Giants 40-14, lost to the Bears and Gayle Sayers' four touchdowns 45-37 and then went to San Francisco. The curfew bloodhounds weren't as active in those years. Flatley was invited to a party by old friends and obviously lost track of time. When he looked out the window it was daylight, and he was miles from the Vikings' hotel. He was also in the first stages of a hangover. He arrived undetected a few minutes before the team breakfast and devoted the next three hours to avoiding eye contact with Van Brocklin. "It was the culture of football at the time," he says today. "Dutch had been part of it himself when he played. Bobby Layne of the Lions and the Steelers was the champion. Paul Hornung and Max McGee couldn't have been far behind. You didn't have the constant media surveillance you have now. It was just another time. People did that and still came ready to play. Most of the time."

Flatley was ready. Bloodshot but ready. He was motivated not by the vision of glory but by raw fear of reprisal if it came out. So he played what was practically the game of the century, making impossible grabs, catching eight passes for more than 200 yards and two touchdowns. The Vikings won 42-41 and were primed, with a 5-3 record at midseason, to get over the hump. The language was Van Brocklin's. He meant it rhetorically but the hump might just as well have been the Himalayas. The Colts hammered them 41-21 and the next morning the Dutchman called a press conference to announce he was through as the Viking coach. The owners sagged. Some of the players held a victory party.

Two days later at the Vikings practice site at Midway Stadium in St. Paul, Bedsole walked into the meeting room, last as always. "You're not going to believe this," he said. "I just saw The Dutchman driving up in his car. He's back." Some groans ensued, but not overwhelming groans. The guy could coach. Life around him was constant turmoil, which was why the team never struck a rhythm, but it was hardly boring.

Van Brocklin walked in, apologized and resumed coaching. For three weeks he was practically mute. The Vikings lost three in a row and he was raging again. They finished 7-7, but it was never going to be the same. He was not the same domineering autocrat in the team meetings

Ball players of the '60s came into pro ball without huge amounts of sophistication. They were rough-cobbled customers, like linebacker John Kirby from Nebraska. They charged into the nearest tavern for beer at the end of two-a-day workouts and played ball with grime in the nostrils and blood on the arms. Nobody got much money. The John Kirbys were around for a few years and left. For them, the memories were worth more than the money.

and on the field. He was less convincing to the players and down from the mountain. They won only four games in 1966 and a few months later, Tarkenton wrote Van Brocklin a letter announcing his retirement. Their frictions had deepened. They argued on the sidelines. In a game televised in Atlanta in Tarkenton's home state, Van Brocklin benched him and played Bob Berry at quarterback. His explanation was transparent fiction. He said he wanted to see Berry in a pressure situation. What pressure? The reason, of course, was to make Francis squirm by depriving him of his audience in Georgia.

Van Brocklin started Bob Berry ahead of Fran Tarkenton in a game in 1966. The act ignited a rumble that led to the departure of both Van Brocklin and Tarkenton.

The fairest judgment of The Dutchman's six years with the Vikings would have been close to this: Not many coaches could have taken them further the first five years. His football team was competitive from the beginning. It played violently and creatively and it was practically always entertaining. That was a verdict he would have settled for some 18 years later, when he died of a brain hemorrhage on his farm near Atlanta.

A few days after Tarkenton quit the Vikings in 1966, Van Brocklin followed. The melodrama left the Vikings (a) without their best player and (b) without a head coach.

The situation, general manager Jim Finks decided, demanded a stroke of international thinking. He picked up a telephone, dialed Winnipeg and in a few moments had issued an invitation to Harry P. (Bud) Grant to coach one of world's most confused football teams.

Going with Grant to the Land of Oz

If you watch a man hunt pheasants, you might learn a lot about how he runs his life and how he sorts out his values. Just incidentally, you can also get a pretty good read on the condition of his eyesight and his trigger hand.

"You didn't have to hunt with Bud Grant more than a couple of times to get the hang of why he lasted in coaching so long and why he won so much."

The speaker is Mick Tingelhoff, former all-pro football player, rancher, barnyard philosopher and, today, suburban investor and stock market player. Because of the way he made his living in football, Tingelhoff has to be credited as a man of uncommon insight. When you play center in football, your view of the world is different. The quarterback's paws are always in close proximity to your vulnerable parts and sometimes you get the feeling you're upside down. A day in the duck blinds or cornstalks with Bud Grant, Tingelhoff said, usually restored him to normalcy.

"On our day off in the football season, some of us went hunting with Bud. Wally Hilgenberg and Roy Winston and I and one or two others did it pretty often. Bud hunts just about the way he coached football. He'd get out there and glance over the field and get everything under control. Then he'd give the terrain a closer study. Some guys just sort of stumble out there. Bud was like a guy checking the football field an hour before the kickoff. He looked to see the way the wind was blowing and where the sun was. He found out what time of day the birds were eating. He'd get local information and he'd work that in with the last time he hunted that kind of country and I'd be surprised if he didn't check the almanacs and the pheasants' won-loss record for the last two years."

There's one other thing.

"He didn't waste any gunshot."

And yet the Tingelhoff and Ed Sharockman and Jim Marshall who stood amazed at Bud Grant's entry into their lives in the summer of 1967 would have safely predicted only two events in their foggy futures: 1. Their team was so screwed up that nobody on it was going to live long enough to get into the Super Bowl. 2. Bud Grant was no Moses.

In three years they were playing in the Super Bowl.

Grant made no claim to being able to divide seawater. For one thing, he didn't have enough hair to look credible. What casting director would install a man with a crewcut and a headset in a Cecil B. DeMille epic?

For the players, the contrast between the Van Brocklin of their first six years and the glacier from Canada made them almost catatonic. The shock was that great.

"Old Dutch," Tingelhoff said, "he yelled and swore. He threatened to fire you every other week. Even after you played a few years for him, you never knew where you stood. He could coach. He could also drive you nuts. When Bud came in, everything all of a sudden went very quiet. The first team meeting he held, it was practically over before it started. He didn't say much. He didn't say much on the practice field, either. In the early years, we never really gave him enough credit for what he was doing. What he was doing was watching. He was observing. Before I finished playing, I found out that no coach I ever played for knew as much about his players as Grant did – I mean things both on the field and in their personal lives that might affect the way they played. He didn't go snooping around. He could actually tell whether something was wrong by the way they acted on the field.

"We weren't ready for his practices, either. Van Brocklin's workouts

Shifting from Van Brocklin to Bud Grant in 1967 practically traumatized the Vikings players. Van Brocklin was verbal and acidic in thought and word. He was dictatorial and sometimes hilarious. Alongside that kind of open passion, Grant was almost monastic. He didn't talk much. His meetings were quiet. He put in some Boy Scout rules. It took a year for the players to recognize the iron in him, but once they saw it they didn't forget it. There was another difference. Van Brocklin was an offensive wizard. Bud's first year offense had all the diversity of a shuffleboard game. It got better when Jerry Burns arrived to coach the offense.

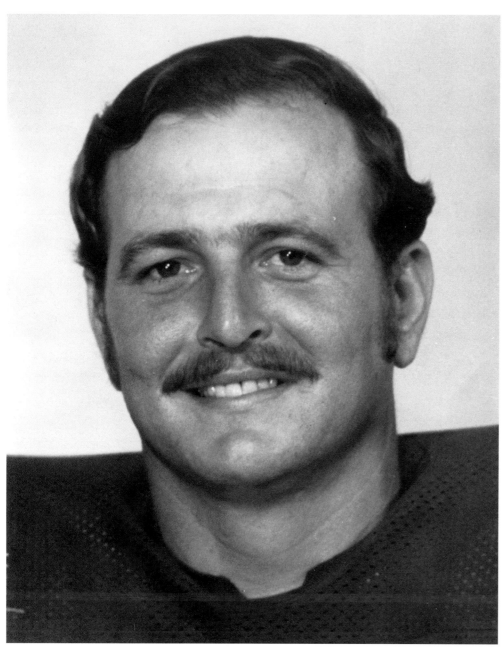

It took awhile for Roy Winston and Bud Grant to understand each other. Winston was a drawling, emotional linebacker from Louisiana, conditioned to Van Brocklin's tantrums and style. He resisted Grant's training camp rules. But they grew to understand each other, and they became hunting companions.

were wars. You beat on each other for two hours. Bud's were shorter. You worked. But you didn't need an ambulance when it was over. Pretty soon, though, Bud began putting in some of those rules or procedures. I don't know what you call them. He told us he wanted us to start looking like we're together. So the first thing we did one day was to line up on the sideline, holding our helmets on our hips, and standing at attention for the national anthem. Milt Sunde, one of our offensive linemen, had some National Guard training and he was conscripted to be a sort of drill sergeant to make sure we did it right.

"Nobody could believe what was happening."

Locker room comics mimicked the sideline tableau. They also groaned when Grant decided they could smoke in rooms where the ceiling was 12 feet or higher, but not otherwise. Grant detested the smoking habit in athletes. He also was annoyed by the rather universal practice of drinking a cup or two of coffee to start the day. So for a while he experimented with removing the coffee pot from the locker room, the theory being that active athletes about to go to work didn't need hot coffee in their gut to launch them into blitzes and drive blocking. That one, though, eventually petered out when the grumbling reached the coach's office. Grant didn't win four championship Grey Cups in Canada by strutting his power. His discipline and organization were calmer. Whatever worked. What he didn't want on the field, in the locker room or on the planes, was a mess. If your preparation habits were sloppy, he said, you were going to play that way. Teams that win are unified. You can get unity in a dozen different ways, including the fundamental one of looking and acting like a team.

Another way is to start winning.

The Grant theory, of course, was that one would follow the other. By no special accident, it started to happen in Grant's second season. By then he had athletes who were beginning to find belief. Grant's first season in 1967 was pretty much a fiasco, 3-8-3. The offense seemed borrowed from the days of the drop-kick. Compared with the Van Brocklin-Tarkenton offensive circuses of the mid 1960s, it commanded all of the electricity of the November freeze-up on the Minnesota lakes. Players conditioned to the volatility of the Van Brocklin years were baffled by Grant's stony calm and seeming aloofness. The Xs and Os looked simpler. To a few of the players they looked unworkable. One of Van Brocklin's playing loyalists, linebacker Moony Winston, stood up in a team meeting one evening in camp, probably after a few beers, and ripped into what he decided was Grant's zombie style and frigging rules. He was finally persuaded to yield the floor, but not before he got sympathetic nods from some of the other regulars.

Eventually, Grant made a friend and a convert of Moony Winston. One reason for this conciliation was Winston's obvious ability to play major league football, a gift that was Grant's first perception of Moony Winston. The rabble-rousing he could forgive and change. He and the

Joe Kapp was a quarterback who in another life – or maybe in this one – could have been a tavern bouncer. Or maybe a shotputter, considering his throwing technique. But he played football without fear and without a shred of doubt that eventually Joe Kapp and his allies would win. Running with the ball, he attacked, with knees, legs, forearms and helmet. Passing, he had no vanity about how the ball advanced from the quarterback to receiver. Spirals weren't obligatory. Knuckleballs were OK, even common. In 1969 his personality created a team unity and fire that lifted the Vikings into the Super Bowl. He was Chicano Joe, Zorro, a dozen other things. The ball players of all colors treasured him, and fought beside him. Grant treasured him also, although he would have preferred a few more spirals.

Vikings needed people like Roy Winston to win in the NFL. So Moony stayed, despite his outburst. The skeptics that Grant didn't need he removed from the team. Time ultimately produced mutual respect between the coach and players like Winston, Marshall, Eller, Alderman, Brown, Kassulke, Sharockman and Tingelhoff – veterans who gave him blank stares in the early months. That respect grew to the level where it became lasting and even emotional. Years later, at the funeral of Jim Finks, Grant and Winston embraced and cried together. The scene was not only an expression of their loss in the death of Jim Finks. It affirmed the fondness they felt for each other and, of course, the times they'd shared.

Up front in the NFL. It's a grinder. Willful men hitting head-on. Bones and torsos in collision. Joe Kapp hands off against the Lions. Grady Alderman blocks. Bill Brown barges toward a Detroit linebacker. It was a standoff, meaning Brown and the linebacker both eventually got up.

The effect of Grant's arrival on the team's public chilled as the winless weeks of 1967 deepened into the Minnesota frost. Expecting liberation from the bickering mediocrity of the Dutchman's last season, the fans got tiresome mediocrity instead.

"Fans think and act that way," Grant said later. "The season wasn't discouraging at all as far as I was concerned. We knew we had some players who weren't going to stay in the NFL because they couldn't play for a contending team. Good guys, but transitional guys."

What was new began with a battle-stitched character from Canada named Joe Kapp, a quarterback on the roster but a dockwalloper in his heart. Where most quarterbacks mince and stride going back into the

pocket, Joe slogged. He gave the impression that most of the time he was playing in two feet of mud. He had big hands, an unsinkable heart and a huge scar on his jaw from where he stopped a beer bottle in Canada. Even in casual conversation, Joe's voice sounded as though it had been dragged through four layers of sand. He became downright lovable in Minnesota. But because he was so obsessed with the idea of team play, because he played like an angry wrangler shagging after horse thieves, the Minnesota fans underestimated Joe's head for the game. He had that, in addition to all of those warrior's instincts he brought to the ball game. He had it substantially enough to coach the University of California, his alma mater, years after he left the pros. What he had mostly, he said, was machismo, a word he heard in the Hispanic neighborhoods of California where he grew up. He played manly football. He was the proud Chicano and everybody's crony in the locker room. The black players loved him. There seemed to be something of their heritage in his, something of their struggle,

and a lot of their pride.

Occasionally, he threw a spiral. He didn't throw it often enough to crash the NFL all-star teams.

"But playing with Joe," Dale Hackbart once remarked, "was like getting back into the sandlot again. It was 'hail, hail, the gang's all here' kind of football, bloody-nose stuff. If you get hurt, don't rub it. It was hard for anybody to think about his own stats when he played or knocked around with Joe."

They loved him, a little bit for what he did but mostly for what he was. "He was a piece of work," John Beasley, the tight end, said. "He was big and loud and fearless, old Chicano Joe. I'll never forget him coming back to the motel the week we played in the Runner-up Bowl in Miami. He rolled in about two or three hours after curfew, beating on my door. He looked like he had run into a school of sharks. His shirt was ripped off and his pants were mangled. I asked what happened. He said, 'somebody on the highway called me a goddamned Mexican.' He figured that was explanation enough for the way he looked, and I guess it was. I'd hate to see what happened to the guys he ran into."

With Tarkenton gone, the incumbent quarterback was Ron VanderKelen, a popular fellow who had authored a near-miss,

Jim Finks' skillful drafting and trade strategy steadily built the Viking talent levels in the late 1960s. In the eighth-round of the 1967 draft the Vikings found John Beasley (above), a tight end who couldn't run much but blocked hard, caught passes in a crowd and led the team in free-thinking. On the first round of that draft they collected Clint Jones (right) of Michigan State, in part payment for the Tarkenton trade to New York. Jones broke some long ones for the Vikings and played productively for several years.

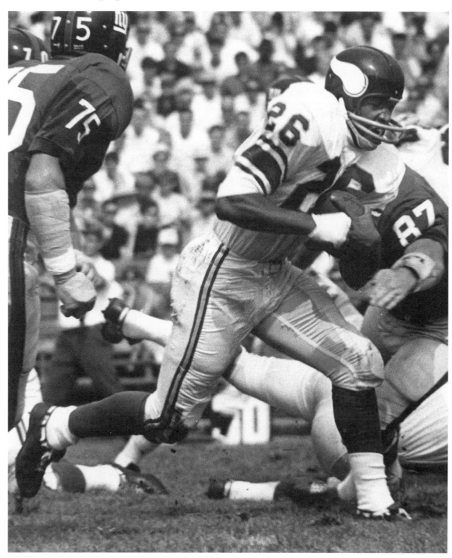

historic comeback by Wisconsin in the Rose Bowl early in the 1960s. His success in the NFL was limited, though, and Finks and Grant were both educated Kapp-watchers from their days in Canadian football. Joe did nothing momentous in 1967 except to arouse the puzzlement of Viking fans, who couldn't imagine what was all the urgency about getting Joe Kapp through customs to win three games.

What they didn't see was one of pro football's more remarkable collections of athletes evolving.

The process was sped by Tarkenton's departure. In the next three years, this is what Finks' trade with the New York Giants produced for the Minnesota Vikings:

Clint Jones, one of Michigan State's best running backs of the decade, was drafted in the first round in 1967. Although not part of the Tarkenton trade, with him from Michigan State came receiver Gene Washington, also a first-round choice.

Bobby Grim, a receiver from Oregon State, was drafted in the second round in 1967.

Ron Yary, who would become a habitual all-pro offensive tackle, was drafted in the second round of 1968.

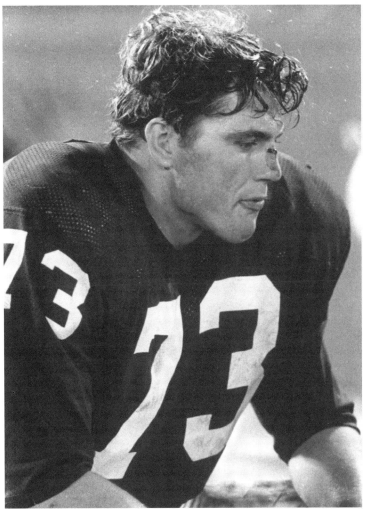

One more harvest from the Tarkenton trade to New York was Bob Grim (above) who caught passes and ran back punts. He was one of those available people who are invaluable in a business where depth of talent is critical. But the biggest coup of that trade was Ron Yary (left) from USC, drafted on the first-round in 1968. He played for 15 seasons as an offensive tackle, tall, powerful and moody. Every play was a private war for Ron Yary. Most of them he won.

Ed White, who for years would be an all-pro offensive guard, was drafted in the first round in 1969.

In the midst of the bonanza from the Tarkenton trade, Finks and his drafting accomplices acquired one more first-round draft choice in 1967 in a deal with the Rams. They traded Tommy Mason, the running back so valuable in the Vikings' early struggles, and the temperamental receiver, Hal Bedsole. When it came time to translate the trade into a first-round draft choice, the Vikings decided that the All-America from Notre Dame, Alan Page, might find a place in the National Football League.

By then they had also acquired Gary Larsen, the ex-Marine from Minnesota and Concordia in Moorhead who had begun life as a pro

The arrival of Alan Page (crunching a quarterback above) from Notre Dame in 1967 completed the ensemble for what became one of the storied defensive lines in pro football history, the Purple People Eaters, or the Purple Gang. Minnesota native Gary Larsen (right) had come to the Vikings two years earlier in a trade with the Los Angeles Rams for the rights to receiver Jack Snow. He was a stereotypical Norseman, big, powerful, blonde and ready to pillage all available quarterbacks.

with the Rams. Larsen came to the Vikings in a trade for a first-round draft choice, Notre Dame's Jack Snow, who preferred to catch passes near the California beaches rather than dodging the Met Stadium icicles. This meant that by 1967 the Viking roster included Jim Marshall, Carl Eller, Alan Page and Gary Larsen, a.k.a. the Purple People Eaters, the team's defensive line. In 1967 they had drafted a defensive back from South Carolina named Bobby Bryant and in 1968 they drafted another from Texas-El Paso, Charlie

West. Their draft harvest in 1967 and 1968 also included a tight end from California, John Beasley; a running back from Colorado State, Oscar Reed; and a quarterback from Pacific, Bobby Lee.

Bill Brown and Dave Osborn were already seasoned players. So were linebackers Lonnie Warwick, and defensive backs Ed Sharockman, Earsell Mackbee, Dale Hackbart and Karl Kassulke. Karl was a wild hitter and punt blocker who played defensive back in the finest tradition of the suicide squadrons. Also there were offensive linemen Grady Alderman, one of the originals, Tingelhoff, Milt Sunde, Doug Davis and Jim Vellone, kicker Fred Cox, running back Jim Lindsey and defensive lineman Paul Dickson. In 1968 they brought in linebacker Wally Hilgenberg, quarterback Gary Cuozzo and receiver John Henderson with trades. They also added the scowling leprechaun from Vince Lombardi's staff in Green Bay, Jerry Burns, to run the Viking offense. Grant's coaching staff now filled the circle. It had veteran and compatible people working in a relaxed relationship with Grant and the athletes – Burns coordinating the offense, Bob Hollway the defense, John Michels coaching the offensive line, Jack Patera the defensive line and Buster Mertes the running backs.

With the critical addition of the pass-intercepting safety, Paul Krause,

The Revolutionaries – a.k.a. the Purple People Eaters. Down the line, from left, Marshall, Page, Larsen and Eller. In the same way that cavalry changed open field warfare centuries ago, the speed and mobility of Marshall, Page and Eller changed line play in pro football. Man on man blocking, at least against the Vikings, was usually futile. Marshall, Page and Eller were too quick for that. Opponents had to double on them or block in zones. Larsen's heft and durability, laying back, watching for delayed line smashes, opened the gates for the other three to mount their assaults on the quarterback.

this was the team that reached the Super Bowl in the 1969 season. That was just two years after Grant heard the subdued whistles of the Mickey Mouse Song, sounded mischievously by some unknown ballplayer as a commentary on Grant's rules.

From the safe distance of years later, the unknown whistler was revealed to be Jim Marshall, who became Bud Grant's all-time favorite football player.

In the late 1960s, he was a reclamation project. Although he'd been a pro football regular for years, Marshall's spectacular quickness and his leadership abilities had not been fully harnessed. For one thing, Jim believed in juggling his agendas. Football was one. Partying was another. Walking around with enough gunnery to outfit a Marine patrol was another. His fantasies were one more. Jim's romance was adventure. He parachuted.

Oscar Reed's (above) dependable work in the Viking backfield alternating with Bill Brown, Dave Osborn and Clint Jones gave the Vikings major league running when they needed it.

Bobby Bryant (right) looked fragile, as though the pro monsters could break him in two. But in the 14 years he played defensive back, he was one of the most valuable of all Vikings. Four times he led the team in pass interceptions. For his career, he picked off 51, including eight in 1969.

He dabbled in Oriental philosophy. He envisioned mountain climbs and deep sea adventures. Between those times he accidentally shot himself and almost died in a January blizzard when the snowmobile party he and Paul Dickson joined was marooned on a savage night in the mountains of Montana east of Yellowstone. If a pro football player were destined to pick up a 49er fumble in Kezar Stadium in San Francisco in 1964 and run it 66

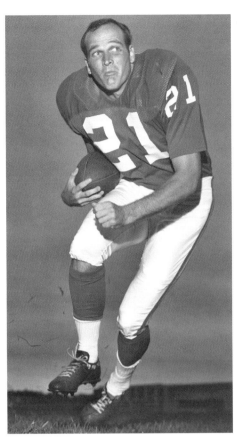

yards into the wrong end zone, the man would be Jim Marshall by the acclamation of fate.

He did it, and the humiliation of it nearly destroyed him, until his bouncing nature saved him and he rolled with all of the horse laughs and lampoonery. He did remember that awful moment in the end zone when the gyrations of the Vikings on the sidelines suddenly made sense. They were leaping and waving their arms as he ran past them en route to the goal line. For some loony reason, a few of them were pointing in the other direction. He paid no heed. Jim Marshall was running wide open and in gulping strides, and he was going to get six.

He got two, for the other guys.

Bruce Bosley, a 49er lineman, was the first to break the news by putting his arm around him. Thanks, buddy. You ran into your own end zone. It's a safety. Nobody bothered examining the circumstances later on, how the fumble happened in the middle of a mixed-up play involving changes of direction. And if you looked at it that way, Jim Marshall's wrong-way run could be excused. The Vikings didn't have any trouble excusing it. They won the game 27-22. Grant never thought about it. He wasn't the coach when it happened. And Marshall the Unhinged Spirit represented a huge resource.

"The first thing I did was to ask him to let me keep the guns while he was in training camp," Grant remembers. "He didn't think that was such a hot

Nobody from the Pro Bowl came calling on Jim Lindsey (left). He was one of those running backs who tended to be obscured by the stars. But he stepped up when the stars went down, or out.

Teammates called him Hackie. Dale Hackbart, defensive back (49). He was an untamed one, Hackie. He was tall, bony and belligerent, an uncommon resume for a college quarterback. For a couple of years he specialized in unnecessary roughness and hitting out of bounds. Grant talked to him. Then he benched him. The second strategy worked better. Hackie reformed, almost.

idea, but he did. He did his partying after games, but he cooled it after a while and he got himself under control. He was a football player who was just out of this world in what he contributed to his team. His skills were only part of it. He had speed and instincts. A lot of players have that. What he had that nobody I've ever seen could equal was a quality a lot of fans don't think about. He just refused to go down with an injury. He got hurt a lot. But it was almost as though there was something different about how he was put together, his physique. He'd get his leg twisted under a pile, really bad. But it never broke. He never pulled muscles so bad they took him out of the game. It was eerie. When he got cut, he didn't seem to bleed as much as most players."

The bionic pass-rusher?

"If you coached him, you had the feeling that he almost willed himself to keep those injuries to a level where Fred (Fred Zamberletti, the Vikings' trainer from the beginning of time) could handle them and he didn't have to go into the hospital. Playing on Sunday was a bigger deal for Jim Marshall than anybody I ever met. He loved the game and it was his identity. There's a danger in that. What happens when you can't play anymore? Every pro athlete has to deal with that in his own way, and some of them never do it. Jim just decided someplace that he was going to play forever, and he almost did. Think about it. Twenty years in pro ball, the highest level, playing defensive end, exposed all those years to big bodies hitting you on every play. We went through so many years and so much football together. I'll say this. We use love a lot. But if it's possible for a man to love another man, that's the feeling I have for Jim Marshall."

The numbers were only part of that, but they were pretty astounding numbers – 270 consecutive games played for the Vikings after his apprenticeship with the Browns, 270 games started, 19 seasons, 1961 to 1979. By football standards, that's a millennium.

Practice, though, was literally another ball game for Jim Marshall. As the years lengthened, Grant and Marshall developed an understanding about practice. Everything being

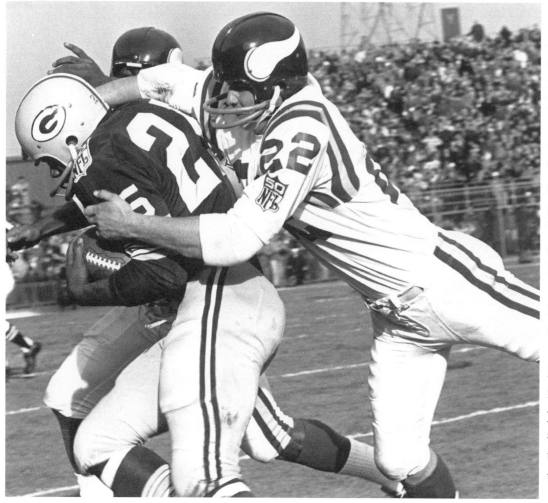

The rap on Paul Krause over the years was that he wasn't overzealous about sacrificing his body as a defensive back. First of all, why should he? They paid him to intercept passes. He did it at a level never equalled in the NFL. He also, incidentally, made tackles when required, including this one against the Packers.

PURPLE HEARTS AND GOLDEN MEMORIES

equal, they decided, it was a good idea for Marshall to be out there when the Vikings put in their defense for the next game. It was also a good idea for him to go through the drills. But Marshall very often sounded and looked like a victim of bubonic plague in the middle of the week. He wretched and gagged and coughed and his temperature crept past 100. Grant routinely assigned him to locker room duty and Marshall spent the next couple of hours in meditation in the sauna.

"How's his temperature?" Grant would ask Zamberletti.

"It's up to 103."

Grant nodded with approval. "Good. He'll play a helluva game Sunday, 103 and all."

He did, every time.

By then Jim Marshall knew Bud Grant, stares, quirks, schemes and all, and so did most of his players. Quirks and schemes? Oh, sure, he had them. He had also had some streaks of mischief along with a mean memory that demanded a moment of settling-up when somebody crossed Bud Grant. But the fans in those icebox seats never saw him up close. And it wasn't because those ski masks gave them a narrow field of vision.

Grant's persona on the football field was the one everybody always saw in November, the scene now graven in nostalgia for thousands who sat there in the dumpy old Met and millions pigging out on chips and beer in the living room. Grant is standing mummified on the sideline, vagrant snowflakes falling on his billed cap and his earphones. He doesn't move an eyebrow. Around him, there is a strange ballet going on. His players are jumping up and down with their hands hooked around their belts, tucked inside their pants. Their eyes are glazed and they are staring covetously down the sideline to the Rams' bench. There, blowtorch sounds can be heard from stacks of hot-air blowers. The roar overpowers the slow thumping of the stadium fans, who also are jumping up and down in their snowmobile suits. Rams' players congregate around the blowers, grasping for a shaft of warmth in a tableau of Darwinian survival. But Grant is oblivious. He hasn't moved for 10 minutes. Chuck

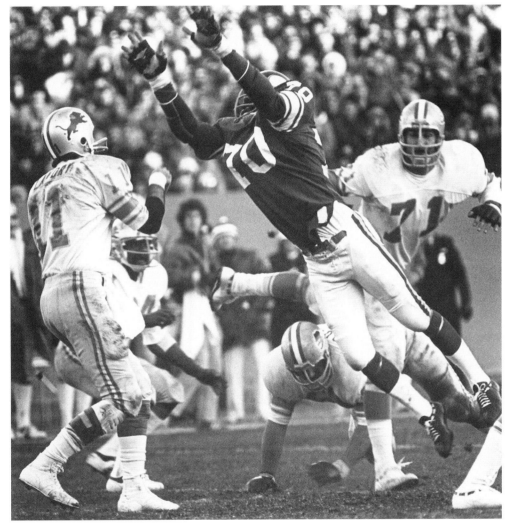

Jim Marshall's war cry for the Purple People Eaters defensive line was "let's meet at the quarterback." They didn't all get there at once. They didn't always sack the quarterback. But when Marshall threw that panther frame into the quarterback's eyes, the ball tended to fly out of there in a hurry, sometimes into the fifth row.

Marshall grabs a breath between plays. They didn't play "situational defense" in those days. Marshall played every down healthy or sick. He did it for 20 years.

Foreman pounds into the end zone. Grant doesn't move. The Vikings win. Grant removes his headset. That is his version of a celebration. Nobody on the Viking bench yells and screams. They all run across the field with their hands in their belts and throw themselves in the hot showers.

How much of this version of Grant was really to be believed? Someone asked him about that not long after the Hall of Fame of 1994.

"Well, it wasn't an act, if that's what you mean. I couldn't coach stalking back and forth and blabbering. If I looked intense, it's because I was. I didn't mind the blabbering around me. I had to get something out of that. Burnsie was going a mile a minute from the coach's booth. He called the plays and swore a blue streak. Between that and the action on the field and all the rest, I just wanted to be free to make good decisions. That means I wasn't going to get into all of that ranting and yakking some coaches do. I didn't say they shouldn't. A coach does what he thinks is right for him. My style was just to screen out everything that didn't matter. All I took in was what I needed to stay in touch with what the players were doing, how they were doing it, and what we ought to be giving them.

"People get hung up on coaching philosophy. To me, a coach's philosophy is pretty well summed up in the coach's personality. It's how you approach the job of coaching with the nature you have, and then let that nature work for you. In his way, Van Brocklin was an outstanding coach with all of his temper and badgering. I think he got practically all of the mileage out of his teams that he could. Of course, with that kind of nature, a guy can self-destruct as a coach. Vince Lombardi was an absolute tyrant. He's eulogized now by most of his players and there's no question he was a great football coach. But people who were the closest to him still have a hard time making Vince the football saint we see today. He was ruthless about getting what he wanted on the football field."

The description, of course, might just as well be applied to Bud Grant and to Denny Green, for that matter, or to any coach with a truly disciplined mind for winning. The difference is in how that ruthlessness is applied, particularly in the tough decisions on personnel. Grant did it quietly and surgically. Lombardi did it like Napoleon. Green does it like an amiable but corporate CEO, breezy and talkative but a gut-fighter inside.

What links successful coaches?

"The first thing is competitiveness," Grant said. "I think the most competitive people in sports are the ones who become coaches. They have to be. You can make money in coaching today, but think of another job less secure. You're at the mercy of the fans, players, the writers and broadcasters, the talk show characters, owners and a ball that bounces crazy. My way of being competitive was to stay disciplined. I think the best thing I did as a coach was to observe. On the practice field I did it all the time. I didn't mean putting players under a microscope or making them feel uncomfortable. But I did keep my eyes open. I could tell if a player was trying to cover up a limp. I got to know the players psychologically. I could tell you by his body language if some guy had a fight with his wife.

"I wasn't fascinated by the psychology. I wanted to win. People asked me what makes a winner. Wanting it is only part of that. Using everything in your head and body to do it is the other part. But both as a player and coach, I'd do anything I could, anything that was allowable. I could outlast you. If you wanted to scrap, I think I could outfight you. If you wanted to play dirty, I'd do it any way you wanted, but I'd beat you. That was my attitude. I didn't project that. I didn't want to. If I had to show you how much I wanted to win, it got in the way of winning. So why show it?"

Was that impassivity something he learned playing football under that monument to grimness and emotional isolation, Bernie Bierman of the University of Minnesota?

"I'd be the last guy to give you that theory. I did play under some coaches who were known as great men in their field, or were at least

Grant sometimes smiled – usually when he got a new fishing rod.

pretty famous. People like Bernie, Paul Brown when I was at the Great Lakes naval station, Allie Sherman and Dave MacMillan, the Minnesota basketball coach. But whether it was under them or somebody else, most of the valuable things I learned were the things I didn't want to do if I ever coached. I mean they all taught. Most of them were smart and made me a better player, although some of them taught me indirectly by showing me how not to coach. No matter how good they were, sometimes they'd

do something I knew was self-defeating: how they approached this player or that, how they talked, how they organized, how they prepared. I'd tell myself: 'You can't coach it this way. It's not going to work.' I remembered that. And I didn't repeat the mistake. If successful coaching is partly avoiding mistakes, I had a pretty good book of what to avoid."

So it might not have been altogether shocking that in his second season as the Viking coach, in December of 1968, Grant brought his team into Philadelphia for the final game of the season with a chance to win the Central Division championship. It should be even less shocking that they won, 24-17. Mathematicians weren't especially impressed. The Vikings won eight games and lost six. Mathematicians don't give game balls and live and die with each other on frozen football fields. "We can beat the Colts," Joe Kapp said. Joe's picture of paradise was a bunch of grunts, of whom he was the grunt-quarterback, busting into the Super Bowl together, yelling and stomping with blood on their pants and a quarterback who occasionally threw a spiral.

He threw well in the playoff game with the Colts, the team destined to become an infamous part of the history of the old-guard NFL in its rivalries with the new American

Behind Dave Osborn's blocking, Joe Kapp, the roughneck, drops back to throw. Note the single bar face mask. Joe thought even that was excessive. Helmets he tolerated. (Photo credit: Herb Weitman/NFL Photos)

Someplace beneath Alan Page (88) and Jim Marshall (70) a quarterback sags into oblivion. It could have been worse. Eller might have joined the mayhem.

PURPLE HEARTS AND GOLDEN MEMORIES

Football League. By 1968 the leagues were merging, but they were now Super Bowl rivals. The Colts were Establishment. John Unitas, Don Shula and selected immortals. None of it fazed one Joe Namath and the New York Jets in the Super Bowl of January 1969. But a month before, the Colts were more than Kapp's Grunts could handle. The Colts hammered them in the mud 24-14, but Joe was substantially heroic. He threw 44 times and completed 26. His lumps mounted with the tempos of the Baltimore rush as the game ran down. But Joe played it to the end like a battered heavyweight, slugging, refusing the hand of a Colt lineman who wanted to pull him out of the mire. He even refused the consolation of his coach afterward. Joe sat there with muck clots on his face and blood seeping out of his cuts. Grant thought he could have beaten any other team that day.

The trouble with that, Joe mumbled, was that they weren't playing any other team.

There just weren't many heroic ways they could finish their first Central Division championship season. After the Colts, they played in a game between playoff losers in Miami, and lost to Dallas, 17-13.

Yet they were now plainly a maturing and contending football team. They didn't expect what happened in the opening game of 1969 against the New York Giants. What made it all the more grievous was the quality of the opponent. The New York Giants of 1969 were mild-mannered and essentially inept. At one stage they were capable of losing seven straight. They did have one uncommon asset, a quarterback with a harried look but an inventive brain. He also had evasive feet and, on this particular day in Yankee Stadium, the most tenacious guardian angel on God's green earth.

Skinny cornerbacks aren't supposed to make open field tackles. That news never quite reached Bobby Bryant.

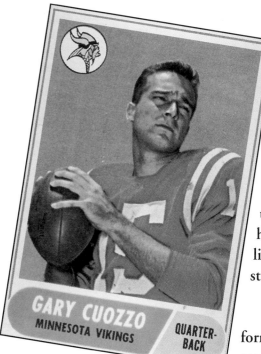

GARY CUOZZO
MINNESOTA VIKINGS
QUARTER-BACK

Gary Cuozzo threw with precision. He was never great (except the day he threw five touchdown passes for Baltimore against the Vikings). But when he played, he did it with brains and toughness.

Page and Eller (right) break through the offensive line. Eller was ungainly and some days unblockable. Page was nimble and almost always unblockable.

There's no other explanation for what happened. The Vikings loosed the Purple Gang on their old playmate, Francis Tarkenton, and for most of the afternoon it was the lions headup on the Christians. In the 1970s the defensive line of Carl Eller, Jim Marshall, Alan Page and Gary Larsen would be known as one of the most disruptive in pro football. This was the Purple Gang's formal coming-out. Afterwards Tarkenton admitted that for most of the game he considered it a moral victory when he was able to complete a hand-off before the avalanche flattened him. When he passed, he usually did it in a flight of total panic. When that wasn't available, he did it falling down or escaping decapitation. The Giants' offensive line offered hope and prayers but no serious resistance to the Viking stampede.

Tarkenton later confided:

"If I wanted to get a pass off, I'd tell Greg Larson at center (the former University of Minnesota Rose Bowl star) to double up with the guard on Page. I'd double on Marshall with the left tackle and fullback. Against Eller I told the tight end to stay in and block with the right tackle. That meant I was doubling on everybody on their defensive line except Gary Larsen, who almost always stayed back looking for draws. So I never sent more than three people out on pass plays, a back and the two wideouts. That's all we had downfield and the Vikings were sitting back there with four defensive backs, including guys like Krause and Kassulke and Bobby Bryant, and we assigned six people to block three of their defensive linemen. I never saw a more clear confession on a football field in my life. We were saying 'you got us surrounded. We need pure luck to

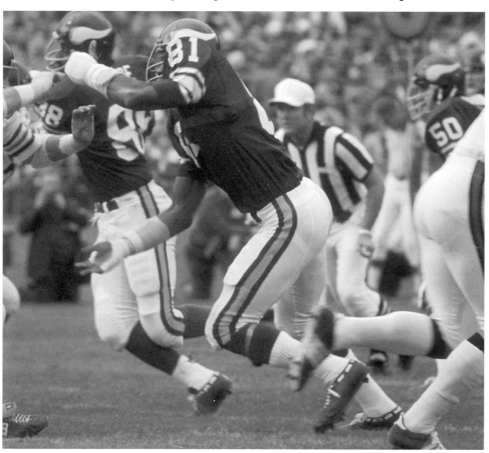

beat you.'"

It materialized.

With six minutes of the game remaining, the Vikings led by 13 points, a modest figure that was a minor marvel in itself. Tarkenton remembers: "We were in some ridiculous third-and-17 situation on our own 43, something like that. While I was going through my cadence behind Larson I glanced at Eller and I nearly fainted. He was pawing the ground and practically snorting. If he ever got through he was going to tear my head off. Good old Carl, my ex-teammate. Right there I thought, 'My daddy was right, I should have entered the seminary.'"

Larson snapped the ball and the chase was on. Tarkenton rolled one way and then the other. When he got near the sideline and the monsters were upon him, he planted his feet and threw. Eller insisted later that the way Tarkenton was located on the field and with the Viking bodies where they were, it had to be impossible for Tarkenton to see a receiver downfield.

"Eller was right," Tarkenton said. "I didn't. All I saw was the stadium seats past the end zone. I just threw the ball as far as I could toward the goal line. That's all I did, and I'll tell you why: I was scared to death of Eller. I figured if I got rid of the ball, he'd probably have to stop."

Tarkenton threw and Eller did stop. The ball came down 55 yards downfield near the goal line. No Giant was in a position to catch it. Two Viking defensive backs, the closest to the ball, both knocked it down. It was perfect pass defense. Before the ball hit the ground, however, it landed

Anybody care for some privacy? The textbook says when you hit the line, put two hands on the ball, keep your legs driving and watch for land mines. Dave Osborn is the guy on top, two hands on the ball and legs working. In that mess, he didn't get much. But he managed to avoid land mines.

on the exposed chest of a Giant receiver, Butch Wilson, lying flat on the ground. Pleasantly surprised, Wilson welcomed the ball and put his arm on it before it rolled off his chest. The Giants were stirred by this outbreak of offensive brilliance and scored on a Tarkenton pass a couple of plays later. When the baffled Vikings fumbled after the kickoff, the Giants went in for another touchdown in the last minute and won the game 24-23.

Sorting through the mess the next day, Grant and his coaches decided none of wacky events were particularly the fault of their chosen quarterback for the day, Gary Cuozzo. Cuozzo had come to the Vikings from New Orleans for two first-round draft choices. It was

Above: Grant always ranked stability close to godliness. He might have made it a dead heat. He usually had it on his coaching staff, in this case (from left) Jerry Burns, Neill Armstrong, Bob Hollway, Jack Patera, John Michels and Buster Mertes.

Right: Kapp winds up to throw. It was always an adventure, for both sides. (Photo credit: Malcolm Emmons/NFL Photos)

assumed that his steady skills and craftsman's style would probably be more suitable for Grant's football than Kapp's lusty, Three Musketeers' bravado. Cuozzo's toughness wasn't in question. He'd led a long touchdown drive against the Lions in 1968, playing with what was later diagnosed as a broken collarbone. He was more impressive than Joe in the 1969 exhibitions, and became the starting quarterback for opening day against the

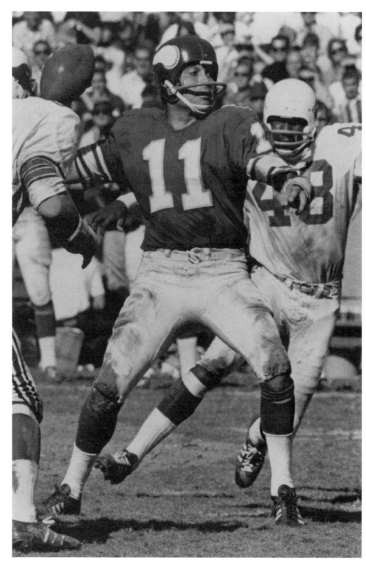

Giants. So the oddball loss to the Giants couldn't be laid at Cuozzo's hand. But Joe Kapp started the next week against the Baltimore Colts in Metropolitan Stadium. With the possible exception of Don Quixote, nobody with roots in Spain had the kind of day that Joe Kapp had against the Baltimore Colts in September of 1969. The Colts came with their NFC championship of the previous year and with the predicted gang assaults on the heavy-footed quarterback they had plastered in the mud in the playoffs in Baltimore a year before. They never got there.

Kapp was throwing. People were catching. The others were blocking and suddenly the crowd started going nuts. No one, not Tarkenton, not John Unitas, not Norm Van Brocklin, had ever thrown more touchdown passes in one game than Joe Kapp of the Minnesota Vikings with his beer bottle scar.

He threw seven.

He threw one to Dave Osborn, two to Gene Washington, to Bobby Grim, to Kent Kramer, to John Beasley and to Jim Lindsey. When it was over there was a serious question about who were the neediest candidates for an asylum, the statisticians or the Colts. Remember, this was the team that was supposed to begin and end the day with defense, with the rampages of the Purple Gang on the line of scrimmage and the piracy of Bobby Bryant, Paul Krause, Earsell Mackbee and their confederates in the secondary.

Would you expect a football team with Joe Kapp passing and Bill Brown and Dave Osborn running to score 50 points three times in 14 games? Those gate-crashers?

The same. They actually only needed ten weeks. It was 52-14 over the Colts, 51-3 over the Browns and 52-14 over the Steelers. The gate-crashers on some days were almost incidental. The team had

Gene Washington (left) was one of those slick and controlled receivers who ran tight patterns – and scared the trousers off cornerbacks who had to cover him one-on-one.

Karl Kassulke (below) played full throttle every play and reveled in it. A lot of players compared pro football to war. For Karl, every play was a celebration. (Photo credit: George Gojkovich/NFL Photos)

disciplined power on the offensive line, Washington and John Henderson roaming deep or slicing through the secondary for Kapp's passes. It had a defense that accounted for almost as many points as the offense, either by getting into the end zone itself or strangling their opponents into futility. The team was stable, all right, but some days it played like a wild hare. It gave you sound reliability in Grant and in its offensive line. The offense played with sure hands in the close games. But this was also a team of uncorked characters like Kapp, Lonnie Warwick, Dale Hackbart, Karl Kassulke, Marshall and Mackbee. In one game, in a snowstorm against the Lions, these people played as though they had just been let out for recess. The culminating play was a gleeful romp downfield after a fumble recovery, Page and Marshall lateralling to each other in full gallop in the falling snow.

They won 12 in a row between their opening loss to the Giants and a 10-3 defeat by Norm Van Brocklin's Atlanta Falcons in a monsoon in Atlanta. If the Dutchman felt any special elation beating his old stiffs – the name he invariably gave them when they lost – he made no production of it. The game was played in a slop with no special enthusiasm by either side. In the post-game press conference, Van Brocklin offered some compliments to his punter, made a few other joyless remarks and ended the discussion quickly. He and Grant had enjoyed a cordial relationship in the early 1960s when Grant came down from Winnipeg between games and asked to look at some of the Viking films. Van Brocklin made them available courteously. "Then one day in the mid-1960s I was doing that," Grant said, "and Dutch came into the film room. He just exploded. He wanted to know what the hell I was doing hanging around. He swore and carried on, and I had no idea what provoked it."

Yet when the Vikings reached the Super Bowl at the end of the 1969 season, Van Brocklin sent a message of congratulations to Grant and his old team.

En route to the Super Bowl, they nearly blew themselves out of it in the first playoff game. If they had, it would have been a pretty grotesque anticlimax to Joe Kapp's speech. The speech took place at an awards banquet following the regular season. The banquet sponsors asked Joe to come up to accept the Most Valuable Player award.

Joe was the guy who always signed autographs the same way when somebody pushed a photo or a scrap of paper in front of him. "Best wishes from ALL of the Vikings," he'd write, and then sign his name. Some folks might snicker at a gesture like that and call it hangover from the Frank Merriwell days, when heroes were fairy tale characters ready to give life, limb and the keys to the Model T for the benefit of the team.

Kapp wasn't that kind of Boys Life hero. On days off, he bar-hopped and roughhoused. But when he played, The Team First was Joe's religion.

He walked to the podium that night and turned down the Most Valuable Player award. He explained why. The Vikings, he said, were a team of 40 players, a different kind of team because he didn't see any selfishness on this team. He was the quarterback, but he was one of 40 guys. It was an award, he said, that shouldn't be accepted by one player. There wasn't any most valuable player. There wasn't any Santa Claus, either, and no red-nosed reindeer. If the red-nosed reindeer is a myth, he was saying, so is the most valuable player.

What looked like a myth on a Saturday afternoon in December was the Vikings' prospect of reaching the Super Bowl. The Rams came into Metropolitan Stadium with Merlin Olsen, Deacon Jones, Roman Gabriel and a quality supporting cast marshaled by George Allen, the relentless schemer. George looked on the game confidently until he found out to his horror that his players were going to be sequestered in a Bloomington motel on Christmas Eve, two days before the game. George flung himself into a hysteria of worry. He was afraid that a Christmas Eve away from children and their families would plow the Rams into depression. He asked the Rams' public relations man what he could do to line up some kids to make the evening more familial. The PR man contacted a Minneapolis journalist, who contacted the management of a boys' home. On Christmas Eve, a half dozen homeless kids were enjoying the holiday with professional football players, who hugged them and gave them presents galore. Everybody in the room was having a great time except George Allen, who had discovered a small crisis in the Rams' game plan and spent Christmas Eve doing Xs and Os on a tablecloth while the carols rang around him.

For two quarters, whatever revisions George made worked. The day was chilly, but it was bearable for the California sunbathers and they looked unstoppable. The score was 17-7 for the Rams at halftime and Grant and his staff did the usual technical talk about adjustments. When they were about finished, the shaking began.

"It was the fans in the stadium," Grant remembers. "They began stomping and yelling a few minutes before we came out for the second half. We'd played a pretty mediocre first half, but they were trying to tell us they were in it with us. They were saying the Vikings were their team, and they believed. You know, the stadium was a little decrepit even then and you could feel the walls rattling. The noise was that big. And then when we ran out there it all broke loose. I've never

Quarterbacks have always believed the Geneva rules of humane warfare should protect them against being publicly garroted. Wally Hilgenberg never traveled to Geneva. His tackle here may not have been humane, but it did stop the hostilities.

had much trouble keeping under control. But that roar and togetherness was so great, the unity of the fans with the team, that it just lifted you off the ground. Almost literally. I've never ever experienced a moment like that in all my years in athletics."

On their first defensive series of the second half, the Vikings stopped the Rams. The offensive line started hitting hard. Kapp got the offense together. "Get me that seed," he screamed to the defense. Marshall, Eller, Page and Larsen hounded Gabriel. The Vikings started scoring and Kapp nearly brought the upper deck down by scoring from the two-yard line to give the Vikings a 21-20 lead. And in the final minutes, Eller crashed into the end zone to tackle Gabriel for a safety, and the Vikings won 23-20. A week later they crushed the Cleveland Browns 27-7 to win the National Football League championship and head for the Super Bowl against Kansas City.

Oscar Reed, put that ball away before the bad guys eat it!

In the locker room, they uncrated champagne after the Cleveland game. From one corner, Carl Eller bellowed across the room through the chaotic tinsel of discarded tape and jock straps hanging from the lockers.

He waved a bottle of champagne, clamped in a grimy hand. Years later, out of football and freed from his dependency, he would not wave a bottle of champagne, anywhere, anytime. But this was National Football League championship in January of 1970, and the open door to the Super Bowl. Eller called to Joe Kapp, who was pouring two bottles simultaneously, one on the head of Bill Brown and the other on Oscar Reed. This was the Joe Kapp who, during the game, had run out of the pocket on a pass play. The Browns' linebacker, Jim Houston, came up to tackle him. Kapp did not slide. He didn't head for the sideline. He headed straight for Houston and tried to hurdle him. Joe could never have made it in track. His knees got no further than Houston's helmet, which was a source of regret for the Cleveland linebacker. The collision knocked him out of the game.

"Hey, Moose," Kapp yelled in the locker room. "You're the man."

Eller lifted the champagne a little higher.

"Joe," he said. "You got soul, Joe. You're my brother."

He was, and at that moment, so were most of the people in that room, mud thawing on their skins, tape wrapped around their chests, blood on their jerseys.

It was a kind of grubby, rowdy sanctum for men who played football. They were people who bled and cried together and sacrificed for each other, and it took them hours to leave.

And a week later, they were in shock.

Las Vegas said they were going to beat the Kansas City Chiefs of the American Football League by two touchdowns. The spread made some sense. The Vikings were clearly the class of the older and more prestigious league, and never mind Baltimore's loss to Joe Namath and the Jets. Kansas City barely escaped the playoffs. The Chiefs came into the Super Bowl with Lenny Dawson and Mike Garrett and Buck Buchanan and Willie Lanier and Bobby Bell, but the Vikings probably had more stars and they had the carriage and aura of a winner.

"I think what we did wrong tactically," Alan Page said later, "was to change our defensive schemes to adapt to this 'offense of the 1970s' stuff that Hank Stram kept talking about at Kansas City. It was a waste of time. We took what we'd been doing all year and tinkered and diluted it with things we put in overnight, and it just didn't work." The offense of the 1970s never got much past January of 1970. Stram gushed about moving pockets and man-in-motion variations. During one memorable passage during the game – he was wired with a micro-phone for posterity – he got positively jubilant: "They're running around like a Chinese fire drill." Eller did get hoodwinked on a damaging reverse. But it was the Kansas City ground game that punished the Vikings, that and Jan Stenerud's three straight field goals in the first half. Combined with Garrett's five-yard touchdown run, they built a 16-0 Kansas City lead at halftime. Dave Osborn scored for the Vikings in the third quarter, but Dawson's touchdown pass a few minutes later buried them, 23-7. The last bell sounded when Kapp went out with an injury in the fourth quarter.

Joe never wore the uniform again. He was gone the next year in a con-tract dispute, confirming his gruff assessment of reality vs. fairy tales: There really is no red-nosed rein-deer.

Wally Hilgenberg, though, was less glum about reality and probably better at prophecy: "We'll be back in the Super Bowl," Wally said, "if we have to play until hell freezes over."

Meteorologists might have been sur-prised that this event occurred in just three years.

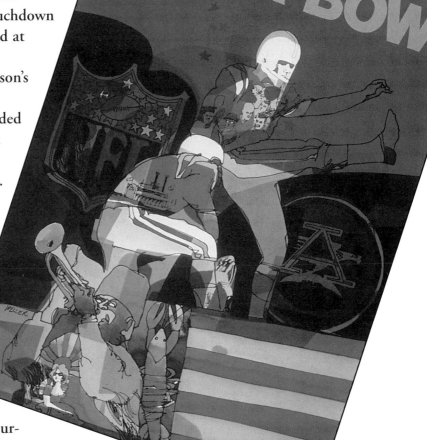

They played the Super Bowl of January, 1970, in New Orleans. Vikings vs. Kansas City. The fans got hot licks in the jazz emporiums and hot toddies on Bourbon Street. The Vikings got hot compresses after the ball game. Kansas City 23, Vikings 7.

Chapter Four

Suds and Shishkabobs for Miles Around

There's a recorded case of a small party of football fans from Warroad, Minnesota, driving 800 miles round-trip in a motor home for a Minnesota Vikings-Philadelphia Eagles game at the Metropolitan Stadium in Bloomington. The distance was not a record. Others have doubled it. What made that Warroaders' voyage notable was the fact that when the game started they never got out of the motor home or the parking lot.

"We had tickets," the captain of the voyage explained. "But we decided to stay in the RV and watch the game on television. We figured it would be more fun in the parking lot. The thing about it, you got a lot sound effects that you couldn't get from TV. We couldn't have been more than 150 feet from the stadium. There was a terrific roar every time the Vikings did something. People laughed when we told them. But what we really came down for was the tailgating at the Met. It was ten big RV rallies put together."

If winning division titles identified the Vikings, if Bud Grant's iron eyes did, or Tarkenton's scrambles or the Purple Gang's assaults on enemy quarterbacks, they had to share space with the Met Stadium tailgate epics.

In fact, the specter of losing those tailgating klatches explained some of the public anger directed against the dome football scheme. The tailgate argument rarely surfaced in the endless hearings that preceded the Metrodome. But the tailgaters represented a large and fanatical community. They fought extinction for years. In the political brawling over moving the Vikings indoors and into the city, their loyalty to their barbecue ovens burned with a steady charcoal flame. They were the shock troops in the resistance movement to stop indoor football. Their revolt gave aid and comfort to the more prominent indictment against dome football, the one about God never intending that football should be played under a roof.

The tailgating passion at Metropolitan Stadium was a triumph of geography and the human instinct to bunch up in times of excitement or thirst. The Met Stadium tailgatings got so notorious that in time they

This is not the tailgate version of the human torch. This is a cook who needs a gas mask. Someplace under that column of smudge are three hamburgers on the edge of incineration. (Photo credit: Star Tribune/Minneapolis-St. Paul)

achieved the status of a social phenomenon. Psychologists were called in to analyze them. One of them decided that tailgating was a modern version of the old circle-the-wagons urge of the frontier. Another one thought it was an extension of the 19th century prairie quilting bee. There was more. Somebody said the Swedes and Norwegians did it. The tailgate was an expanded smorgasbord.

Some of those theories were romantic. None of them had to be taken seriously. The tailgate mania evolved for the same reasons the crowds came when they made a baseball stadium in the cornfields of Iowa. If you build a football arena, and if you lay enough asphalt for the biggest block party in town – enough to accommodate thousands of cars and RVs – they will come.

They came not only on land but by sea. Don McLaughlin, a promoter of fishing tours and adventure travel under the less-than-original pseudonym of Don the Beachcomber, would wheel in a fishing boat to create the most exotic tailgate party in the lot. His was a South Seas motif that included palm trees. McLaughlin didn't have the guts to test his credibility beyond October. Nobody ever heard of a luau in a snowstorm.

For 20 years the tailgaters came. They came with cookers, iceboxes, rotisseries and barbecue spits big enough to roast a cow. They came with vast stores of sausage, burgers, steaks, rolls and grandma's cookies. They added booya, goulash, keggers and cases of Scotch. They came under the heat of the sun, in rainstorms and in driving snow. Somebody figured out that a typical tailgate crowd brought enough food on a given Sunday to feed the first day invasion force on the North African beaches. There

The fierce dragon at the head of the Viking longboat has the well-fed look. He should. Tailgaters in the Met Stadium turned the deck into a buffet. (Photo credit: Star Tribune/Minneapolis-St. Paul)

weren't many rules. The tailgaters were supposed to limit their picnics to the boundaries of their parking stalls. But social customs usually blurred the lot lines. An hour or two before the kickoff it got to be a moveable feast, a Utopia for strolling noshers.

Originality was prized. So was excess. A bunch of Croatians from South St. Paul, celebrating their ethnicity, put on a lamb roast every year before the Green Bay game. It started as a neighborhood party. By the third year the chef had to send out for more lamb because the Croatians from Wisconsin were horning in.

The official entertainment was the Viking band, arrayed in a Nordic longboat, blasting out all registered forms of music from bluegrass to John Phillip Sousa. There was no ordinance, though, against walk-on musicians. Semi-trailer trucks, regulation 18 wheelers, were rented for polka parties before and after the game. Ching Johnson's semi-trailer blowouts were the most popular. Ching hired five musicians to play in what he called the skinniest version of the Prom Ballroom. Most of the partiers eventually found their way into the stadium. Some preferred to dance and stayed in the trailer. A few couldn't find the way.

The most romantic musical interlude in the parking lot, though, occurred on a warm August evening during the exhibition season of 1970. Most of the picnickers showed up in jeans and t-shirts and hauled in the usual armament of Hibachi cookers and footlockers of ice. A young man and woman threaded through the thick fumes on a motorcycle, he wearing a full tuxedo with boutonniere and she in an ankle-length peach gown.

While the munchers looked on, fascinated, the couple drew a folding table out of the motorcycle's baggage rack and then two candelabra.

On the table they placed an immaculate white linen tablecloth. They lit the candles and brought out a bottle of French champagne and two wine glasses of expensive crystal. To these they added a setting of plates with silverware. With great chivalry the young man helped seat the

The dancers called this the Purple Shuffle. If anybody else in the tail-gate crowd knew the steps, they were either bashful or wanted to stick closer to the barbecued ribs. (Photo credit: Star Tribune/ Minneapolis-St. Paul)

PURPLE HEARTS AND GOLDEN MEMORIES

woman in one of two chairs he snagged from the stall next door. They then sat and turned up a cassette player he pulled out of his backpack. He also set out the evening's entree. And there, with the chords of Rachmaninoff's soaring Second Piano Concerto floating in the Hibachi fumes, they looked imperishably into each other's eyes, above the rims of their wine glasses. They then bit off tasteful chunks of Polish sausage held in their free hands.

Never has young love been expressed so tenderly. Or, as a matter of fact, so impatiently. As soon as they polished off the sausage and chugged the champagne, they vanished into the upper deck, barely taking enough time to stash the silverware and crystal. The Rachmaninoff was still playing in the backpack, but the mood was smashed all to bits when the piano concerto collided with the Viking band in the longboat.

Not all love in the parking lot was invoked so privately. The most celebrated social event in the history of Met Stadium tailgating was a wedding in the Kansas City parking lot before a Viking-Packer game. Scores of friends showed up in formal dress. Hundreds of others from neighboring lots, uninvited, crashed the party without resistance. The nuptials united a bartender at Duff's Bar and Lounge in downtown Minneapolis with a beautiful receptionist. A municipal court judge, Scoop Lommen, was hired to legalize the alliance. After a wedding brunch, catered by black tie waiters, the wedding party proceeded into the stadium to watch the football game.

Not included were the bride and groom, who retired to their Winnebago and later announced to friends that they may have been the only newlyweds to have their honeymoon at halftime.

With a few vocal exceptions, the Twin Cities clergy fretted about the tailgating mania. Their objection had nothing much to do with tippling and indulgence. The tailgate's worst offense was the havoc it wreaked on attendance at the late Sunday service and to the collection basket. For years the good shepherds would look out on banks of empty seats at 11 a.m. and silently ask for deliverance. A few devised practical strategies. One of them was the Rev. Arvid (Bud) Dixen, then the pastor of Edina Community Lutheran Church. Dixen advertised a tailgate party of and by members of the congregation. The venue was the church parking lot immediately after the 11 a.m. service. At the cost of enormous personal sacrifice, Rev. Dixen managed to end the service by 11:45 a.m. By holding his sermon to under ten minutes, the Reverend was able to give his flock both theology and a potluck tailgate in time for the 12 noon kickoff. Extension cords from the pastor's study enabled the devout to watch the first half in the parking lot before driving home. It was one of the few tailgate parties of the day where the strongest beverage was apple cider from Lund's.

But the Armageddon in the ministers' silent struggle came on a Christmas Day in 1971, when the Vikings met Dallas in a first-round playoff game at Met Stadium. The NFL subsequently changed its policy and prohibited playoff games on Christmas Sunday. But in 1971 it led

Characters of all shades rolled into the Met Stadium tailgate bashes. Santa Claus came to this one with his personal bell ringer (left). He also managed to drag in the Lone Ranger's bratwurst-loving brother (right). (Photo credit: Star Tribune/Minneapolis- St.Paul)

off with one of the blockbuster games of the year, between teams that were both contenders for the Super Bowl. The game was sold out and on national television. It was a direct collision between an observance of the biggest day of the Christian calendar and the new quasi-religion of millions of American football watchers.

"It's contemptible," a minister said. "But we can't do anything about it."

The Rev. Dick Smith of St. Patrick's Episcopal Church in Bloomington disagreed. "At least most of the people will be in their homes watching the game but surrounded by Christmas," he said. "The people we've got to care for are the season ticket holders who are going to be in the stadium. They get there early. They're probably not going to church. What we ought to try is to give them some kind of on-site service before the ball game."

He proposed the idea to a Minneapolis newspaper columnist, whose friends included Walter Bush, then the chief operating officer of the Minnesota North Star hockey team and the Metropolitan Ice Center. The hockey arena stood a few hundred yards from the football stadium and seated 15,000 people. The journalist offered Bush a rare opportunity. "You have the chance to turn your hockey building into a cathedral for a day. You can score points with the big commissioner in the sky."

Bush agreed, conceding that he was one of those who had to score such points when they were available. So he opened the arena for a non-denominational church service at 11 a.m. All sinners were invited. The service was tasteful and melodious. Smith appeared at center ice in the standard robes and gave a five-minute sermon, taking his text from St. Paul's well-quoted epistle about running the good race. More than 3,000 people attended. *The New York Times* reinforced its game-day reporting staff to cover the service. The *Times* gave the usual coverage to the playoff game but thought the church service in the hockey rink was so sensational it put the story on the front page. Why not? Smith had invited a small vocal group from a Catholic church to lead the congregational singing. It was the first time in nearly 2,000 years of Christianity that the choir sang in the penalty box.

Most tailgaters considered it a point of honor to stretch the parking lot action into December and beyond. The creed was that anybody can tailgate in Bermudas but it takes a practicing zealot to do it in a polar gale. Once the snow flew and the wind-chill dropped to Yukon levels, nobody made a fashion statement at the Met tailgates. There was one basic fashion, the snowmobile suit. It cut across all lines of demographics and blood thickness. The snowmobile suit was quilted and zippered from hood to leggings. Its secondary virtue was that it had unlimited storage space, which could accommodate all supplies from portable radios and TV sets to expedition mittens. The standard footgear was snowmobile boots or Canadian Sorrels. Long winter underwear and two sweaters separated by silk liners were often worn under the snowmobile suits. Full ski masks usually rounded out the ensemble. Special tailgate decals bearing such folk axioms as "Don't Eat the Yellow Snow" enjoyed wide popularity. The ski masks presented special challenges to etiquette buffs. The simple mechanical act of transferring bratwurst from hand to mouth became a major project, especially when the face mask froze.

The Vikings' cheerleaders (left) are always ready to fire up the fans. Some fans (below) don't need to be fired up.

Once the bitter weather set in, most tailgaters were good at maintaining the harmless deceit that they were actually out to get fed in the parking lot. What they were doing was hanging out to stay warm. The car was nearby. Once they got into the stadium, all routes to warmth were cut off. If the sun was out, it wasn't out long. Much of the stadium was in shadow by noon. By midafternoon the sun

had disappeared beyond the big scoreboard. For all of the advertised virtues of the snowmobile suit, the usual method to avoid frostbite was stomping and leg-crossing. That and frequent expeditions to the rest rooms.

The third strategy was dicey. Getting up and inching to the end of the row in a snowsuit and Sorrel boots invariably exposed the incher to hazards. He could spill somebody's beer or go up in flames making contact with a carton of hot coffee. Fist fights sometimes developed. Gallons of beer and coffee, casually spilled on the concrete floors of the stadium concourses, usually froze to form glaciers, dozens of feet long. This meant that if the customers managed to escape from their seats during the action, they often found themselves skating wildly out of control on

Crazy George (above) never misses a beat on game day. He, like the guys below, truly bleeds purple.

their way to the john. Once there, they usually found the restroom bulging with standing room only because half of the stadium had the same idea.

The more disciplined fans were the most successful when winter football struck. One lawyer maintained a spartan diet the day of the game, virtually shutting off all food and drink. "Some people yelled and jumped up and down and carried on the whole game as though they were actually enjoying that miserable weather," he said. "I had season tickets and I'll be damned if I was going to stay home and watch TV. I hated those snowmobile suits. They were big and floppy and made everybody look like a dope, and I refused to wear them. What I did was put on every piece of wool I owned, sweaters, socks, jackets, the works, and when I got into the stadium I slipped into the best sleeping bag money could buy. It was one of those tapered cocoon jobs with sealant and the works. I sat in the seat for practically three hours without moving, except to sip coffee from my thermos, and I did that carefully because no way was I going to fight 10,000 desperate guys to get to the men's room."

They asked him years later if he looked on the comforts of dome football as his liberation.

He said hell, no. He said it was the football fan's inalienable right to be miserable at the ball game.

They could have used that as the old Met's epitaph.

The ultimate gate crasher, Hub Meeds, walked past the guards during Super Bowl IV in full dress and they figured he was part of the team. He was immediately asked to be the Vikings mascot and did so from 1969 to 1989. Hub was the epitome of the Vikings spirit.

A Future Judge Makes a Case

They threw the flag on Alan Page on consecutive plays. It happened early in a game with the Detroit Lions in 1971, and the formal indictment was "encroachment," also known as offsides. Page never believed it and the ensuing two hours became historic.

The ultimate victims of those two offsides calls were not the Minnesota Viking defense or Alan Page's personal stats but the somewhat innocent Detroit Lions. The Lions never relished playing the Vikings in the 1970s. They lost endlessly and a large part of their misery was tied to their futile attempts to deal with Alan Page. But it was one thing to face Page when he was playing as a normal, all-pro defensive tackle. It was quite another to face Page when he was driven to wrath and destruction.

One of the stricken Lions said after the game: "Watching Page, I kept thinking about the old Four Horsemen of Notre Dame (where, coincidentally, Page played his college football). What was all that bad stuff in the Bible they were named after?"

Pestilence, famine, things like that.

"That's right. They got a fifth horseman now. They could call this guy murder. We couldn't block him. He played like we weren't even there. He was unreal."

He was also en route to a lineman's season of a lifetime in the National Football League, climaxing with the Most Valuable Player award they gave him when it was over. It was the first ever to a lineman.

The Detroit game produced Page converts in droves. Page's hair-trigger reaction time and his instincts sent him charging into rival backfields faster than any lineman of his time. Officials generally understood that when Page was moving, and everybody else appeared to be standing still or squatting still, it didn't mean Page was offside. It usually meant that the center snapped the ball, Page was a blur, and he was also legal. Occasionally, though, they dropped the flag.

When they did, Page thrashed his arms and yelled about the injustice. Sometimes he would stomp around.

They dropped the flag once in the Detroit game. He waved his arms and demanded justice.

On the next play they dropped it again. Page went amuck. He roared and stomped and denounced his persecutors. Grant removed him from the game momentarily, allegedly to calm his raging lineman, but actually to save innocent lives.

When Page got back into action, he destroyed the Lions. He did it in the heat of passion and without serious resistance. He hounded the quarterback and chased halfbacks from sideline to sideline. He caused

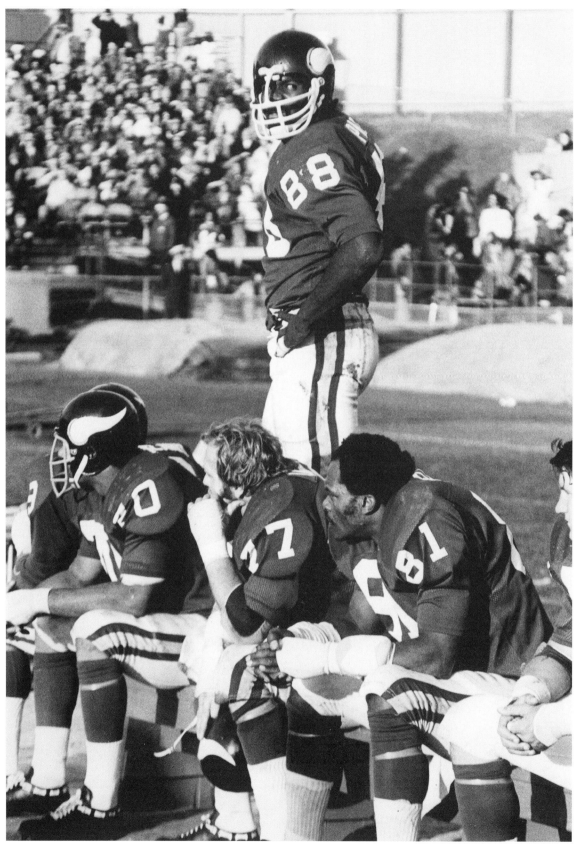

fumbles and wrecked the Lions' passing game. In most games, when the offense has to punt, it's considered a tactical surrender. In this game, it was an act of mercy. It permitted the Lions' offense to escape and got Page off the field. Rival coaches who saw the game on film later called it an open-and-shut case of one lineman dictating the flow of a game all by himself.

With due tribute to Fran Tarkenton's stunning numbers and his impact on the Viking franchise, Page may have been the team's most extraordinary personality and player. He played beside two authentic superstars and vivid characters, Jim Marshall and Carl Eller. The fourth member of their defensive line during their best years, Gary Larsen, was unavoidably obscured by those three. Larsen was nonetheless a quality player who completed a defensive line that became historic in pro football. In the early `70s, it was unmatched in the National Football League. The battle in the pro football front lines in those years was still fundamentally man-against-man. The defensive end went head-on against the offensive tackle, the defensive tackle against the offensive guard. Page, Marshall and Eller were among the first to force major tactical changes. Almost no offensive lineman could handle them singly. That dictated double-team blocking and changes in the passing schemes. The net effect was that in most of the Viking games of the early 1970s, it was the Minnesota defense and not the opposing offense that was on the attack.

Eller had a kind of ungainly menace about him when he came on the pass rush. He was all arms and legs and terribly intimidating, and he might have been a biblical avenger if they had played ball back in Isaiah's

Alan Page and Jim Marshall were the lightning bolts of the Viking defensive line. Carl Eller (81) was Thor's hammer, the thunder. "Add Gary Larsen," Page said. "We played with respect for each other. Each had something unique to give."

ALAN PAGE
VIKINGS
DEFENSIVE TACKLE

time. Marshall brought out metaphors from the animal world when the ballplayers talked about him. He was the panther or the greyhound. He would pivot inside or out and flash by the tackle with a long jump that put him either in the face of the passer, or in the face of Eller or Page. Sometimes all three of them converged on the miserable quarterback. Page never weighed much more than 240 pounds. In his later years, after he decided he would play at the weight that pleased Alan Page and not the coaches, he weighed less. He had great power in his upper arms but it was his speed and his anticipation that produced the critical free first step for him. It got him into the backfield. It defeated a block on running plays. Yet none of those fundamental assets were as critical to Alan Page's game as the private zeal with which he played it.

It was private because, apart from his occasional tantrum over an official's call, Page was never much for public postures and melodrama. He was a union politician in the locker room, all right. He walked picket lines during disputes with management and, long before pro football players liberated themselves from the NFL's feudal control, Page was an unapologetic maverick. He talked militant union talk that most of the players didn't want to hear or believe in.

But in the football game, or in the preparations for it, Page conducted his own war.

He recognized the divided faces of football. One was football as the player's business. Page knew that and he preached it. But when the center came over the ball, and the knuckles went into the ground, and the heavyweights stared at each across that foot of electrically charged air called the neutral zone, Page was transformed. Adrenalin poured through him.

Against the Lions one day, Page (above) and Marshall ran downfield in the snow, frolicking like kids, after a pass interception. Almost nobody saw it on TV. The snow was too thick.

The thought of being defeated on that play, any play, was repellent to him. He competed savagely. Intelligently, yes; under control practically all of the time, yes. But still savagely.

"Winning the football game was always the most important thing," he could say later in his chambers of the Minnesota Supreme Court. "But I can't say that winning the game, winning a championship, trying to win a Super Bowl was the biggest motivation in football for me. I wasn't afraid of losing a game. But I was afraid of failing at the most personal and intense level there was. Did I do what I was capable of doing? Did I make a play I should make? If it was a contest between the other guy and me, did I win that?

"If there was anything in football that drove me year in and year out, it was that. The fear of being less than I should have been."

That is a long way from defining selfishness. It is very close to defining Page, then and in his uncommon life after football. The idea of acquiring public popularity never crept very far into Page's priorities or ambitions, although it's a paradox of his life that he was a political creature, an advocate, both during his football career and afterward. To fans, he tried to be civil or coolly polite. He didn't always make it. Marshall and Eller liked the crowd contact. Tarkenton reveled in star status. Page was Page. He was driven to excel both in football and in what he saw as a far more critical test of his excellence and agendas after football. Some of those got mixed into his philosophies when he was playing. Fans and writers sometimes puzzled over the modest role that Page assigned to the Super Bowl on the scale of cosmic events. Some of the fans were positively appalled. "If you play as hard as you can in a Super Bowl and you lose," he'd say, "why should you be all torn up about it afterward? Starvation in the world is something to be torn up about. Inequality. Kids not getting the education they need."

But there were fans who not only wanted to get torn up about losing Super Bowl games but insisted on it. The fans weren't so bothered when Bud Grant – from whom Page eventually parted resentfully – walked away from the post-Super Bowl hysteria with as much abruptness as Page

Against the Lions on another day, Page was unstoppable. By himself, he changed the course of the game. Offensive linemen held him, officials threw penalty flags on him, and the Lions' strategists double blocked him. It didn't matter. He destroyed the Lions' offense and became the first defensive lineman named the league's most valuable player.

Many quarterbacks, such as Miami's Bob Griese, found it difficult to throw around the brick wall known as Alan Page.

did. But Bud used different language. It didn't sound quite as defensive. It might have been a little more tactful.

Being a football star didn't inspire Page to become a diplomat. But what made him truly belligerent was the football owners' arrogance in trying to preserve a baronial policy of keeping the players in legal bondage. Some of his teammates thought he was a troublemaker, rocking boats.

He was. He was Page. He saw goals and adopted codes. They were his goals and if they coincided with the comfort levels of his employers or teammates, that was nice but it wasn't necessary. He followed the straight lines as he drew them. While he was still playing he studied law. While he was still playing he decided to become a marathon runner and lost weight. He refused to see any connection between his slim contours and his strength as a tackler or rusher of quarterbacks. It got to be a point of contention between Page and Grant, and eventually Page went to the Bears to finish his career.

If you watched this man closely in his later years as a player, you knew this was one football star who was not going to drop out of sight for long. He might not stay famous. But he was

PURPLE HEARTS AND GOLDEN MEMORIES

going to be heard, and he was going to matter. Page was an odd and intriguing mixture of idealism, athletic greatness, social evangelism, and a passion to fulfill himself. He was opportunistic and ambitious. He was conscious of race, and never bashful about striking at racism in football or society. He wasn't even shy about making use of the establishment's racial guilt to advance himself in life after football. But he never yelled about racism frivolously. What he got as he advanced, he deserved. He didn't wait for people to open doors for him. He opened them himself. If there was resistance on the other side of the door, and the resistance seemed foolish or self-serving, he kicked the door down.

He went into private law practice, then served in the state attorney general's office for a few years. In 1992 he decided that it was time for both Alan Page, lawyer with agendas, and Alan Page as a person of color to be sitting on the Supreme Court of the state of Minnesota. One of the court's more elderly judges, two years from his retirement, wanted his term extended by act of the governor instead of standing for election. The governor extended it. That's illegal, Page said in a lawsuit. Page is right, said the court that heard the case. Page ran for election and won easily.

And now, sitting in robes in his aerie in the highest court in the state of Minnesota, does the judge remember pro football as something transitional, nothing profound, a game?

"It was something powerful in my life," he said. "I'd be foolish and wrong to say anything otherwise. Mostly it was good. It was good for the life it gave me, for the moments in it I'll never forget, and most of all for the people who came into my life as a result of it."

The men who came into his life were people like Jim Marshall, Carl Eller, Joe Kapp, Charlie West and Bobby Bryant, teammates like that and hundreds more, as well as guys on the other side of the line, like Art Shell, Larry Little, Ken

JIM MARSHALL
MINNESOTA VIKINGS
END

It's hard to be heroic playing defensive back. You are wide open, vulnerable, a target for sniping quarterbacks and sniping critics. Charlie West (40) played a creditable defensive back. His heroics, though, usually came on kickoffs, and he hauled a lot of them back 50 yards and more.

Stabler, Franco Harris and hundreds more: the brotherhood of the professional athlete.

"Not all of them were lovely guys," he said, "but a lot of them were great and most of them were memorable. Playing with Moose and Jim Marshall was a special reward. And you don't want to forget Gary (Larsen). What happened with our defensive line was a coming together of people who had common goals but different abilities. Moose was powerful and created happenings. Jim had that tremendous durability plus speed and athletic skills I have rarely seen in a pro football lineman. Individual sacks didn't mean much. It's not how you judged the player then. Winning his match with the guy across the line, winning the game, that's how you made the judgments."

Who can tell you that more accurately than a judge?

Yet even with the Purple Gang, with Kassulke and Warwick and Krause and Bill Brown and Dave Osborn and Mick Tingelhoff and the rest, the Vikings in the early 1970s got sucked back into the post-season malaise that began with their Super Bowl loss to Kansas City. The departure of Joe Kapp may have been a reason. Joe was one of those honest-in-the-guts, warts-and-all heroes the public can't resist. But he was more than a football mercenary. There was the sulfur of the political revolutionary in Joe. He didn't like the legal

Jeff Siemon (below) came into the league as a studious kid from Stanford, mature, strong and devout. He became known as the Minister of Defense. Hearing this, a Bear running back said, "maybe our guys better get a minister to preach peace. This guy is killing me."

GARY LARSEN
VIKINGS NFC
DEFENSIVE TACKLE

servitude imposed by the National Football League contract. He also didn't like what the Vikings offered him for the 1970 season. Joe was thinking of security and something in the million dollar range. The Vikings weren't sure that at his age, and given the kinky spiral on his forward passes, that Joe warranted a major investment.

They were probably mistaken. Their dispute graduated into impasse.

With sidelines howling him on, Ed Sharockman (45) carries an intercepted pass towards the end zone.

Joe refused to sign and later in the season was dealt to the Boston (later New England) Patriots for a 1972 first round draft choice that became Jeff Siemon, the all-pro linebacker. The Vikings played the 1970 season with Gary Cuozzo and backup Bobby Lee at quarterback. They started with a tour de force in the Revenge Bowl at Metropolitan, a season-opening game with their Super Bowl conquerors, the Kansas City Chiefs. The Vikings breezed 27-10 without Joe Kapp, with Cuozzo and with all of the other dependables. They rolled almost unstoppably toward a Super Bowl encore. Cuozza drove them to a 54-3 demolition of the Cowboys; Ed Sharockman carried a pass interception in for one touchdown and ran back a blocked punt for another; the defense choked the Rams on five first downs, 13-3; Clint Jones scored three touchdowns in a 24-20 victory over the Lions and the Vikings finished the season with a 12-2 record, identical to 1969. They did it with consecutive victories at the finish over the Bears, Boston (quarterbacked by Kapp), and the Atlanta Falcons (coached by Norm Van Brocklin). It was the Vikings' third consecutive Central Division championship. Nothing in the National Football League was tougher than the Minnesota Purple Gang defense.

So? Let's go to the big bowl and be super, the Met Stadium customers sang.

Stay home, said the 49ers.

While Joe Kapp (above) looks with some anxiety, Clint Jones (26) threads his way into a thicket of defensive players. Clint ran with speed and finesse. Joe would have gone in there with elbows flying and a knee in somebody's gut.

The Washington Redskins traded Paul Krause (right) to the Vikings allegedly because he didn't hit like a gorilla. Bud Grant scoffed. "We don't need the guy to pound his chest," he said. "We want him to intercept passes." Nobody has ever done it like Krause.

They met in a playoff game at the Met two days after Christmas. The temperature was nine degrees. The 49ers installed their hot air fans. The Vikings came on looking like creatures from the Greenland Ice Cap. The customers showed up in their face masks and snowmobile boots, and the scenario was perfect for another Viking sweep through the permafrost. It looked even better after Paul Krause grabbed a 49er fumble and

PURPLE HEARTS AND GOLDEN MEMORIES

ran it into the end zone. But John Brodie had the 49ers ahead 10-3 at halftime with a touchdown pass and a field goal by Bruce Gossett. They added 7 more in the second half before Cuozzo passed 24 yards to Gene Washington for a fourth-quarter touchdown, but the Vikings disappeared in the first round of the playoffs.

That was disheartening, but not quite as hard to swallow as 1971, when these things happened before Christmas Day: The Purple Gang scored three shutouts, over Buffalo, Philadelphia and Green Bay. The Vikings went nine consecutive quarters without surrendering a point. Their defense forced 33 fumbles and 27 interceptions, including seven by Charlie West and six each by Paul Krause and Ed Sharockman. It created a modern era record for smothering the opposition. In 14 games, the Vikings' defense gave up 139 points, an average of nine points a game. The offense had its interludes. But nobody took charge at quarterback. Cuozzo alternated with Bobby Lee and Norm Snead, and none of them threw more than six touchdown passes. By midseason, when the Vikings' offense ran onto the field the crowd was yelling, "OK, offense; hold 'em." The crowd wanted the offense to help by giving Eller, Page and Marshall good field position to crush the quarterback.

Good field position for the Viking defense was anything outside its own end zone. The Purple Gang devoured practically everything in sight. Nobody played much situation football in those years. You kept the same offense and the same defense on the field and shifted the formations. Any offense that had to deal with Eller, Page, Marshall, Larsen, Sharockman, Bryant, Kassulke, Hilgenberg, Winston and Krause wasn't going to do it by changing formations. It needed something closer to Mace and elephants. The Vikings won 11 out of the 14, and they did it partly with an infusion of young players like defensive back Jeff Wright, a 15th round draft choice from the University of Minnesota; defensive tackle Doug Sutherland and defensive back Nate Wright, who came to the Vikings by trade from St. Louis; and two of their young reserves from the drafts of the 1969 and 1970, offensive lineman Ed White and

One December day in 1975, Nate Wright (below) was victimized on the play now known as the Hail Mary pass. It was a lousy fate to befall Nate, a God-fearing guy and a first rate defensive back for years.

tight end Stu Voigt.

All of which produced a dilemma. The Vikings were matched against the Dallas Cowboys at the Met on Christmas Day, the first round of the playoffs. Who starts at the quarterback, the customers demanded to know. Cuozzo, Lee or Snead?

Harry P. Grant decided to withhold this vital news for a few days. He wasn't worried about giving the Cowboys any tactical comfort. Getting a football team ready was filled with so much routine that Bud Grant of all people – the tip of the iceberg, the Grant's Tomb of the sideline – felt an itch to puncture some of the pre-game folderol. He teased or needled and generally tried to confound the analysts. "Sooner or later everybody takes themselves too seriously in this business," he said. "I didn't have to keep everybody guessing about the quarterback. But it was fun doing it."

Cuozzo had more minutes and more passes and was the nominal No. 1 quarterback, although he completed only 44 percent of his passes that year. Lee and Snead did better. Lee had been drafted on the 17th round from Pacific in 1968. Often in his relief roles he showed an ability to move the team and to energize the offense. Snead was a vet, but a lumbering vet. Cuozzo was a vet who could throw and had a first-rate mind for the game but lacked consistency.

Grant decided on Lee. The decision might not have been crucial because one way or another it was assumed that the Viking defense, playing at home on a frozen field, would decide the game.

It didn't. What decided the game were two interceptions thrown by Lee and two more throw by Cuozzo later in the game. The Viking offense gained more than 400 yards and the Purple Gang held Dallas to 181, but Dallas had a quarterback named Roger Staubach and a halfback named Duane Thomas. Both of them produced touchdowns and the Cowboys won 20-12 en route to their first Super Bowl championship.

In his general manager's office a few weeks later, Jim Finks chain-smoked and did some major league deliberating.

This team shouldn't be heading for the trade winds in January, he said. It ought to be back in the Super Bowl. He asked himself some questions: Who plays defense any better?

Nobody.

So why aren't we in the Super Bowl?

Well, we need more offense.

The old quarterback asked a last question.

So where does the offense start?

He picked up the phone and called New York.

"I understand," he said to Wellington Mara of the New York Giants, "that Francis is not happy there. Maybe he needs to change time zones."

Francis Tarkenton didn't need a change in time zones to improve his disposition. What he wanted more was an offensive line and a chance to renew friendships in Minnesota. It was just a coincidence that these friends included people named Carl Eller and Jim Marshall.

He was back in Minnesota before the thaw.

The decision for Bud Grant in a 1971 playoff game with Dallas was whether to start Gary Cuozzo, Norm Snead (above) or Bob Lee (below) at quarterback. The Dallas defense didn't care. It intercepted four passes and went to the Super Bowl.

35 Years With The Minnesota Vikings

Sir Francis the Unflappable

Francis the Disenchanted Knight drew up a list in New York City. It was the end of the 1971 football season, and Francis indexed the pro football teams on which he would enjoy future employment.

In the custom of the times, popularized by Bo Derek, he created a sliding scale of 1 to 10. To the worst teams, those on which a life-loving young plutocrat from Georgia and Madison Avenue could get beheaded for want of an offensive line, he assigned the usual 1. To the heaven-on-earth situations – championship contenders that could use an experienced, prosperous quarterback – he gave a 10. To the Minnesota Vikings, he gave an 11.

Francis Tarkenton was going someplace for sure. It was written, if not in concrete slabs, then certainly in the daily columns. There were two excellent reasons why Tarkenton had played his last for the New York Giants in 1971, five seasons after his trade from the Minnesota Vikings produced a talent harvest big enough (Ron Yary, Ed White, Clint Jones and Bob Grim) to help push Minnesota into the highest levels of the National Football Conference. First, Francis' preseason walkout over contract terms in 1971 generated friction with the Giants' owner, Wellington Mara. It wasn't exactly smoothed over by the Giants' 4-10 finish. Secondly, the Giants had a lousy football team and Francis decided all sides deserved more harmony in their lives, particularly Francis. Francis was a man of capitalist impulses who believed in the best use of resources. This meant that Tarkenton's resources deserved a new environment. His contract agitation in New York may not have been plotted with that in mind, but it certainly moved him that way. Mara made Tarkenton available. A half dozen teams called.

One of those calls came from Jim Finks, the Viking general manager who had concocted the first Tarkenton trade. Mara and the Vikings negotiated. They agreed tentatively. Finks then called Tarkenton and asked if coming back to Minnesota appealed to him. Tarkenton asked for the number of the first flight to the Minneapolis-St. Paul airport. Finks expressed his joy. He also offered Tarkenton a pay cut.

"You know the picture, Francis," Finks said affably. "Size of the

Tarkenton launches one more toward the end zone. In his first game in the pros, he threw four touchdown passes. When he finished 18 years later, the total stood at 342, the highest in pro football history.

market, all that stuff."

Tarkenton said market sizes don't throw touchdown passes, and the Vikings weren't getting many of those. They wrangled a little and Tarkenton took a minor salary hit. It still gave him slightly under $125,000 for the season. He quotes that figure today with a mild blush. Quarterbacks today would look at $125,000 the way gourmets look on sunflower seeds. But that was in 1972, before free agency, before the cables got into the network bidding war. The deal was made. The Vikings gave the Giants their reserve quarterback, Norm Snead, Bob Grim, Vince Clements, a reserve back, a first-round draft choice for 1972 and a second-round choice the following year.

By then, Tarkenton had played pro football for 11 years, six in Minnesota and five in New York. He had made his original splurge as a renegade scrambling quarterback on a Viking team where he was convinced scrambling was the door to survival. He probably did it excessively. But he did other things excessively, such as throwing touchdown passes in record numbers before his 18-year career was over (342) and compiling record yardage passing (47,003) as milemarks on his way to the Hall of Fame. But the Giants had fewer redeeming virtues than the early Vikings. With New York, therefore, Tarkenton still scrambled until — approaching 30 — he decided that scrambling in the National Football League was an unlikely way to achieve dignity in old age. So he either threw in a hurry or threw it away when no receivers were in view. He hardened as a competitor and learned the craft of quarterbacking as few had before or have since. After more than 10 years in the league, calling plays in the huddle, cramming in the film room, changing at the line, defying the rush, finessing the rush, throwing in wind, cold and rain, Francis Tarkenton concluded there wasn't much that would ever surprise him at the line of scrimmage. The guys on the other side of the line knew it, too. His prestige grew in pro football, although he'd played all those years for teams that offered him little chance to win.

He wasn't universally loved. He seemed to have a well-developed concept of Francis Tarkenton's interests. But since when is that a shock in competitive athletics, competitive business or competitive anything? He'd quarreled with his coach in Minnesota in the '60s and quarreled with management in New York in the 1970s. That is commonplace among the stars and their overseers in the 1990s, but it wasn't then. Tarkenton was independent enough and good enough to risk it 25 and 30 years earlier. For a man who looked fragile among the behemoths, Tarkenton was an uncommonly tough and well-muscled 6-footer. He took poundings year in and year out without serious injury until late in his career. When they did hurt him, he camouflaged it. His arm ached some seasons and the sportswriters berated it, as they did most arms that couldn't reach the second deck from 75 yards in a headwind. That was supposed to be the way to define a great arm, by velocity and distance. But Tarkenton didn't talk about the aching arm. "What the hell would I be doing throwing into the second deck? What's wrong with hitting a receiver?"

By the time he returned to Minnesota, he was an accredited celebrity. His venues weren't confined to the huddle and 3rd and 18. He read the *Wall Street Journal* as avidly as the scouting report. He owned real estate in Georgia and Minnesota. He bagged big money with commercial endorsements for merchandise ranging from shirts to pasta. He got into television as a weekly host and as a peddler, into learning centers, advertising and promotion, and ultimately, behavior management. He got invitations from the Republicans to run for office.

It was a dilemma. There didn't seem to be enough days in the week. He explained: "The problem I had with life in the middle of my football career is that I had more things to do and wanted to do than I had time to do them. I spread myself around. But I never had the feeling of being harassed by outside activity. When it came time to concentrate on football, I blocked the rest out of my mind. The first thing I have to do in any activity I get involved in is to believe in what I'm doing, and to know what I'm doing. You can overdo endorsements. I know that. I did. It's money you make fairly, cashing in on your prominence, and it's also an ego ride. It measures the credit you have with the sellers and with the public. That may not sound noble, but it's reality. But when I talk about creating something in business off the field, I'm talking about a deeper involvement than just putting your name together with a carton of spaghetti. I found that out in a van I lived in for 16 to 18 hours a day years ago. I motored around the South, finding out what assembly line workers were doing and saying. I loved it. And I think I was able to make a difference in some of those lives with the things I tried to put together to bring management and its employers closer to their goals."

A substantial fellow, Francis. Later, after football, some of his business interests soured and brought the inevitable lawsuits.

One of his more pertinent goals in 1972 was the Super Bowl.

It didn't happen. He played superbly. But he didn't get close.

To begin with, he didn't get close to a man like Alan Page. Page had won the NFL's Most Valuable Player award the previous year. He wasn't especially jubilant, although he was hardly surprised, to see a Tarkenton commercial playing on all of the local stations within hours of the trade announcement. Page always had regard for Tarkenton's quarterbacking skills. He had no reason to dislike him personally, and didn't. It was the old caste system, alive and flourishing. Defensive lineman, black and independent, gets Most Valuable Player. Quarterback, white and persuasive, gets the endorsements. Somebody asked Page for a comment on Francis' return. Page said the Vikings were getting a quality quarterback, "but I don't think this team needs a savior."

Both had successful individual seasons in 1972. So did some of the others. But if the Vikings didn't need a savior in 1972, they might have needed something with more practical attributes. What happened, in fact, was pretty startling. With Tarkenton back, with its powerful defense still in place, with Eller, Page, Marshall, Alderman, Tingelhoff, Sharockman, Kassulke, Krause and the others at the peak of their games, the Vikings went 7-7.

There'd been no measurable dissension. Players didn't yap around on

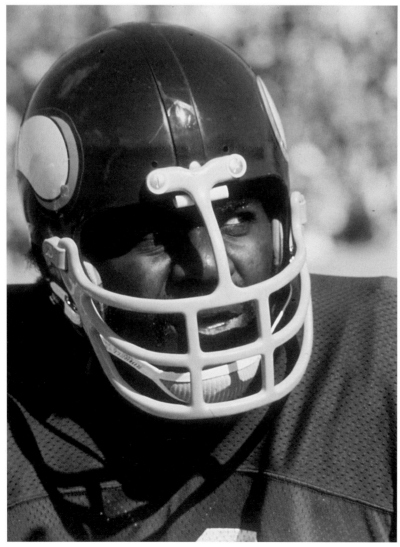

When Tarkenton returned to the Vikings from the Giants, Alan Page (below) applauded, politely. But he didn't regard Francis as the rescuing knight of the Minnesota Vikings. He didn't think they needed a knight, although he thought they needed a quarterback who could score. That, Francis was.

all channels the way they do today, especially with Bud Grant coaching. But three of the veterans, Gene Washington, Charley West and Clint Jones, had negotiated their contracts as a coalition. Finks wasn't crazy about that process, and the other players didn't exactly hide their own irritation. Page played part of the season with a bad leg. Others got hurt. They played a streak of games where goofy bounces killed them or the laws of astrology seemed to intervene. One way or another, with their roster full of Super Bowl vets and one of the pricey players in the league at quarterback, they fell on their cans. John Beasley, a kind of large troll who played tight end, remembers the consternation of that year.

"With Tarkenton coming back, we all had this unconscious feeling that we were just going to walk on the field and everybody was going to concede us the Super Bowl. As the season wore on, it was 'migawd, what's happening.' And after awhile it was, 'let's get the damned thing over with.' As for Francis, I had him measured wrong before he came in. Football players gossip like anybody else. I heard from some of the Giants that he was a pretty hard guy to talk to and kind

Grady Alderman (left) played in one Super Bowl game knowing he had cancer. Mick Tingelhoff (below) was one of Tarkenton's long-standing bodyguards on the offensive line. They were Francis' closest friends on the team. The friends of Francis were more numerous than some critics alleged.

of selfish and wanted to run the show. I never saw that. He knew he was under pressure rejoining a team that was filled with winners. He never showed that or talked about it. He was fun in the huddle. He was spontaneous and smart. You knew this guy was going to win sooner or later."

If Beasley knew it, he had company. Grant looked at 1972 for what it evidently was, an oddball spasm made up of bad luck and a little bad chemistry. He was sure he had another winner. Tarkenton and Grant were a match from the start. Grant liked Tarkenton's mind, his decisiveness and his ad lib verve. He wasn't like Grant's other quarterbacks. You didn't have to give him lectures or put shackles on him when he lined up in his own end zone. From the first day, he'd developed a breezy, hands-on relationship with Jerry Burns, the noisy little offensive coordinator. For his part, Tarkenton liked Grant's calm authority. Two things Grant wouldn't have on his team were dumb guys and bad guys. And he was a gut fighter. He never announced it but you could feel it. A winner. Tarkenton had been playing for losers for ten years, and he was sick of it.

What was new about 1973, among other things, was Chuck Foreman. They'd drafted him on the first round from Miami, but the Vikings promotional flacks had to sell him hard to skeptical media people in the off-season because his numbers at Miami didn't set the scouts drooling.

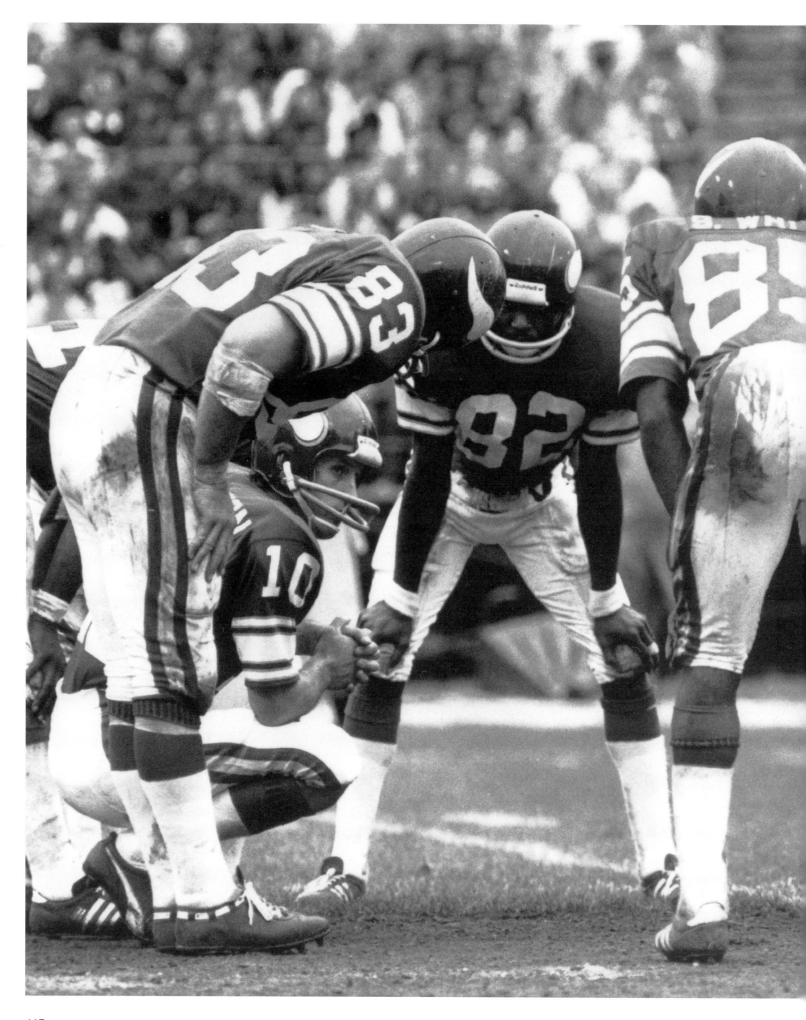

In the mythology that grew up around Tarkenton, it was assumed that he concocted a lot of his plays off the top of his helmet, inventing as he went along. He actually did call some scramble plays in desperate situations. One of them beat Vince Lombardi and the Packers.

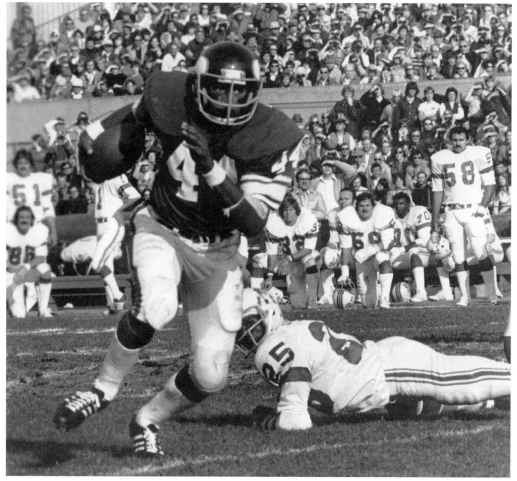

And Miami in the 1970s wasn't the Miami of the 1990s. If anything, he was undersold. From his first season Foreman was an offensive force unlike many of the decade in the NFL. He ran with big-striding power or with whirling impulsiveness when he got trapped. He caught the ball anywhere on the field, deep or wide. He gained over 800 yards in his rookie season and averaged nearly 4.5 a carry. He was a perfect complement to Tarkenton with his versatile skills and his playground knack for improvising. What also was new for the Vikings was the emergence of the second-year middle linebacker from Stanford, Jeff Siemon, as a defensive star. He was perceptive and disciplined, with

In the 1970s, the Vikings assaulted NFL rivals with an offensive circus. Tarkenton threw to a half dozen receivers, including Chuck Foreman (above) a running back of classic versatility. He ran with speed, power and resourcefulness. He had one move, an open-field 360-degree pivot, that put defensive backs into the seats. He caught passes with the best. He was an all-pro, one of the superstars of Viking history.

While Tarkenton was throwing and Foreman running, the team was not exactly chopped meat on defense, and it wasn't only the Purple Gang line, Jeff Siemon (tackling a Lion runner, right) ran the defense on the field.

a sense for the ball. He was also a catalyst in the locker room for the devout players on the club. Inevitably he became known as the minister of defense, one of the first of a dozen or so who have held that portfolio in the NFL. Not quite new but more comfortable was John Gilliam, a sleek wide receiver who had replaced Gene Washington as the deep threat. John had played for New Orleans. He talked like a riverboat gambler and, with his mustache and chiseled good looks, could have taken the role. He ran routes of precision and with speed. It didn't take Tarkenton long to develop a happy relationship with John Gilliam. But like a basketball point guard, Tarkenton distributed the ball, to Gilliam, to Foreman, to Ed Marinaro, the Ivy Leaguer drafted a year earlier, to Oscar Reed, and to the chugging but savvy tight end from Wisconsin, Chainsaw Voigt.

Karl Kassulke, though, was gone; Karl the hard-living, reckless hitter in the secondary. He got on a motorcycle the day before

In the pros, the wide receivers are the smooth as satin guys, the gliders, whippets and gazelles. John Gilliam (above) was all of that for a couple of starring seasons with the Vikings. He was the long-strike receiver who could break up the game. The guy who lined up a few yards away was the tight end, Stu Voigt (left). Sometimes it took Stu months to get downfield. Sometimes it looked as though they could cover him with one of the Budweiser horses. But he caught the ball when they threw to him. He blocked. He was Chainsaw, the guy who kept cutting wood.

On the field for a decade, Karl Kassulke (covering a receiver above) played without inhibition and without heed to the future. For years, he ran his life off the field the same way. One day his motorcycled flipped and he was paralyzed for life. The crowd gave him its admiration and love when he reappeared one day. But what happened to Karl privately was more important. He found bigger things in life than football. The accident, he said, salvaged his life (right photo, credit: Daniel Dmitruk/ NFL Photos).

practice started in the summer. There was an accident. Karl was paralyzed for life. In some providential way, it changed his life for the good. He accepted God and discovered a calm he'd never had. He learned from the broken marriage his wildness had caused, and met a nurse who cared for him, loved him and married him.

From the beginning, the first exhibition, the

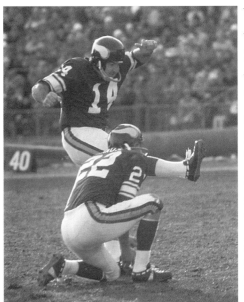

Vikings were convinced the season wasn't ending until they reached Houston and the Super Bowl. They won all five of their exhibitions. They ran off nine straight in the regular season before losing to Van Brocklin and Bobby Lee in Atlanta. They won another, lost badly at Cincinnati and finished powerfully to end the regular season 12-2. They drew Washington in the first playoff game at the Met, and for two quarters they were duds. The Redskins were the defending league champions. But one large and prominent member of the defense considered that no excuse. The team came in to the locker room trailing 7-3, and Carl Eller went ballistic. He grabbed a chalk board and threw it against the wall. He raged and stalked and gave ultimatums. He pounded his fist on metal doors. He wanted more guts, more drive, more brutality and above all more points. The players stared. Nobody said much. "What we really wanted to do," Tarkenton said later, "was find a place to hide from Eller."

They might have still been occupied doing that in the third quarter, because they trailed 13-10 early in the fourth. But Tarkenton hit Gilliam with two touchdown passes, Fred Cox kicked his second field goal and the Vikings won 27-20. It was easier in Dallas, where another Tarkenton-to-Gilliam bomb and a Bobby Bryant interception and touchdown sealed it, 27-20, for another run at the Super Bowl.

Miami was waiting in Houston, the Miami that had won 17 in a row a year before to win Super Bowl VII. It was the Miami of Bob Griese, Larry Csonka, Mercury Morris, Paul Warfield, Nick Buonocanti, Manny Fernandez, Dick Anderson, Jake Scott, Larry Little, Jim Langer, Garo Yepremian and, of course, Don Shula. Grant thought there was a fair chance his team might squeeze through

Some things were predictable when you watched the Vikings in their championship years. Freddie Cox was going to kick a few field goals with Paul Krause holding (left) and Bobby Bryant was likely to intercept a pass (below). Oh, and somebody in the stands was going to start a chant that would implore Eller to "Kill, Carl, Kill."

that impressive minefield. He wasn't as sure about the sparrows. In most of the Vikings' Super Bowl games, Grant found a semi-loony subplot to create a distraction for the hounding journalists. Although he looked to be a Gibraltar of patience, Grant disliked the droning repetition of the daily press inquisition at the Super Bowl. So did most of the players, at least the veterans. The Dolphins' defensive tackle, Manny Fernandez, delivered a scornful indictment in the middle of the week. Sullenly he listened to the what he thought was the hopeless inanity of the endless questions. Some of them, like "do you find yourself building a hatred toward Mick Tingelhoff," he simply ignored and closed his eyes in incredulity. Finally somebody got down to the inner sanctum of cliche-dom. "Is this going to be the biggest game of your life?"

"What big game?" he barked. His was the exasperation of a man caught in a cell with idiots. "Every game I ever played was a big game. What do I have to do to show that I'm emotional? Run out on the field with two rockets strapped to my ass?"

For Grant, sparrows were a handy substitute for rockets. He stewed about the sparrows in his team's shower room. He said the facilities his team got in the bowels of Rice Stadium would have been rejected by the old-timers in a company picnic game. He blamed the National Football League for not upgrading them. The journalists got three days worth out of the story and Grant got some private satisfaction because he DID think somebody could have put hot water in there for the price of a monkey wrench. Beside, he liked the idea of getting his players fired up. He reminded them they were pretty much being treated like dogfood alongside the glamour of Miami.

It didn't work. How could it? Miami in the early 1970s could have beaten the hordes of China if you could have put all of them on one side of the line of scrimmage. Csonka ran so hard and so much that Griese needed only seven passes all day. Miami's defense strangled the Vikings despite Tarkenton's 18 completions, and the Dolphins won 24-7.

"It's not the end of the world," Alderman said. "We'll be back next year."

It was an ironic statement. All season he'd harbored the knowledge that he was carrying a cancerous growth in his lower body, potentially fatal. He played every game with that knowledge, undergoing treatment but playing his usual high-level, dependable football. None of his teammates was aware until after the Super Bowl, when he confided in Tarkenton, his best friend on the team. Tarkenton cried when he told his wife about it. Shortly after the Super Bowl, though, Grady underwent an operation and the cancer was removed.

So it made sense for Alderman to talk about next year, the Vikings, and another Super Bowl. The world may have started to dread that possibility, but Alderman was right.

Photo Credit: Vernon Biever/NFL Photos

Chapter Seven

The Occasionally Incredible Mike

Mike Lynn actually arrived without a 100-piece brass band.

That should surprise Viking followers of later lineage, the ones who came to identify The World's First Million Dollar Pro Football General Manager with big deals and a bionic ego. Mike never quarreled with that description. Most days he relished it. And that partly explained the Vikings' adventures of the next 18 years in the National Football League.

Most of them were touched with success, a lot of it attributable to Mike, ego, bombast and all. Mike is the guy who put cardboard livestock on the field to make an honest man out of Chicago's Mike Ditka after Ditka called the Metrodome a barnyard. Mike's the one who sent the football team into an expensive Camp Skywalker in the desert caverns of the Southwest to teach teamwork and togetherness, with results not noticeable in the won-lost ledgers. Mike is the guy who divested the Vikings of a horde of draft choices, five players and a fair amount of common sense for the Cowboys' Herschel Walker. The goal was for the Vikings to win the Super Bowl, propelled there by Herschel. It didn't happen. But Mike is also the man who scavenged and spent, while his competitors stood around looking startled by his gall. It's the way he corralled a half dozen star quality football players like Keith Millard, Anthony Carter, Gary Zimmerman and others to recycle the Vikings as a major force in the NFL in the late 1980s and early '90s.

When he arrived in the summer of 1974, though, he had no more heraldry in town than a fishbait salesman from the muskeg swamps. Mike kept a low profile, in defiance of all of his instincts. It happened that he arrived when the Vikings were in the middle of a pretty extraordinary year. The team was en route to its second consecutive Super Bowl and its third in six years. One of the primary architects of that success, Jim Finks, the general manager, left the Vikings in the spring of 1974 after being denied ownership of company stock. The episode defined a shift in power on the Vikings' board.

In the earlier years a trust made up of John Skoglund, Bill Boyer and Bernie Ridder controlled Viking management decisions. Ridder was popular with most of the others and a figure of respect from the years of the Vikings' origins. He was the catalyst in most decisions. But he was also a full-time newspaper publisher in St. Paul and, while he technically was a part-owner, it was actually the newspaper organization (Knight-Ridder) that held the stock. Ridder gradually receded as a force on the Viking board. Max Winter became the full-time president and the team's de facto chief executive officer. He brought with him decades of experience in sports management and promotion. He'd run the Minneapolis Lakers during their championship basketball seasons. He hadn't enjoyed an obscure role in the Vikings' early years, and when he became president he wasn't going to be a figurehead president.

Finks was a man the Viking media and the community trusted. It was the same wherever he went after leaving the Vikings: Chicago, New Orleans, anywhere. His posthumous induction into the Hall of Fame years later confirmed his achievements as well as his integrity. In Minnesota, he enjoyed an ideal relationship with Bud Grant.

He'd been a pro quarterback and coach, and he knew talent and player negotiation as well as anybody in football. Moreover, he was successful. His trades and most of the Viking drafts paid off. It was a performance, he thought, that merited something more than employee status with the Vikings. He thought a small part of the company stock represented a fair tradeoff for his value.

Winter said no.

Finks resigned.

It happened about that quickly. It was a contest of wills and values in which the general manager had the public support and a logical argument, but the company president had the leverage.

Winter looked around for a replacement. The NFL's confidential memo wire to the owners, which kept them posted on the random schemes to start rival leagues, often mentioned the name of Mike Lynn of Memphis. Lynn was in the discount store business in Memphis, an extroverted pitchman and manager. But once he got the pro ball fever, his passions and ambitions quickly went from markdowns to touchdowns. He wanted to bring an NFL franchise to Memphis and he got to

Mike Lynn came to the Minnesota Vikings in 1974 as the designated gofer of the management, headed by Max Winter. By the time he'd left 18 years later, he was running the store, the waiver wire, the board and the fake-animal menagerie he installed at the Metrodome one day in honor of Mike Ditka. Ditka's sin was to call the Metrodome a barnyard. Lynn had critics all over town. He was bombastic and egocentric. But he knew football management. The team usually won and it always made money.

be the ringleader of the Memphis campaign. As such he was a familiar figure at NFL meetings. Winter paid little attention to him, however, until his name started to hog the memo wire as a man who looked aggressive and seemed to have some savvy.

That wasn't a bad description of Lynn's modus operandi the next 18 years. In the summer of 1974, though, the Vikings had a potential championship team, a crowd of veterans who were mostly unsigned. Max had personally signed Tarkenton to a contract that was to eventually reach $400,000 a year. Somebody had to get the others under contract, although the job then wasn't all that daunting. The players had no effective union to contest management and no real leverage. But somebody had to sign them, and Winter hired Mike, not as the general manager he became in a few years but as Max's assistant in charge of small print and contract signings. Lynn was too quick and motivated to be anybody's gofer very long. In any case, the Mike Lynn regime was launched. Within a couple of years he knew pro football administration and the locale of his organization's skeletons as well as anybody in football. A few years after that, he knew them better. He read the contracts. He knew the procedures. He knew the small escape hatches and the loopholes. In time, he used them to grab football players his opponents were convinced were out of reach.

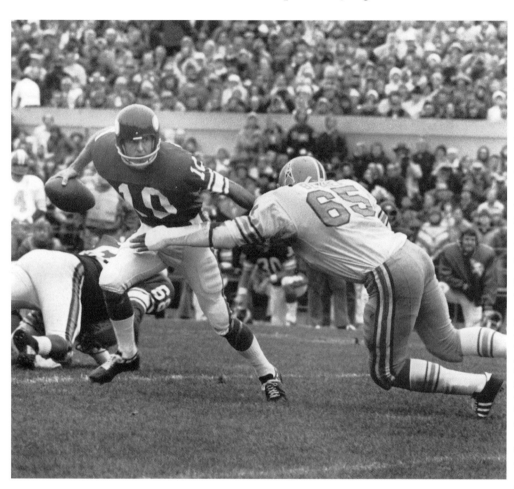

Tarkenton played in three Super Bowls. The team won none of them. Detractors later sneered and said he couldn't be called great because he didn't win the big one. Tarkenton seemed unbothered. So did the Hall of Fame selectors.

Beyond negotiating contracts during summer camp, though, Lynn contributed only in minor ways to the team's third appearance in the Super Bowl as the NFC's 1974 champion. And although the team may not have been Bud Grant's best, it probably had the best chance of all of his teams of winning the Super Bowl. Tarkenton played most of the season with a sore arm. It wasn't just a crick. It was something severely painful and limited his passing options. It came on in the Vikings' early season victory at Dallas, which got to be historic for another reason. Fred Cox kicked a winning field goal that seemed to bisect one of the goalpost uprights. Dallas grumbled so much about it that the league decided to extend the uprights to the current height. Tarkenton never bellyached about his sore arm. "Actually, I had a good season, 17 touchdown passes,

VIKINGS TE
STU VOIGT

2,500 yards, good for those days," he said. "Everybody was always peeing and moaning about my not being able to throw the ball deep, anyway. The sore arm made them accurate about that, as well as mean. The soreness went away but I put up with that weak-arm business for the rest of my career. It got me mad but it never changed my game. What we had in 1974 was a team and a style that made it easy for me to move the ball around. Foreman and Marinaro and Dave Osborn could take the ball out of the backfield. We had John Gilliam and Jimmy Lash to go deep and Old Chainsaw (Voigt) in the middle when I got desperate. He was one tough football player, Chainsaw, one of the most dependable receivers I had. The point is, if we really had to go deep, I went deep. I did it that season or any season. You don't throw more than 300 touchdown passes in a career by dinking around."

The Vikings won 10 and lost 4, mauled the St. Louis Cardinals with the running of Foreman and Dave Osborn in the first playoff game and then beat the Rams 14-10 at Metropolitan Stadium in a football game memorable for its unbuttoned brutality.

"I remember it," Mick Tingelhoff said. "The Rams were just about as good as we were. They led us in one thing for sure. Nobody yelled and screamed on the line of scrimmage like Jack Youngblood, their defensive end. Maybe he had something to yell about. He was a helluva football player." So was Yary, the man against whom Youngblood threw his muscle and kamikaze howls all day. It was one of those epic caveman confrontations, unlike any the snowmobile hordes at the Met had seen in years. Yary and Youngblood finished about even. But the Vikings intercepted one pass more than the Rams, recovered one more fumble and flew south one week later.

He came out of the Ivy League with huge ground-gaining statistics. Ed Marinaro (below) never approached those in his few years with the Vikings. One reason was the presence in the Viking backfield of a player named Foreman. But Marinaro caught the ball impeccably. He had his moments and he later made tons as one of the stars of a cop series on TV.

New Orleans of January 1975, accosted them with Bourbon Street, Al Hirt, Pete Fountain, the actor Pat O'Brien and the Pittsburgh Steelers. They got through the French Quarter with great aplomb. They weren't so lucky with Mean Joe Greene, L.C. Greenwood, Ernie Holmes and Dwight White of the Steeler front four.

They did score at least one victory in advance of the Super Bowl.

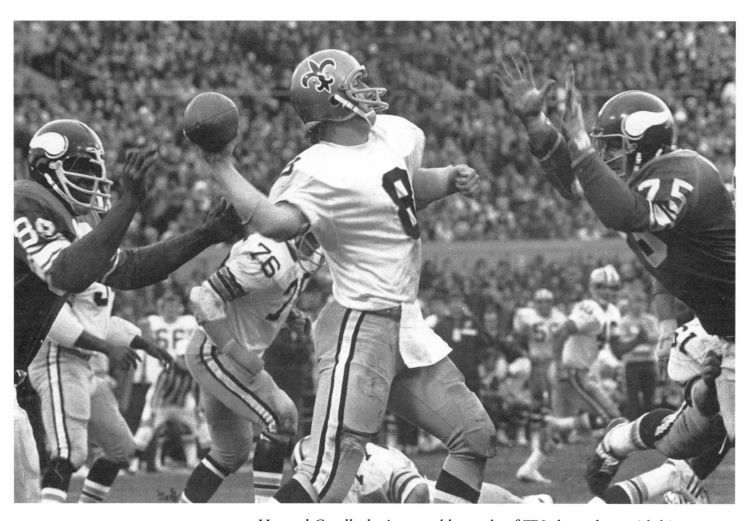

It was Archie Manning's predictable fate (quarterback, New Orleans Saints, awful team) to get himself bookended on this play by one of pro football's superstars (Alan Page, 88) and a man who later became a sort of Dogpatch TV idol (Bob Lurtsema, 75). Manning had a right to ask a question: "Lurts, what are you doing on the field? Get back to the bench." That was Lurts' venue on TV: Benchwarmer Bob, everybody's favorite nonentity. But, incidentally, he was a good football player.

Howard Cosell, the inescapable oracle of TV, showed up with his canary blazer and broadcast crew to tape an hour with Tarkenton at the motel where the team was staying. Midway through it, Wally Hilgenberg spotted the proceedings from a balcony where he was out for a stroll. Hilgenberg later acquired the maturity of the reborn, but at the time he was an avowed hell-raiser. His conception of some harmless hell was to dump a wastebasket of water on Cosell's head. He got one from his room and was about to perform the act when he was interrupted by Bob Lurtsema, the backup defensive lineman who later got rich and lionized as "Benchwarmer Bob." Lurtsema demanded to know why Hilgenberg should hog the glory of splattering Cosell. Hilgenberg told him to get his own basket of water. He did. They were about to unload when they were interrupted by Alan Page, later to become a judge but not unknown for random acts of nonsense in those years. Page was instructed to get his own water, which he did. At the snap count of three, they all pitched their water on Cosell's defenseless head. Cosell could have withstood the cataract like the old show biz trouper he was, except that the deluge skewed his hairpiece and broke up the broadcast.

It was the unpardonable offense. Cosell broke out with language unheard of on Monday night TV. "Howard," yelled Hilgenberg, "It's the first time I understood a word you said."

The Pittsburgh defensive line and the Viking defensive line graded out about evenly for the Super Bowl. Regrettably, they weren't playing against each other. The Steeler backfield was headed by young Terry Bradshaw at quarterback and Franco Harris. They did no special violence to the Viking defense. What was happening on the other side, though, was depressing.

Pittsburgh's Steel Curtain knocked down six of Tarkenton's passes, Greenwood accounting for three of those alone. With the Steelers leading only 2-0 on a safety, the Vikings moved toward a score. Tarkenton threaded a pass to Gilliam near the goal line. A catch would have given the Vikings the lead, halftime momentum and perhaps the Super Bowl. The ball and defensive back Glen Edwards hit Gilliam at about the same time. The ball came loose, Pittsburgh intercepted and the Vikings were

Offensive lineplay is not for egomaniacs, John Michels, the line coach, used to say. Offensive linemen spend a lot of their lives defending people like quarterbacks, falling back, taking the whacks of glory-hunting defensive linemen. It's why offensive linemen love to block on running plays, because then they're delivering whacks of their own. Chuck Goodrum (below) was one of those linemen who pleaded with Francis in the huddle: "Let's run. We can move them." But when it was a pass, Chuck got into that crab position and backpedaled. It was a living.

effectively finished. The day was ugly enough when it started, dank, gray and mucky. It got uglier. The Curtain and linebackers Jack Ham, Jack Lambert and Andy Russell choked the Viking offense in the second half. At the end, Foreman had gained only 22 yards in 12 carries. Tarkenton completed only 11 of 27 passes. The Vikings' only score came on Terry Brown's recovery of a blocked punt. The Steelers began their remarkable run of Super Bowl victories, 16-6.

Afterwards, Page grumbled about the disappearance of the Viking offense. The Viking offensive vets showed scant sympathy for those sounds because they were mystified themselves. The impartial viewer didn't have much trouble identifying the source of the mystery: Greene, Holmes, Greenwood, White, Lambert and Ham.

Gary Larsen tried being philosophical one more time. In Houston the previous year, he tried to put losing the Super Bowl in some kind of perspective that didn't smell of corn or bad grapes. He tried again

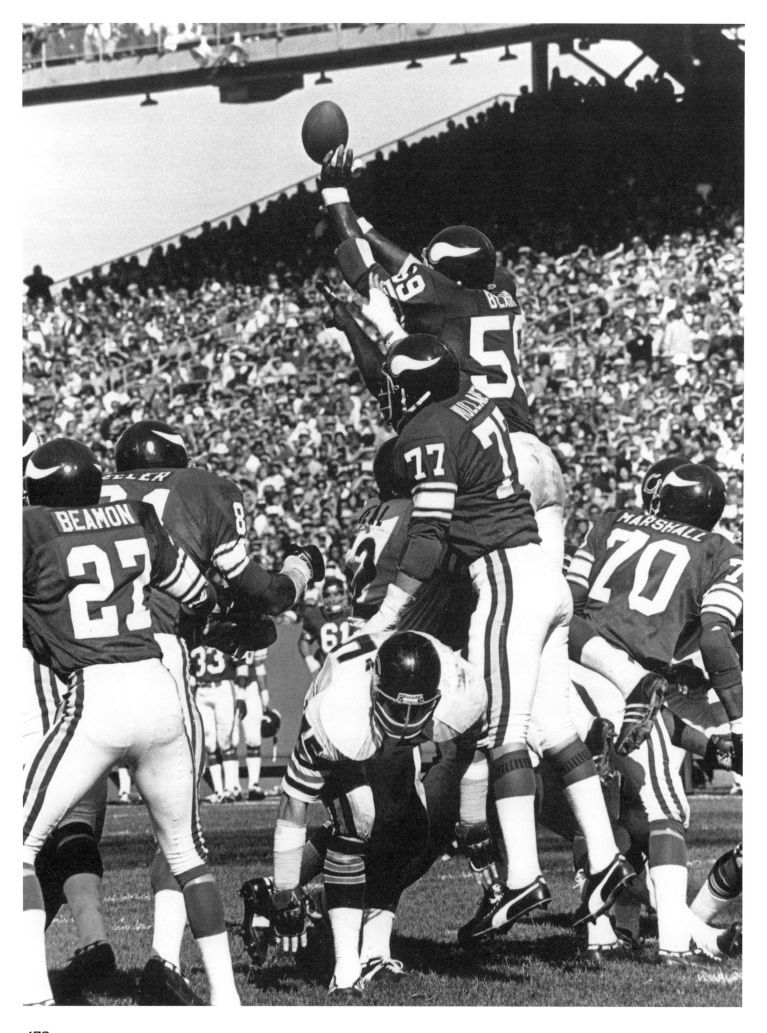

in New Orleans. "Tomorrow," he said, "eight hundred million Chinamen are going to get up and not give a damn about who won or lost the Super Bowl."

It wasn't quite convincing in Houston.

It wasn't any more convincing in New Orleans.

And yet they might have broken through the next January. They could have won the grail that kept vanishing. They could have, if they had gotten to the Super Bowl. The old heads, Tarkenton, Yary, Tingelhoff, Marshall, Eller, Page, Krause, Bobby Bryant and the others were still good. Foreman and Siemon had become stars. A young dynamo named Matt Blair, tall and gymnastic, had joined the linebacking corps along with Fred McNeill. The younger offensive linemen, Chuck Goodrum, Steve Riley and John Ward, gave them depth. Jeff Wright balanced some of the age in the secondary.

They didn't reach the Super Bowl in January of 1976 because of one play that became the indisputable moment of horror in the team's history.

The Vikings came into the playoffs on fire. Tarkenton had his career season: NFL's Most Valuable Player, 273 completions in 425 attempts, 25 touchdowns. Foreman scored 22 touchdowns, four of them in the final game against Buffalo when he outdueled O.J. Simpson in the snow in Buffalo. The team opened with 10 straight

victories and finished 12-2.

The weather on December 28 at Metropolitan Stadium was passable, literally. It was nippy and it gradually got dismal, but neither Tarkenton nor Roger Staubach of the Dallas Cowboys felt any special handicap from the weather. They'd met before. Their matchups of the 1970s did not generate quite the media frenzy of a meeting between Joe Montana and Dan Marino 20 years later. The explanation was that in the 1970s there weren't a jillion information agencies cramming the story into cables, faxes, Internets and global syndicates. But Staubach vs. Tarkenton was something memorable every time. For the

There's something about the yammering and hostilities of pro football that leads some of its people to consider the profession of law as a natural sequel to it. When he removed his bandages and shoulder pads, linebacker Fred McNeill (above) became a lawyer.

In street clothes (or Prairie buck-skins) John Ward (left) had the look of an Oklahoma cowboy. That may not be a coincidence. The Vikings drafted him as an offensive lineman on the first round from Oklahoma State. He played well when healthy. As they did for hundreds in this business, injuries smothered his potential.

Viking watchers, none of those memories was as ghastly as the one of December 28, 1975.

It materialized out of the half-darkness of late afternoon, a scene out of a spook show more than a palpable event because at the time the Dallas Cowboys looked dead. They came in as a wild card team and for much of the day looked the part, although they did finish with the stats as well as the ball game. Fred McNeill's recovery of a muffed punt near the Dallas goal line made it easy for Foreman a few plays later and the Vikings led 7-0. But the Viking ground game was chilled by Too Tall Jones, Harvey Martin and Lee Roy Jordan. Tarkenton's attempts to hit deep strikes to John Gilliam were messed up by Cliff Harris, the bald-headed and homicidal free safety, and the rest of the Cowboy defense. Dallas tied with a long drive and Doug Dennison's touchdown and took a 10-7 lead on Toni Fritsch's field goal early in the fourth quarter.

But Tarkenton herded the Vikings 70 yards with Foreman and Brent McClanahan running,

The glamour of pro football tends to disappear on the line of scrimmage. Chuck Foreman gets dumped on his can. Brent McClanahan (33) heads for daylight, which disappears along with the glamour.

Francis throwing and Yary, White, Tingelhoff and the others sledging away at the Cowboy line. McClanahan scored from a yard out and it was 14-10. With less than a minute to go Dallas stood 4th and 16 on its own 20. Drew Pearson made a living being slick and heady out on the flank. He told Staubach he could beat Nate Wright with an out ball. Staubach bobbled the center pass but got it off. Pearson caught it falling out of bounds at the 50, but the official said he was shoved and allowed the catch. Staubach had 37 seconds left. Preston Pearson dropped a pass and there were 32 seconds left. Staubach threw again, deep, toward the sidelines. Drew Pearson and Nate Wright were going shoulder to shoulder. The ball flopped in the wind and came down awkwardly. Pearson slowed. Wright adjusted. They touched and Nate fell. Pearson, stepping around him, caught the ball on his hip. It seemed to get there with a half pound of glue. There was no other earthly explanation for a catch like that. Pearson looked almost as startled as the crowd. He loped into the end zone, and it was Dallas 17-14.

What followed was even uglier.

Wright confronted the official, Jerry Bergman, and said Pearson had interfered. Tarkenton charged onto the field with Page and a half dozen others. They swore and demanded justice, called names and screamed. The touchdown stood. From the stands a whiskey bottle hurtled onto the field and struck another official, Armen Terzian, in the head. He was bleeding. Chuck Foreman, who'd been hit by a rock-filled snow missile in Buffalo the week before, ran to the grandstand and yelled for the fans to knock it off.

The game ended a few seconds later. For Tarkenton, the horror wasn't over. Shortly after the game he learned that his preacher father, Dallas Tarkenton, had died of a heart attack while watching the game.

Sammy White was a scamperer. He had speed and instincts and a habit of hanging onto the ball when the headhunters in the secondary committed their assaults. All those qualities are endearing to a quarterback. Tarkenton threw often to Sammy, who was the Rookie of the Year in 1976 and played for 10 seasons.

When Sane Men Went Bonkers in Pasadena

Nobody put Chuck Foreman in Winston Churchill's class as a public speaker. But late in the 1976 season, Chuck Foreman asked the Viking captains for permission to make a speech.

Powers of oratory were notably missing from his resume. What you found confirmed that Chuck Foreman was one of the two or three best running backs in American football, hugely skilled, strong and intuitive. He caught the ball as well as he ran, and in 1976 he was destined to become the first running back in Viking history to surpass 200 yards in one game. It happened in Philadelphia in a season when the Vikings won 11 games, lost two and tied one for yet another division championship. Moreover, they were going to win the two playoff games and, despite howls of protest from the millions of pro football watchers around the country, crash their way into a fourth Super Bowl in eight years.

All this, Chuck Foreman prophesied when he stood in the Viking locker room and produced The Talk. There was no doubt about Foreman's intellect. He was a perceptive guy but not renowned as a polished speaker. What he said was "let's go crazy."

He added some four letter words to remove any idea that this was a talk borrowed from Dale Carnegie. What he meant was: We've got great players. But we're getting old. We've got maybe one more shot at it with guys like Tarkenton, Marshall, Eller, Page, Krause, Yary, White, Cox and all the others. Everytime we go into a Super Bowl, we go under control. Discipline. That's us. Calm. No screaming and jumping up and down. Emotion? Emotion is for the Bears and the tailgaters. We're cool pros. Everybody says that.

Put all that stuff in the can, Chuck Foreman said.

"Let's go crazy. Let's get wild. Let's have fun. Let it hang out all the way from here to Pasadena."

The NFL was playing the Super Bowl in Pasadena's Rose Bowl in January of 1977. H.P. Grant, the father of calm, disciplined and non-screaming football, heard about this and entered no objection.

"As long as they make the plane to California before they go crazy," he said, "I'm OK."

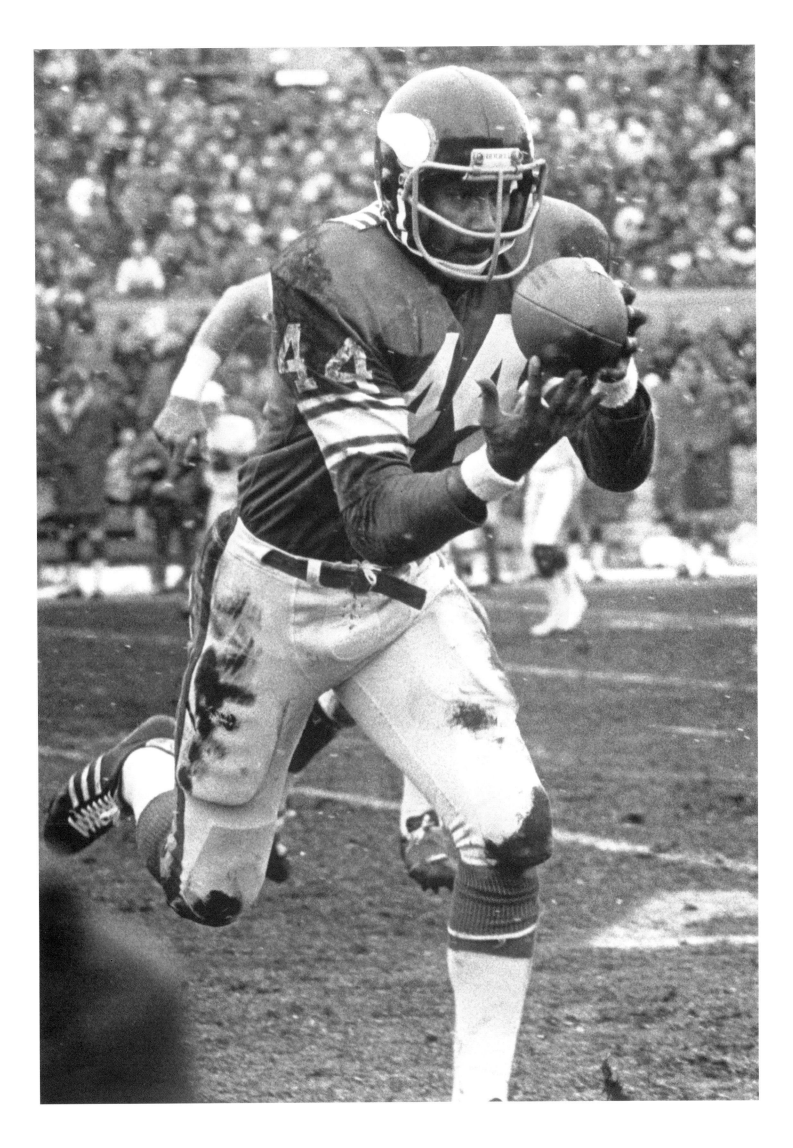

Psychologists might have sided with Foreman. Maybe it was time to try something different with this team. Despite Grant's gospels about the hazards of eccentric behavior and individualism, the players who were winning Central and NFC championships practically every year weren't automatons. Far from it. Tarkenton ran the offense on the field and called the plays. He bitched at bad blocking and improvised plays.

And, of course, he was the man who maneuvered his way out of Minnesota to New York and back to Minnesota when New York started looking dangerous for independent-minded quarterbacks. Alan Page followed nobody's drum beats but Alan Page's. Marshall was a man-sprite. Eller played throughout his career as a man who was almost invincible when paired against great players but dawdled and smelled the dandelions when his opponent was mediocre. Hilgenberg was often an unguided missile. Foreman's running style was pure invention. And then in the middle of the 1976 season, little Sammy White, a rookie, grabbed a pass from Tarkenton against the Lions and was bolting toward the end zone when he raised the ball in a gesture of impending triumph.

By today's standards of burlesque celebrating, Sammy's act was mild. Two things about it were different for 1976. Nobody EVER celebrated like that on Bud Grant's teams. Nobody spiked the ball. Nobody danced the hula or wiggled like a snake. That was one difference. The other was that Sammy dropped the ball before he got

The most hideous moment of Sammy White's life was followed by some quiet advice from his mother. Sammy exuberantly spiked the ball – before he reached the end zone. The Lions recovered. "Son," his mother said over the phone after watching TV, " you learned something today." He did. He hugged the ball for the rest of his career.

into the end zone.

There were no demonstrations from Grant on the sidelines. There was a glare that could have pierced a battleship's armor plate. White felt it from the back of the end zone, where the Lions recovered the ball for a touchback, to the back of his skull when he got to the bench. Grant spoke briefly. "There's a difference," he said, "between show biz and showboat."

White never performed the act again in ten years of pro football. What he did for most of the rest of the game was to pray for a chance to atone. He got it later in the game when Tarkenton lofted another long

one near the goal. Sammy caught it. The
Vikings won and Sammy was spared seven more
days of the Bud Grant glare.

It might not have been a coincidence that
one of the additions to the team for 1976 was
Nate Allen, a jivey defensive back. Nate played
with a rollicking recklessness and, on some days,
a supernatural nose for the ball. He'd been lost
in the 49er secondary, but when he was traded
to Minnesota, he recognized a chance. The
Vikings needed depth. They also needed some
off-the-wall spontaneity. He wasn't sure what he
was getting into, coming to Minnesota. "Nate,"
his 49er pal, Cedric Hardman told him, "you're
gonna freeze. Up there they wear earlaps on the
4th of July. December, you're gonna look at the
other teams and everybody is standing around
the hot air blowers like they're pumping
lifeblood. No hot air blowers for you, Nate. Oh,
you're gonna learn about Minnesota."

"Hey, baby," Allen said. "Those guys win. I
got 11 months to thaw out."

Nate discounted any serious designs on
football immortality. "Call me Nate the
Trashman," he said when he arrived. "I pick up
blocked punts, lousy passes and anything they
don't want to nail down or paint. I'm not particular. All I am is available."

So the team had plenty of free-floating personalities, some of whom
were ready to unload that stiff professional veneer. The ones who didn't
see any need for a character change humored the idea and went along
with it. "I don't know that you can turn it on and off, having one kind
of attitude as a team and then wanting to tear down walls," said Jeff
Siemon. Siemon's calm, intelligent off-field reserve could make a Tibetan
monk look hysterical. But he also hungered for a Super Bowl
championship. Like Page and Krause and some of the other more
restrained veterans, Siemon said: "Sure. If the locker room is going to
get noisier with boom boxes and guys yelling, 'get crazy,' let's see what
happens. It may be fun."

What didn't change much was that the Vikings kept winning. One
reason was the arrival of Ahmad Rashad, the onetime Bobby Moore
who'd been having an uneven career in pro ball. Nothing much in St.
Louis, strong performance in Buffalo, and not much rapport with the
former Viking assistant, Jack Patera, in Seattle. When the Vikings got
him he brought a reputation. "Probably bad news," an NFL coach said.
"Individualist, questionable work ethic."

When Grant saw him the first day, he wondered where that gossip

The supporting-cast players are
often the most intriguing ones.
Nate Allen was a defensive back,
verbal and jivey, a guy who usually
had a wagonload of fun playing
football. Nate could cover receivers
and block kicks but he never put
on airs. He called himself "The
Trashman." He hit or picked up
anything that moved. Whatever
Nate's identity, it got him to the
Super Bowl.

Ahmad Rashad's football was a kind of relaxed art and a form of self-entertainment. He rapped with opposing players. He pretended to be terrified by homicidal linebackers (hey, not always pretended). And he generally wrung every ounce of camaraderie and joy out of football. Players on all sides admired and liked him. Rival players liked him less when he went downfield for a pass, because he usually caught everything in sight and did it with style – terrified or not.

came from. After a couple of passing drill sessions with him, Tarkenton also wondered. When Rashad finished as a Viking six years later, EVERYBODY who played on his team or spent any time with him, on or off the field, had the same response:

"Where are you going to find anything better than this guy?"

Rashad was a man who played with precision and guts when he needed it. Underneath, he had a kind of unshakable amusement at the idea of grown men striking all those fierce attitudes in a game that to him was invented for fun. The villains of his life were linebackers. "Those guys," he'd say, "they're angry people. I don't know why. Big and tough like that, why do you have to play mad? I go down there on pass routes, and I let those guys know in advance I mean them no harm. I might even wave to them. Tell them what fine human beings they are. Ask about the missus and the kids. And those big guys, they stare and look sour, and when I run into their zones they want to squash me. I ask you: Could you go through life being a linebacker?"

He quickly became the most popular man on the team, a sort of effortless confidante to both white and black players. His network of friends among the great black athletes of America was remarkable. When the Vikings arrived in Los Angeles, Kareem Abdul Jabbar would be waiting for him to have dinner. He'd get telephone calls all over the country from Muhammad Ali. But what counted most to Grant and Tarkenton was that he teamed with young White to create a legitimate two-way deep threat in the passing game. Still, for all of the multiple sets that sprang from Jerry Burns' nervous mind, Tarkenton's improvising flair and Foreman running and catching, it was the Viking defense that drove this team into the Super Bowl again. The Steelers' Bradshaw thought it was the best he'd ever seen in stopping an offense with a yard to go. "I never saw a team with that kind of penetration," he said. He made the statement after the Vikings beat the Super Bowl champions in the regular season. The havoc came from the Viking special teams as well as the Purple Gang. For most of the game, the Steelers were actually unable to kick the ball in the face of the Viking rush. Pittsburgh scored a touchdown and Page blocked Roy Gerela's conversion try. Gerela attempted a field goal from the 22 and Eller blocked it. Gerela kicked from the 33 a few minutes after that, and Page creamed it again.

When he hit the open field, Chuck Foreman "created." He ran with moves. But he was a different character hitting the line. He drove with high legs and forearms, and he usually found a way.

Later in the game the Steelers' Bobby Walden, the former Viking punter, badly rushed his kick because Page's intimidation forced center Mike Webster to snap the ball high. Not long afterward, it happened again. Walden tried to run with the ball, but fumbled. Nate Allen, who'd intercepted Bradshaw twice in the game, recovered. Foreman scored from short range and the Vikings won.

Before the playoffs, Grant surrendered to Foreman's go-crazy proposition. He told his players all the signs for it made sense. There was the day in Detroit when the Viking team bus got snagged in a pre-game traffic jam on the way to the Silverdome in Pontiac. Grant always insisted that the team bus should arrive at the stadium no more than an hour before game time. Players who had to kill time before the kickoff were likely to be edgy players or distracted players. He never used dead reckoning to plot the bus' drive time. He sent the driver out on a dummy run the day before the game if the stadium was new to the team, and he drew on previous trips if the team had played there before. Grant thought he had Pontiac pretty well figured out, so he ordered the bus to leave the motel an hour and 15 minutes before kickoff. It rained that day in Pontiac. Approximately 80,000 people left late for the game. Most of them left at the same time and practically all of them were on the same road as the Viking bus. By the scheduled kickoff time, Mike Lynn, the head administrator himself, was out in the medians trying to direct traffic to give the two Viking buses some wedging space. He had as much success as old King Lear trying to slow the ocean. Riding the second bus, Tarkenton needled Lynn ruthlessly:

"Hey, Lynn," he yelled through the open window, "How about another pre-game meal? Your men are dropping like flies from starvation. You want these guys to go into a game with the Lions' undernourished? Their lives will be on your hands, Lynn."

Lynn sweated until the Lions blew a conversion in the second half and the Vikings won, 10-9.

That kind of year. The auguries were right for something wild and non-traditional in the Super Bowl, such as the Vikings winning. In the first NFC playoff game, Grant himself got into the act. The National Football League was and is obsessed with the idea of micro-managing its annual tournament. All blades of grass have to be in place, all press conferences on time, all contingencies covered, including the possibility of a typhoon in Minnesota in December. Grant never made his peace with the super planners. When the league directed the Los Angeles Rams to fly into Minnesota on Christmas Eve for the NFC final that year, Grant bellowed against this heartless act of bureaucracy. He said it deprived the Los Angeles players of the holiday with their families. It didn't seem to bother the Rams all that much, since there was a pretty standard league policy requiring a team to be safely installed at the play-off site two days before the game. But Bud did his deadpan hassling with or without provocation. A week before, as the first playoff game with Washington approached, Grant insisted that the FBI or somebody of that ilk ought to investigate Mark Mosely's shoe.

Mosely was the Redskins' field goal kicker. Insiders generally believed that as his career ebbed, Mark was putting some hidden weight in the toe of his shoe to give his kicks extra oomph. The Vikings' Freddie Cox admitted experimenting with a toe shank himself, although he never used it in a game. Grant concocted an elaborate scenario, pretending he might unleash Cox with his toe shank if the league didn't do something about Mosely. The Redskins' George Allen – who once assigned his football spies to climb a tree high above his opponents' practice field – replied in a burst of wounded dignity.

"How could anybody suspect an organization like the Redskins of violating a league rule?"

He threatened to bring a butcher's scale to weigh Cox's shoes.

If Allen brought the scale, it was never used. If Mosely used a weight, it was never found. If the Redskins had serious intentions of winning, they were misguided. Brent McClanahan got off a long run early in the game. The Vikings scored. Their defense stormed quarterback Bill

Kilmer from start to finish. It may have been their best game in five years until the fourth quarter, when it didn't matter any more and the Redskins scored twice. The Vikings won 35-20 and the Rams flew in on Christmas Eve for the NFC championship game.

This time, Jack Youngblood vowed, they weren't going to be sidetracked by the weather. They weren't going to think about it or worry about it. So they came out for the pre-game exertions in shirtsleeves. No warm-up jackets, and the wind-chill was close to zero. "I thought they were nuts," Jeff Siemon said. "But I guess they thought they had to make a statement." They did, early in the game. With less than a foot to go for a touchdown, the Rams decided to kick a field goal instead of taking on Page, Eller, Marshall and the rest of the Vikings' defense. Tom Dempsey, the club-footed heavyweight who once hit a 63-yard field goal, swung his foot. Nate Allen came tearing off the flank and blocked the kick. Bobby Bryant, cutting in from the other, picked it up on the 10 and ran 90 yards into the end zone, from where he

If opposing runners were headed for Matt Blair's patch (above) they usually ducked their heads, the better to hold on to them.

Quarterback's calling cadence, checking off. The defensive back (Nate Allen, left) better keep his neck on a swivel. They could come from any place.

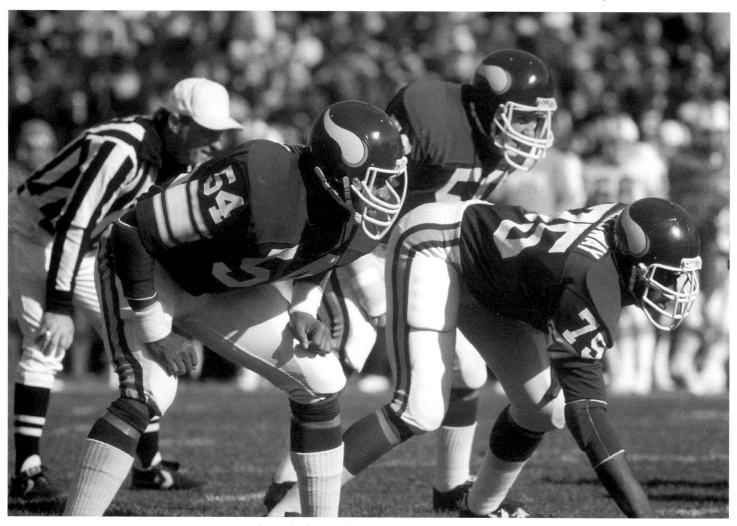

The linebacker's version of Utopia is being unleashed as a blitzer on every pass play in the game. Fred McNeill (54) was a linebacker. He's lined up here to blitz. Would you call this man eager?

thoughtfully blew a kiss to his wife.

The Big Play. Grant and the Vikings lived on it for 15 years.

It got to be 17-0. Pat Haden and Larry McCutcheon brought the Rams back and, with the Vikings leading 17-13, Haden retreated to throw. The Vikings blitzed with Matt Blair and Wally Hilgenberg, turning loose the Rams' fleet pass catchers one on one against Bobby Bryant and Nate Wright. Backpedaling, Haden lofted the ball 40 yards downfield to the speeding Ron Jessie. Jessie was open near the goal line. Near the sideline, Bryant had seen Haden look down the middle. It was worth the risk. Bryant deserted Harold Jackson, the man he was covering. As the ball was about to settle in Jessie's arms for the go-ahead touchdown, Bryant leaped and intercepted. A few minutes later, after Tarkenton's critical third down pass to Foreman, the Vikings scored a clinching touchdown and won 24-13.

The Big Play, again. Why not in Pasadena against the Raiders?

Maybe there was a big play, maybe not. If there was, it went the wrong way. The Vikings were on the Raiders' goal line early. Fred McNeill blocked a Ray Guy punt and McNeill recovered at the 3. That wasn't the big play. It came a few minutes later. With McClanahan about to go into the end zone, Phil Vilipiano hit the ball with his helmet. McClanahan fumbled and Oakland's Willie Hall recovered. Clarence Davis got the Raiders out of danger with a 35-yard run on third down.

SUPER BOWL XI
OAKLAND (AFC) 32, MINNESOTA (NFC) 14

The Raiders ran some more and Ken Stabler passed to Dave Casper. And when they stalled, Errol Mann kicked a field goal.

The Raiders now knew they could run. In a few minutes Stabler also knew he could hit Fred Biletnikoff, a walking gluepot for all the stickum he used for hand lotion.

Art Shell and Gene Upshaw on the Raiders offensive left front tore up the lighter Viking defense. For their own defense, the Raiders had the usual amalgam of cavemen, misunderstood goliaths and miscellaneous Bela Lugosis. All of them could hit and they all played with the Raiders' unholy defiance, jubilantly encouraged by coach John Madden. They had people like Art Tatum, the designated headhunter; a "Doctor Death" named Skip Thomas; and George Atkinson, who was accused of trying to maim players by no less than Pittsburgh's Chuck Noll. They had the tackle from Mars, the bald-headed Otis Sistrunk, the brooding monster, John Matuszack, and Mad Stork Ted Hendricks at linebacker.

The Vikings couldn't molest Stabler when he passed and couldn't handle the defensive villains. Somewhere in the middle of the second half, one of the Vikings cursed on the sidelines: "Jesus Christ, it's happening again."

For the fourth time, 32-14. And this time, maybe even nearly a billion Chinamen were beginning to wonder.

For the fourth time, the Vikings went to the Super Bowl. It was a glorious day in Pasadena. The Rose Bowl was floral. The card sections were flamboyant. The Raiders were insufferable. Oakland 32, Vikings 14.

SUPER BOWL XI

Pasadena

NFL

An Official Publication of the National Football League.
AFC versus NFC for the NFL Championship and the Vince Lombardi Trophy
Sunday, January 9, 1977   12:30 P.M.   Rose Bowl, Pasadena, California $2.00

The firm of Tarkenton and Foreman was one of the NFL's thriving partnerships for years. Chuck could line up anyplace sideline to sideline. Usually Francis found a way to get him the ball. They were the profile players in the Viking offense, but look at the daylight created by the grunts up front.

passing record in the NFL, and yet in the final moments of his final game, he called three meaningless running plays to wind down the clock.

Somebody who suspected his retirement plans asked a question. Why not try to pass for a touchdown in the last minute, something like Ted Williams hitting a homer in his last at-bat?

Tarkenton's response was a mirthless laugh and a shrug. "The first thing that would have happened," he said, "is that somebody might have gotten hurt going downfield on a play that counted for nothing. The second thing is that even if we scored, it wouldn't have made a bit of difference to anybody in the world except the people who put on commercials after a touchdown."

So he stepped away from football. It took the great quarterbacks who followed nearly two decades to approach the records he wrote: 343 touchdown passes, 3,686 completions in 6,647 attempts and 47,003 yards. The man who played in the backfield behind him, Chuck Foreman, left the next season in 1979 after a career in which he was named to the Pro Bowl for five straight seasons, gained more than 1,000 yards in three straight years and scored 52 touchdowns.

But for people who watched the Vikings, 1979 wasn't a year for the mathematicians. It was for the eulogists, because by the end of the 1979 seasons, most of the great players who produced that chain of championships, and filled the unlovely little stadium in Bloomington with all of the memories, were history: Tarkenton; Jim Marshall retiring in 1979 with a victory lap around the field on the seat of a convertible after 19 seasons and 270 games; Paul Krause with his tons of interceptions and Wally Hilgenberg. Both went in 1979. Mick Tingelhoff left a year earlier

An exulting moment for a ballplayer: introductions. The crowd roars. The battle is about to be joined. Sunday afternoon at the ballpark for Carl Eller (81) and Jim Marshall. A is for Adrenaline.

Some ballplayers are born with big league skills. Dave Osborn (41) wasn't. But he came from a town called Cando, N.D., and can-do became his creed.

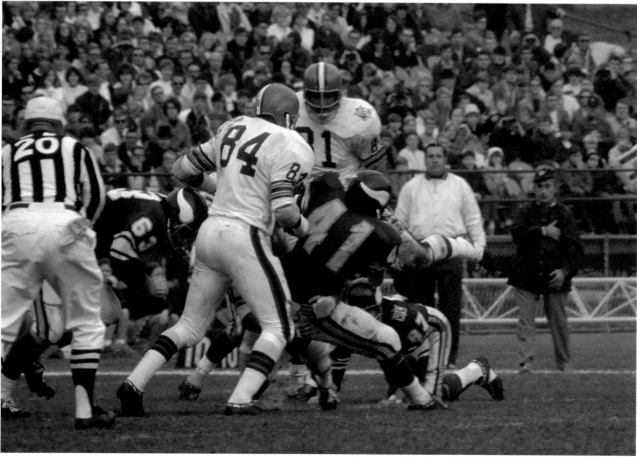

after 240 games. Carl Eller refused to accept Bud Grant's judgment in 1978 and tried unsuccessfully to retread his career with the Seattle Seahawks. Alan Page fared better. Grant decided in 1979 that Page's declining weight had caused declining production, and he couldn't play defensive tackle in the NFL. Page disagreed. He went to Chicago and played three more seasons.

By 1979, a dozen or more of the old warhorses had departed – Roy Winston, Grady Alderman, Bill Brown, Fred Cox, Dave Osborn, Karl Kassulke, Ed Sharockman, Jeff Wright and others.

The transition year, 1979, was not very productive, 7-9, one of those rare Bud Grant losing seasons, but significant because of the emergence of a tobacco-chewing Texan as the next Viking quarterback, Tommy Kramer.

He got to be known as Two-Minute Tommy, a player whose competitive drives and instincts made him one of the most accomplished architects of the late-game scoring drive in pro football. There was one other reason: Although later in his career he got in dutch with the fans for his crude and erratic off-field behavior, most of it drink-related, Kramer played with a mastery of the field. He had a bold and nimble football mind that matched his physical skills. He was, in fact, one of the best quarterbacks in football for six or seven years, until the weight of serious injuries and his trouble with alcohol ended his career.

Grant had a rehearsed answer to reporters who asked about Kramer's feisty leadership: "You'd be feisty, too, if you had nine or ten kids competing at the table for the potatoes and peas." The Vikings drafted him on the first round from Rice. He was the recycling of some of the great Texas passers out of the '30s, '40s and '50s, the Sammy Baughs, Davey O'Briens and Bobby Laynes. On his first day under contract he announced his intention to become the No. 1 Viking quarterback. He didn't specify "when Francis retires." He meant No. 1.

It wasn't quite braggadocio. To

In his big years, Tommy Kramer quarterbacked at the highest levels of pro football. He threw, battled and ran when he was healthy and rode the officials when the calls went wrong. He was, in short, a tough guy to beat.

Kramer, it made sense. He made things happen on a field, and he wasn't afraid to take risks. He played pro football from start to finish that way. And in 1979 he beat the 49ers with a sensational second-half passing outburst that solidified him in the league and with the fans. By then, the Vikings were in the midst of their retooling. Rickey Young, a versatile running back and old-fashioned team player, eased the problem of replacing Chuck Foreman. People like Wes Hamilton, Jim Hough and Dennis Swilley were new to the offensive line,

Coaches hunger for a guy like Rickey Young (upper photo). As a running back he came with all the tools. He could run, catch and block. He was unselfish about his stats, but some days they led all the rest.

The quarterback is free and throwing. It means the people in front of him, including Wes Hamilton (right, 61) have done their job.

Tommy Hannon, John Turner and Keith Nord new in the defensive backfield. Scott Studwell brought all those records he'd broken as Dick Butkus' successor as a linebacking hero at Illinois. Greg Coleman, who pioneered the art form of pretending supreme agony when a rusher wandered into his extended foot, did the punting. He did it well. His kicking and/or acting were directly responsible for at least a half dozen Viking victories over his career.

Rick Danmeier had succeeded Fred Cox as the place kicker. Mark Mullaney, Duck White and Randy Holloway were the youth of the defensive line, joined a year later by the first-round draft choice from Washington, Doug Martin. Ted Brown, a stumpy, barreling running back from North Carolina was drafted

You can debate whether football is a game of contact or collision. Either way, there's not much room for tender feelings. Dennis Swilley lines up a Lion linebacker in front of Sammy Johnson (upper right). Jim Hough and Swilley block (above). Scott Studwell and Tom Hannon (45) crunch a halfback (right).

on the first round in 1979. Dave Huffman, an offensive lineman from Notre Dame and the eventual vaudevillian of the Viking locker room, came with him that year. So did Joe Senser, the tight end and basketball hero from West Chester State, and quarterback Steve Dils from Stanford. For a couple of seasons Dave Roller, a talkative and tubby defensive tackle, played on the Viking defensive line. The fact that he did might have been a wry comment on the damage caused by the departure of Page and Eller. But for those couple of years, every bartender and barroom bouncer in Minnesota who fantasized a life in pro football had Dave Roller as a role model and alter-ego.

This group did not immediately terrify the National Football League.

But by mid-December in 1980 the Vikings stood 8-6 and in a position to win another division championship. At Met Stadium, they faced the Cleveland Browns, who at 10-4 were one of the Super Bowl

For years the TV announcers identified Scott Studwell as the man who broke all of Dick Butkus' tackling records at Illinois. That got old when Studwell began breaking Viking tackling records. Above, he officiates in the burial of a Redskin back.

Almost nobody today kicks field goals the old fashioned way, facing the goalposts, hitting the ball with the toe. But Rick Danmeier (right), Fred Cox' successor, made 70 in 106 tries in seven seasons kicking like an old fogey.

favorites.

It may be the one game the Vikings played in two decades at the Met that left the stadium ghosts stupefied when the team left for the Metrodome two years later.

Cleveland leaped into a 13-0 lead on a touchdown pass from Brian Sipe to Calvin Hill and Sipe's short scoring dash in the second quarter. In the second half, Kramer drove the team with an aerial frenzy that eventually was to produce 456 yards on 38 completions in 48 attempts and four touchdowns. The first went to Senser for 31 yards. But the score was still 23-9 for Cleveland in the fourth quarter. Kramer went five for five and 72 yards to cut the disadvantage to 23-15. The score looked screwy because Danmeier and Don Cockroft of the Browns kept missing extra points or getting them blocked.

With less than two minutes remaining Kramer passed 12 yards to Rashad for another touchdown at the end of a 47-yard drive begun by Bobby Bryant's interception. It was now 23-22 for Cleveland and it looked like the grave for the Vikings when Cleveland recovered Danmeier's attempted onside kickoff at midfield. The Browns moved to the Viking 36 but punted into the end zone on fourth down.

The crowd was yelling that it was time for Two-Minute Tommy. The crowd was wrong. Kramer didn't have two minutes. What he had was 23 seconds, and he was looking at 80 yards with no time-outs.

Twenty-three Second Tommy?

Why not? From the 20 he drilled a pass to Senser, who flipped a lateral to Teddy Brown. It was one of those ancient hook-and-ladder arrangements dug up for this emergency by Jerry Burns and Les Steckel, the receivers coach. Brown ran out bounds on the Cleveland 46 with four seconds to play.

Nobody on the bench or in the huddle said "Hail Mary." They might have, but that one had already been done. Burns and Grant momentarily

Tommy Kramer feathers the ball to Teddy Brown for a line smash against the Falcons.

considered a deep crossing route like one that gave the Detroit Lions a last-breath victory over Baltimore years before in a game that was almost impossible for the Colts to lose. If one of the Cleveland safeties got knocked down, the receiver might score. It wasn't promising.

"Squadron right," they told Kramer. "Squadron right" was a play whose chances depend entirely on the raw congestion of bodies, jumping for the ball. The play has a half dozen names today. Although it was relatively new then, almost everybody uses it now. It's the desperation play of choice. Line up three fast receivers on one side of the field. Send them into the end zone. Throw the ball into the end zone. Something good might happen, a crazy bounce and catch, or our guy outjumps their guys, or the official calls interference.

Sammy White cradles the ball exactly where Kramer aimed it, on the numbers.

Not many interference calls are made on the play today. The officials let natural law take over. The Viking squadron lined up with Ahmad Rashad, Sammy White and Terry LeCount, a young receiver acquired in a trade, stacked near the right sideline. Kramer took the ball and waited for them to charge the end zone. Half of the Cleveland defense was waiting for them. The strategy was for LeCount to lead the Viking posse into the end zone and then leap and tip the ball in the hope that Rashad or White would catch it before it came down. LeCount eventually got near the goal line, but way late. He was delayed on the scrimmage line by the Brown defense. White, however, was there when the ball came down. The man closest to him was Thom Darden of the Cleveland secondary. They went up and Darden got a hand on the ball.

"If I was standing in the end zone," Rashad said later, "we would have lost. Darden would have made a spectacular play. But no way I was going to be standing in the end zone. I'd run that play before. If the ball's tipped, it's likely to come back." So Rashad was not only silky but smart. The ball caromed back into the playing field. Rashad got it in his left hand at the 3 and slid backward into the end zone for a 28-23 Viking victory.

"It was a terrific moment," he said later, "but I'd have to say I've made better catches."

The hell you have, somebody in the Viking locker room yelled. "That catch was worth 5,000 bucks (per man) in playoff money."

Rashad didn't get into network television a few years later by being disagreeable. "OK," he said, "it was the greatest."

It practically was. Somebody did give it a name tentatively: "The Miracle of 78th Street." This was a location well known in Bloomington but not particularly well known among the saints in the sky, so Rashad's catch didn't get enshrined. It did get the Vikings into the first round of the NFC playoffs in Philadelphia a few weeks later. For 15 minutes, they looked like the best there was in the NFC. Kramer threw crisply in the January cold. He hit Sammy White with a 30-yard touchdown strike in the first quarter, and Ted Brown went in for a second score. The Viking defense pestered Ron Jaworski, the Eagle quarterback, through most of the first half until Jaworski found the rhythm and protection. His pass to the 6-foot-8 Harold Carmichael reduced the Viking lead to 14-7 at half-time and Wilbert Montgomery tied the score on an eight-yard run. Matt Blair and Doug Martin mugged Jaworski in the Eagles end zone for a 16-14 Viking lead. But Dick Vermeil's Eagles' offense behind Jaworski and Montgomery dominated the last 20 minutes and won, 31-16.

When it was over and the locker room was emptying, the departing Vikings players had handshakes for each other as part of the usual rituals – but also for two others, Stubby Eason and Fred Zamberletti. They usually did. Stubby was the equipment manager. Fred was the trainer, and remarkably, still is. They were people of special trust for the thousands of athletes who entered their peculiar stewardships over the years. In fact, that season, the players gave one of the game balls to Jimmy Eason after they'd beaten Cleveland. Although their fondness was buried under the usual coarse locker room hazing, giving Jimmy a game ball was no trifling act.

Eason was the little man known to the crowds only as the guy who limped out on the field to retrieve the kicking tee after each Viking kick-off. He ran, but it wasn't very stylish. A man with an artificial leg can't disguise it very well running in the middle of a football field. He lost his leg on the invasion beaches of Italy in World War II. Stubby had been an amateur boxer, and looked it. He had scar tissue on his face and he affected a grumpy style because it seemed to fit into that boisterous parlor of professional athletes. But he was a friend of anyone who needed or wanted a friend. And that meant a rookie headed for the waiver wire after a week in camp, or a Jim Marshall or Mick Tingelhoff. He kept a confidence. He joined the horselaughs and he understood the tears of a 10-year veteran, leaving the locker room after being released, closing the door on something irreplaceable in his life.

Each Thanksgiving Stubby and his wife invited the bachelor players, or the players living away from their families, to a dinner at the Eason

In the beginning, there was Fred Zamberletti. There still is Fred Zamberletti. Fred (left, with Dr. Dave Fischer, the team physician) was the first Viking trainer. He's been the only Viking trainer. That's 35 years of healing hamstrings, consoling, taping, ministering and keeping the whirlpool hot. He's heard the groans and alibis for 35 years, and never lost the players' trust. (Photo credit: Paul Spinelli/NFL Photos)

home. The table was freighted with the usual Thanksgiving provender plus the pasta and sauce the Easons laid on relentlessly.

Dottie Eason was still looking after some of them after Jimmy died, and when her own health had begun to fail.

Observing this at a luncheon gathering in 1994, Paul Krause – one of the Eason's closest friends – said something about longevity. "Jimmy started with the Vikings in 1961," he said. "That seems like a whole different century." It did. But could anybody really imagine Fred Zamberletti?

He was there for the first dislocated thumb in Bemidji in 1961. He was still doing dislocated thumbs and a million other things in 1995. This is The Viking Institution. No one else need apply. He came in with Van Brocklin and Tarkenton and Jim Marshall and practically statehood for Minnesota. He's a big, shambling guy, Freddie, with a quick grin and sensible head. He was the man who in 1964, when Tom Franckhauser suffered a fractured skull in practice at Bemidji, quickly organized the response. He was the man who had an emergency vehicle available daily at the practice site and knew what to do and not to do until the unconscious player was in the hospital. A doctor said later that Zamberletti's cool under duress had saved Franckhauser's life. In 35 years he's heard all of the locker room stories the ailing and the not-so-ailing have ever recited from the forum of the whirlpool room. He learned early that the trick was to be agreeably skeptical when the injury didn't look that bad. You can be too skeptical and alienate the ballplayer. Just skeptical enough to let him know you're not buffaloed, but you're still a friend. A good trainer can win almost as many ball games as a good player. Zamberletti won one in Chicago years ago when he stayed up all night with Fred Cox, and treated his sore back by fashioning a support made up of ice-filled beer cans.

"There's a lot of pain in pro ball that the fan can't possibly be aware of," Fred said. "All of them play in pain one way or another. That's part of the game and part of making a living. They make more money today. They still have to play in pain. But the guys I think I respected most were the guys who went out there years ago, making only a few thousand dollars a year, and played their guts out."

On the road Freddie filled up his time by prowling historical places. In Atlanta one year he decided to visit the federal penitentiary, the residence of a man who was a remote relative of a friend of Zamberletti's. "He'd been in the mob for a while someplace," Fred remembered. "I went to see him as a favor. We had a nice talk. I was riding back to the hotel when I went into my pockets for money for the driver."

It was too bad that visiting hours were over at the pen. The guy had cheerfully lifted some of Fred's cash while confiding the latest from Cell Block B.

And in the season of 1981, the Vikings revisited the homely patches of Met Stadium for the last time. It wasn't a very triumphant hour. They finished 7-9 and missed the playoffs by losing their last five games, although Kramer's offense was one of the more productive ones in the league. Their exit from the scene of all those snow-frosted sagas and the tailgating sideshows had been in the works for a half dozen years. The politics got thick when the Vikings started demanding a bigger and more modern stadium to stay even with the revenue being hauled in by some of their competitors. Lynn publicly called the defenseless little Met "a piece of crap." He may have been right aesthetically, but the language did tend to roil up the Met Stadium romanticists.

There was sometimes a forgotten man in the Vikings' downfield passing assaults. Terry LeCount didn't have the high visibility of Ahmad Rashad or Sammy White, who tended to create open spaces for LeCount.

The campaign came to rival the 30 Years War. Downtown Minneapolis promoters, alarmed at the decline of the city's center in recent years, argued that the city needed the glamor of a major league stadium to regenerate itself. Minneapolis didn't get much sympathy in the legislature. Moreover, the public never expressed any love for a domed stadium in Minneapolis. Bloomington's attempts to keep the Vikings and the Minnesota Twins with a new stadium drew more political support. But eventually Max Winter, the Viking president, aggressively joined the Minneapolis stadium lobby. It made sense. Max's soul was in the city, as a kid on the North Side and later a

As architecture, the old Met Stadium was a well-intended dump. The seats were cramped, the corridors were tight, the views were obstructed and it got ferociously cold in December. But the Vikings tended to prosper in lousy weather, and the fans kept piling in. The Met lasted for pro football from 1961 to 1981. In the minds of thousands of nostalgia freaks, the Vikings lost some soul when they left. What they gained was money and warmer feet.

businessman and promoter with downtown Minneapolis as his base.

But his chief agent at the Legislature, Mike Lynn, was privately holding out for Bloomington.

The several faces of Mike.

"That's right," he said. "On the record and in every statement I ever made to the politicians, I was on the side of the domed stadium in downtown Minneapolis. But I really wanted an open-air stadium in Bloomington, a big and modern one. At one critical stage, John Cowles, Jr. of the newspaper flew to Hawaii to talk Max into supporting a dome for Minneapolis. I knew I had to get to Max before John did. I didn't. Max bought the idea of a Minneapolis dome and eventually he and the rest of the Minneapolis group pushed it through the Legislature. I joined their arguments. I can't say I was very sincere. But the way it turned out, it was a great thing for the Vikings, for the Twins, for major league athletics in Minnesota and for the city of Minneapolis."

In 1982, though, the first year of the Metrodome's operation, the Vikings may have been more lucky than good. They were good enough to get into the playoffs, but even luckier to avoid suffocation. In the first few months of its life, the dome deflated twice.

Bud and the Blizzards Depart Jointly

The Vikings opened the Metrodome Age in 1982 with two rousing successes: 1. They beat the Tampa Bay Bucs. 2. The dome stayed up the whole game.

Neither was a cinch before the season started. The Vikings were unsteady and the dome kept deflating.

In the long run, though, the Metrodome met all of the expectations of its small cult of unpopular but influential supporters. It produced millions of dollars in additional revenue for the Vikings. It turned on the lights again in downtown Minneapolis. In baseball, the Metrodome's quirks of lighting and its bouncy turf baffled enemy players so totally that in the dome's fifth year an event took place to arouse the wonder of all: Minnesota won the World Series.

That may have been the dome's biggest of all cultural dividends. For the first time and for all time, it gave Minnesotans a chance to tell the world: We're No. 1. Not almost, or vice, or semi. But No. 1. Four years later, somewhat more legitimately, the Twins did it all over again.

For the fans, watching ball in the Metrodome was a visit to another planet. The tailgate disappeared. So did the quilted balloon suits they wore to the ball game after October. The temperature was a constant 70 degrees. No breeze blew. No skywriting plane flew. It was eerie. The fans kept looking for Darth Vader. In the beginning, the fans didn't come with much fervor. But they came. And after a while, once the ball game started, who needs frostbite?

For the Minnesota Vikings, nothing was ever quite the same after the dome arrived. Peace and quiet pretty well vanished. It might have been a coincidence. But in the span of less than three years after the Vikings switched from the unlovely duckling of a stadium in Bloomington to the noisy pillbox on Chicago Avenue, these things happened:

A dispute between the owners and players shut down the NFL season for two months in 1982, the first year of the Metrodome.

Bud Grant quit as the Viking coach.

Les Steckel became the Viking coach.

Mike Lynn took full control of the Viking board room.

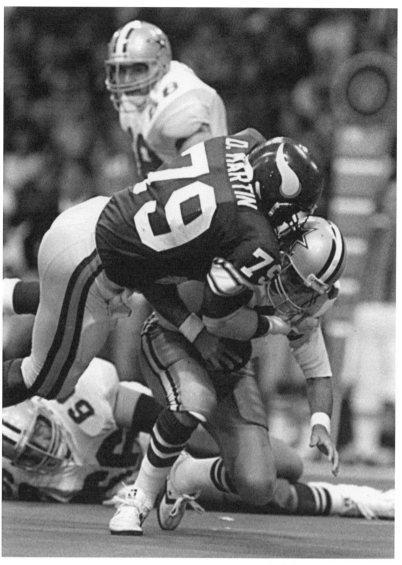

Doug Martin turns a play against the Cowboys into a rodeo. Hog-tie him, Doug.

The Vikings lost 13 out 16 games in 1984.

The more malicious of the Mike Lynn detractors still insist all of these events were related and were probably inevitable. Actually, that isn't fair to Lynn, who took enough of a pasting in his later years to deserve some fairness. Lynn didn't have a lot to do with what was happening on the field until well into the middle 1980s. Which means that the Vikings got back into the playoffs at the end of the 1982 strike season largely without Mike's creativity. The players went on strike after a couple of games into the season and didn't get back on the field until November. The Vikings stood 4-4 for the season the first week in January, needing a victory over Dallas at the Metrodome to make the playoffs.

One play in that game made the rounds of the cable TV highlights for the next 10 years. It's still there. With Dallas backed up to its one-yard-line, the Cowboys handed the ball to Tony Dorsett, hoping for a few yards to give them squirming room. Dorsett dutifully squirmed for a few yards and, surprisingly, found himself still upright. Free of the mess, he broke a tackle in the secondary, reached the sideline and ran 99 yards for a touchdown. It's as far as the statisticians say you can run a ball from scrimmage in football. The touchdown gave the crowd of 60,000 a panic. But Tommy Kramer threw for 242 yards and two touchdowns, Doug Martin forced two fumbles, the defensive line knocked down six passes and the Vikings won 31-27.

With a less-than-Herculean record of 5-4, the Vikings zoomed into the playoffs to beat Atlanta 30-24. The second playoff game, regrettably, was in Washington, D.C. The game was the kind of playoff you'd expect of a strike-shorted season. It didn't have much electricity and it had less suspense. Washington won 21-7 and advanced to the Super Bowl.

The Vikings may have made their most notable advances in 1982 at the draft table, where they picked Stanford's Darrin Nelson No. 1 and a muscular Ivy Leaguer named Steve Jordan No. 7. It was early for either of them to have a major impact, but both became team leaders of the 1980s and Jordan became an annual Pro Bowler. By now, one of the country's brawnier future lawyers, Tim Irwin from Tennessee, had been installed on the Viking offensive line and was going to stay there for more than 10 years. But Kramer went out early in the 1983 season with a knee injury. Steve Dils, his replacement, gave the offense a first-rate intellect but considerably less with his arm. Nelson, with a flitting, stop-and-go running style, led the team in both rushing and pass receiving. This was a credit to Darrin but also an indictment of its wide receiving corps, with Rashad no longer around. Tony Galbreath and Ted Brown, also backs, were the

other most popular receivers. Sammy White missed five games with an injury and Sam McCullum five more, which pretty well shot the outside receivers. All of this added to 8-8 for the season and fourth in the Central Division.

To H.P. Grant, it added one more number to the toll – Bud Grant's. He announced his retirement after the season.

Tight ends don't make the Pro Bowl six straight years by catching the football and admiring their statistics. Steve Jordan (left, 83) was a six-time Pro Bowler. On most plays he was banging his helmet and shoulder pads into a hostile guy on the line of scrimmage, as he does here against the Colts. Among his sweating partners on the offensive line for much of his career were Tim Irwin and Todd Kalis (below, pass blocking).

He gave the expected explanations about having done all there was to do, needing time for hunting and fishing. In general, he said, it was time to put his shovel down. Later in the Metrodome, the Vikings bestowed their unrestrained affections on the departing warrior. They produced enough gifts to start a sportsman's show, including a fishing boat. It was a tidy and obviously deserved haul for the longtime coach.

There's no record of the boat and accessories leaving Bud's dock when he came back to work a year later.

To replace him, the

A former marine, Les Steckel (right), briefly served as head coach of the Vikings in 1984. Steckel was known for his enthusiasm and his attention to conditioning.

Below: Ballplayers talk about their "best moves." Here was one of Teddy Brown's. Teddy was an accomplished stop-and-go runner when an enemy tackler was bearing down. "Teddy was always better going than stopping," Grant observed. He gained 1,000 yards one year doing exactly that.

Vikings chose Les Steckel. Historians gleefully tried to assess blame in later years, because the hill-charging Marine didn't quite succeed in persuading the Vikings that winning pro football games was the same grim deal as war in the Pacific. Once you got a beachhead, you came with flame-throwers, tanks, rockets and barehands. He was exuberant. He was intense. He was devoured by wanting to win in his first shot at coaching in the big show, and he conducted training camp and practice the way the GIs did it in the Marines. He was a decent guy and he was a good receivers coach, but he was not the man to succeed H.P. Grant as the coach of the Minnesota Vikings.

"Les was driven by goals and he was a great assistant coach, very innovative," Greg Coleman said, "but he was following a legend and he wanted to put down his own footprints and run the team by his own concepts. But the ground that old Bud had walked was just too tough to absorb those prints. The worst part of playing for Les was the Mondays after the game. He had set up this obstacle course. It was a Marine-type operation course where you had stations 1 through 6, something like that, and you had to do something excruciating at each station, like a thousand sit-ups and pushups and rope drills and the works. Then you had 400-yard runs and 40-yard dashes, and one of the first things that happened was Darrin Nelson just passed out one day. He recovered, but you could tell Darrin was never going to make it as a Marine general. Then when we finished the stations we had to run over a hill and through the woods. I swear it. That's what we did. And when we practiced Mondays, we usually did it with pads. It was 'oh my God, it's Monday.'

"But one of Les' big mistakes, I think, was that he pretty much ransacked the roster. We did have guys who hadn't performed much the year before and some older guys. But he got rid of people like Randy Holloway and Duck White and John Turner and some other pretty good vets. The team drained itself in the first half of the season and died in the second. Things got rebellious about then."

The evident choice for coach had been between Steckel, the young assistant, and Jerry Burns, who had been the offensive coordinator for more than a decade.

"I was the general manager," Lynn said, "but I didn't make the choice. Bud Grant denies that he did." And the club president, Max Winter, was in Hawaii. Thus the official modesty in the choice of Les Steckel was unanimous. Nobody claimed credit.

Until that summer, when he gained operational control of the club, Lynn looked after a big spectrum of administrative and promotional chores. He did practically all of them well and sometimes theatrically. He was on top of all detail and managed the ledgers so well that by the early 1980s he was drawing more than $1 million a year in salary.

"But Bud Grant was the football guy," he said. "He had the final vote in the critical decisions on players. We had good drafts by and large. Jerry Reichow (who headed the scouting department most of the time) and Frank Gilliam (who became the player personnel director and vice president in 1994) knew what they were doing. When I first met Bud in 1974 I was scared to death. He didn't say much. I had the feeling he was asking himself, 'who the hell is this guy and what's he supposed to be doing?' He just looked at me with those hard blue eyes and there was no doubt he was going make all the decisions when it came to pro football

Playing outdoor football in Minnesota often meant adapting to the misery index. Jeff Wright, one of the team's most dependable defensive backs, adapted better than most. He grew up with the stuff in Minnesota.

players. But I learned how the league ran and I also learned that if you got up early enough and read enough small print and you had enough nerve, you could get some good players outside the draft. It helped to spend money, which is what I started doing after 1984."

That summer, Lynn's contract was coming up for renewal. His relations with Winter had been cordial. Winter and the board had been generous with his salary. Winter's age made it sensible for him to withdraw from day-to-day involvement with the team's management. Lynn was his surrogate. But when the contract came up, Winter balked. It was clear that in Winter's mind, the Minnesota Vikings could survive the departure of Mike Lynn. He refused to renew Lynn's contract and, in effect, asked him to leave.

"I couldn't understand that, and I decided not to accept it," Lynn said. "You don't find a million dollar a year job in football every day. Why should I give it up without a fight? I went to John Skoglund and Jack Steele. I gave them the situation."

Winter had been the club's active, hands-on president during its most successful years. Although he had been obscured in the early years as a kind of outsider while H.P. Skoglund, Bernie Ridder and Bill Boyer formed the majority voice on the board, Winter stepped into the presidency when Ridder removed himself as an active director. When Boyer died, his son-in-law, Jack Steele, spoke for the family's stock. When H.P. died, his son, John, assumed his seat on the board. For years it was Winter, Skoglund and Steele, with Winter as president.

Carrying the ball in the pros can be a lonely life some days. Allen Rice swings around end, looking for tacklers – but probably looking harder for a few stray blockers.

But in 1984 Winter was in Hawaii and aging. Lynn was in Minnesota and the franchise was strong and entering the fast track of the giddy partnership between TV and pro football. The issue for Steele and Skoglund came down to keeping Lynn, or keeping Winter as the decision-maker.

They voted with Lynn. He owned no stock at the time but the board decision gave him complete operational control of the Vikings, making Winter a figurehead.

By the time the convulsion took place, Steckel was conducting summer camp and urging his forces to take all ridges in sight. They did take a few early. After a month, the club stood 2-2. Kramer was the quarterback, supported by Archie Manning, who had been acquired from New Orleans. The team held some promise. It had drafted the manhandling defensive back from USC, Joey Browner, on the first round in 1983, and another defensive back who was going to join Browner as a star of the future, Carl Lee. In 1984 it added two running backs from Baylor, Alfred Anderson and Allen Rice, and got an excellent rookie season from Anderson. He gained more than 700 yards and looked to be the Viking back of the future.

But on successive weekends in mid-season, the Vikings lost by four points to Tampa Bay, three points to the Raiders, two points to the Lions and nine points to the Bears. It was Manning's fate to play for teams that regarded their quarterback as a walking lightning rod. He went for years running for his life in New Orleans. Against the Bears in October of 1984, he wasn't as nimble. The Bears sacked him 11 times. Steckel benched him as an act of pure compassion.

The narrow defeats killed Steckel's team. His flag-and-character appeals seemed a little less than real. And in the last month, the club disintegrated. It lost 42-21 to Denver, 34-3 to the Bears, 31-17 to Washington, 51-7 to the 49ers and 38-14 to Green Bay. For the year the Vikings were outscored 484 to 276, and Les Steckel was simply out.

"I had to do something, obviously," Lynn said. "When the season was over we were facing what could have been rebellion by the season ticket holders. I approached Bud sometime before the end of the season. I told him what I wanted to do. He was the only guy to rescue the situation. He didn't say yes or no. I told him we'd put together a package. Basically, we made him an offer he couldn't refuse. It was a long-term contract that guaranteed him a salary and a deferred compensation arrangement. It gave him the right to end the job after one season which, of course, he did. But he still was going to get paid well into six figures for ten years, until 1995."

The scouting report on the Vikings' secondary was pretty explicit for years: Throw what you have to throw, but try to avoid Carl Lee. It wasn't simple. Lee was one of the best in the NFL.

So Bud Grant came back from the duck blinds and quelled the rebellion with the stroke of a pen. The natives were appeased. Good feeling returned to the cornfields. Farmers began scanning their schedules to be sure they weren't vacationing in Florida the week of the Super Bowl. And for a while, this mass nirvana seemed well placed, although Grant never found love in the Metrodome. It wrecked his image. He publicly disclaimed any interest in how the TV millions reacted to him. But

Alfred Anderson's first was his best (right). In his rookie season, the horse from Baylor gained more than 700 yards, 120 in one of his first games in the league.

Joey Browner (below) played defensive back as though he had a contract out on every opposing player in the stadium. Sooner or later, Browner hit most of them. But he had the speed and instincts to run with the burners, too, and to lead the team in interceptions three straight seasons. He played in six Pro Bowls.

privately he was tickled by that great stone face in the snowstorm, his headset fixed on his head, mouth-piece below his lips, snow falling on his nose.

Privately, Grant looked on the Metrodome as antiseptic and vaguely a crime against nature. No ice formed on the coach's eyelashes. No snowblowers roared on the enemy bench. It was like playing football in a greenhouse, Grant decided. But he didn't complain about it in the early season of 1985, because the Vikings were off to a 3-1 start and seemed headed for their old patriarchal seat as the Central Division champion.

It ended after a month. The reality was that the Vikings didn't have the great veteran players of the earlier Grant years, although his team was certainly competitive. He adapted to the new player attitudes, but reluctantly: What he saw was less

discipline on the field, increasing problems off the field, drugs and the rest, and less commitment to the team. The money in pro football was starting to soar. Agents were intervening. They talked not only about the player's salary but his playing time. But Grant was capable of handling that. What he couldn't deal with was something no football coach can deal with, no matter his style, history or Hall of Fame credentials. And that was mediocrity or inexperience at too many positions.

Ironically, his last team was beginning to shed that mediocrity with young players who a few years later would make the all-star teams chronically. Lynn was gathering potential frontline players from unorthodox sources, mainly from the defunct rosters of the USFL, out-bidding more timid rivals. He got A.C. Carter that way, and Keith Millard and David Howard. The draft provided others. By the end of the season the Vikings had Irwin, Kirk Lowdermilk, Huffman and Terry

Grant thought 1984 was the perfect year to begin his next life of full-time hunting and fishing. He was wrong. The Vikings won three games under his successor, Les Steckel, and Grant returned in 1985 in response to frantic appeals by Mike Lynn. It was a mediocre year, so 1986 became the next perfect year for his next life. This time nobody argued.

Anthony Carter played football with exuberance and a craving to catch the ball on every play. The quarterback couldn't always accommodate him, but when he did, A.C. usually moved the ball a long way. Here he scoots away from the 49ers.

Tausch on the offensive line, Steve Jordan at tight end and Carter beginning to start as a wide receiver. Nelson was the running back and Millard was starting at defensive end. New as a linebacker, and not very comfortable there, was Chris Doleman from the draft. A year later they were going to shift him to the line, and launch his career. Carl Lee, Joey Browner and Issiac Holt were playing in the secondary. Coleman and Jan Stenerud, himself headed for Canton, did the kicking. Leo Lewis was the handy guy, catching passes and running back kicks. Kramer had a middling season at quarterback. It was one of those almost years.

The team might have made the playoffs. In Philadelphia in late season, Wade Wilson produced an astonishing show. He was a young quarterback from Texas with a big arm and ambitions to replace the older Texan, Kramer, in the Viking huddle. In Philadelphia, though, he had to replace a rookie named Steve Bono, who quarterbacked the middle of the game because Wilson, as the starter, couldn't move the team. That made three quarterbacks who couldn't move the Vikings most of the afternoon because Kramer was held out for reasons that Grant officially designated as "wear and tear." Wilson floundered through two quarters. Bono did the same in the third. It got to be 23-0 for the Eagles in the fourth quarter, with only 8 1/2 minutes to play.

And yet the Vikings won the game. At the time, NFL statisticians swore that nobody had come from that far back with so little time left, and they probably were right. Mathematically, it would have stretched the rules of science. But Wilson shot a 7-yard touchdown pass to Allen Rice. Defensive back Willie Teal picked up a fumble a few minutes later and ran it 65 yards into the end zone. Philadelphia stalled again. Wilson cranked it up again and found Anthony Carter with a 36 yard scoring pass. The Vikings were now beyond the reach of ordinary human football players, which, unfortunately for Philadelphia, the Eagles were. Wilson fired again, to Carter for 42 yards and a 28-23 victory.

But the Vikings lost to Atlanta and then to Philadelphia in their replay at the Metrodome, and finished 7-9. Not long afterward Bud Grant folded his play book for good. The ledger: A regular season record of 158-96-5 in 18 years, 10 more victories in post-season games, 12 times in the playoffs, 11 division titles, one NFL championship, three NFC championships and four Super Bowl games.

Not long after he retired, Lynn took a plane to Jamaica, where Jerry Burns spent his winters fishing and drawing Xs and Os on whatever didn't move.

No one spread more fear among NFL quarterbacks in his prime than Keith Millard. He was large, nimble and manic as a pass rusher, a totally disagreeable guy on the line of scrimmage. The Lions' quarterback (below) hears Millard's big footsteps – too late.

Jerry Burns (right) didn't weigh more than 145 pounds. It's hard for a 145-pound man to lose weight simply fretting and scheming. As the head coach, Jerry managed it.

When they gave the ball to Darrin Nelson (which wasn't often enough, Darrin argued), the field tended to stretch out and so did lunging tacklers (below).

Baffling Burnsie the Leprechaun

First day in class for Darrin Nelson, the cool, finger-snapper from the University of Stanford, the No. 1 draft choice. Time for discovery, and never mind the No. 1 draft choice's tardy arrival in camp while his agent haggled with the Viking money-changers. It's part of the perks of being a No. 1.

But the professor was unimpressed.

The subject was the Minnesota Viking offense. The professor was Jerry Burns, then the offensive coordinator. The classroom had a projector in the middle of it but the professor ignored it. This was summer camp and it was a day for indoctrination. The place was Mankato, the Viking training camp. It was Darrin Nelson's introduction to pro football.

And it was chaos.

Burns was talking about formations and line-blocking and the rest of the pro football gobbledygook, and the No. 1 draft choice with the Stanford education looked baffled. It might have been obvious to the professor. But it didn't stop his racehorse recital.

"I didn't understand a word that man said," Darrin Nelson confessed. "It wasn't just the four-letter words that Jerry threw in when he got to something he thought we better remember. It's just that he talked like a tobacco auctioneer and everything came out mush to me. It took awhile, but I did finally figure him out after two or three weeks. I'll say this: I enjoyed playing football for Jerry Burns. He had some unconscious ability to make people laugh and still learn and play for him. If the guy had a major fault as a coach it was insisting that he was going to treat his players like men. With some guys, that can be an awful mistake, and I don't care how much money they make. He figured you were mature enough to get yourself ready to play in the off-season and the day of the game. Sometimes that's a mistake, too. You get a lot of flaky guys in pro football."

He was a squirt of a guy, Burns. He had a pinched face and a sharp nose and a nasal voice that seemed to be bitching most of the time – although part of that was the stage character of a guy of fundamental honor. And he seemed to actually have been born with some permanent memory loss when he came to the names of football players.

"I guarantee this happened," Tarkenton said. "I rejoined the Vikings in 1972. I had more than 10 years of pro ball in by then. I suppose I was as well known as any quarterback in the league. I'd played against Burns' teams when he was with Green Bay and the Vikings. We knew each other well. We met every day after I came back to the Vikings. It was his offense but it was also my offense. We were partners. Right? Well, in practice he'd come over and say, 'On that play I think you might want to set up a little deeper, ah, No. 10.' It happened all the time. The little SOB flat out forgot the name of his quarterback."

With some of the others, Burns was less flattering in wriggling out of his memory lapses, or he just didn't bother.

"I'll never forget the Ron Yary incident," Chainsaw Voigt said. "Burns had generic nicknames for certain position players. They raised some eyebrows in our practices in summer camp where you had hundreds of visitors gawking on the sidelines. They didn't bother the players much. But sometimes he just lost it. He'd call the defensive linemen 'the big

Viking quarterbacks cherished the sight of Ron Yary (73). He was powerful and tenacious and kept them healthy. He did it for 15 seasons. No one in football played offensive tackle much better.

knockers' and he'd call a fullback 'big nuts,' and a guy like Yary, an offensive lineman, he'd call 'hey, big dummy.' Burns didn't think Yary lacked intelligence, or a guy like Ed White. It was just his name for the offensive lineman. One day, though, he and Yary couldn't agree on how to block a play. Burns insisted he was right. Yary thought he was wrong. Burns called him 'big dummy' three times on the same play. The first time, Yary just got back into his stance. The second time, Yary's Polish temper started to heat up. Ron always gave you the impression he was simmering a little. He was a terrific football player, powerful and determined, one of the best I've ever played with or seen. But the third time Burns said 'hey, big dummy,' Yary just went over the edge. He started striding back toward Burns. Big strides. Burns must weigh all of 145 pounds. Yary was 6-foot-5 and weighed 270. Burns had seen that look somewhere before, maybe from his old man when he got sassy.

"Burns started to backtrack. Yary kept coming. Burns was wearing those oversized rubber boots, unlaced, what he usually wore in cold weather. He must have lost his footing because he fell over backward. His clipboard went flying, his cap came over his eyes and he was the damnedest mess you ever saw. Nobody had to restrain Yary. He nearly died laughing."

That kind of guy, Burns. A visitor to one of the Saturday practice sessions the day before a road game in California noticed one of the Viking coaches slowly walking around on the field, examining practically every blade of grass, head down and lost to the world.

Bud Grant happened to be standing near the visitor.

"Isn't that Jerry Burns walking around?" the man asked.

"You got it," Grant said.

"Is he sick or down about something? Did he get some bad news?"

Grant said the crisis wasn't nearly as big as that.

"He's looking for pennies and dimes."

The visitor asked if Burns was down on his luck.

"No, he's superstitious. If he finds a coin on the field he thinks we're going to win."

"Does it work out that way?"

"Sure," Grant said. "We usually win if he finds a coin. But we usually win if he doesn't find a coin."

Burns' bark was thick. He endured practical jokers who had no mercy for his phobia toward insects. Ed White rigged up a fake rubber spider one year and slowly lowered it until it reached Burns' eye level behind the projector. Burns saw it and did the whole full-bore collapse. Simultaneously he went white and speechless. He nearly went into a coma.

But after Grant's second retirement Mike Lynn was aware that Burns was the man to run the Vikings. Although they muddled along in the 1980s, the team had been suc-

Mike Lynn (left) was a schemer. Jerry Burns was a worrier. The combination produced a nice balance of anxiety from September to January, but the Vikings won-lost record for the regular season during their five-year partnership was 52-43 and the team came within one play of reaching the Super Bowl.

cessful for years before. Others from the Viking coaching staff had advanced to head coaching jobs. Over the years, in fact, the Vikings graduated some notable figures and characters into the head coaching ranks either directly or after interims with other coaching staffs. From the Van Brocklin years there'd been Harry Gilmer and Marion Campbell, and later Bob Hollway, Jack Patera, Neill Armstrong, Raymond Berry, Buddy Ryan, Steckel and Pete Carroll. The Viking staff when Burns took over included veterans like John Michels and Paul Wiggin with younger men in Pete Carroll, Marc Trestman and Tom Batta, a mix to which Burns added one of the Viking originals, Bob Schnelker as the offensive coordinator and Floyd Peters to run the defense. Schnelker eventually became the fans' fall guy. It would have happened to anybody running the Viking offense in the years when they might have won a title but didn't. Bill

Walsh would have been hammered the same way. The offense was supposed to be unstoppable, tricky and brutal. It was supposed to produce 30 points a game. Peters, on the other hand, was popular. It helped to have the league's best defensive team. Floyd looked like a man straight out of the warden's guard: bald-headed, rasping voice, gung-ho style. He brought a take-no-prisoners mentality to the Viking defense, and belligerents like Keith Millard and Chris Doleman and Scott Studwell loved it.

So Burns had instant acceptability among the coach-

Chris Doleman's warm breath on his neck was enough to launch any quarterback toward the sanctuary of the sidelines (upper left).

When Doleman was blocked, there usually weren't enough people left to block Keith Millard (above).

Scott Studwell (55) drives a shoulder, leading the Viking posse. In 15 seasons he made or shared in 1,981 tackles, a team record by far.

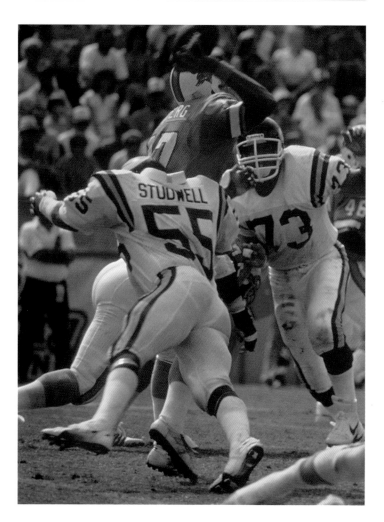

es, among practically all of the players and certainly with the fans and the media. He'd been a head coach at Iowa, with the misfortune of following Forest Evashevski, and a productive coaching assistant for years under Vince Lombardi and Bud Grant. He had a grasp of modern football offense, using the full range of the modern players' evolving skills. And, of course, he had that exotic language. You couldn't categorize it. It was a mixture of pro football jargon, profanity and spurts of literate English.

He also had a developing football team. Tommy Kramer, injured for most of the previous year, had recovered and produced a vintage season. It included a 44-38 overtime shootout that the Vikings lost to the Redskins and Jay Schroeder, a game in which Kramer threw for 490 yards. That made him the first quarterback in NFL history to pass for more than 450 yards twice in a career. This was a year in which the Vikings hit a team record of 398 points and 31 touchdown passes, 24 by Kramer and 7 by Wilson. It was a year in which Steve Jordan, A.C. Carter, little Leo Lewis, Darrin Nelson and Hassan Jones all caught for more than 500 yards. Scott Studwell, Joey Browner and Keith Millard dominated the defense, and Chris Doleman moved in as a partner of

Tommy Kramer barks the count behind the center. Despite mixed reviews from the fans (the fate of all quarterbacks) he was never better than in the crisis of a game. He became Two-Minute Tommy, brash and skilled enough to carry a team from end to end with the game in the balance.

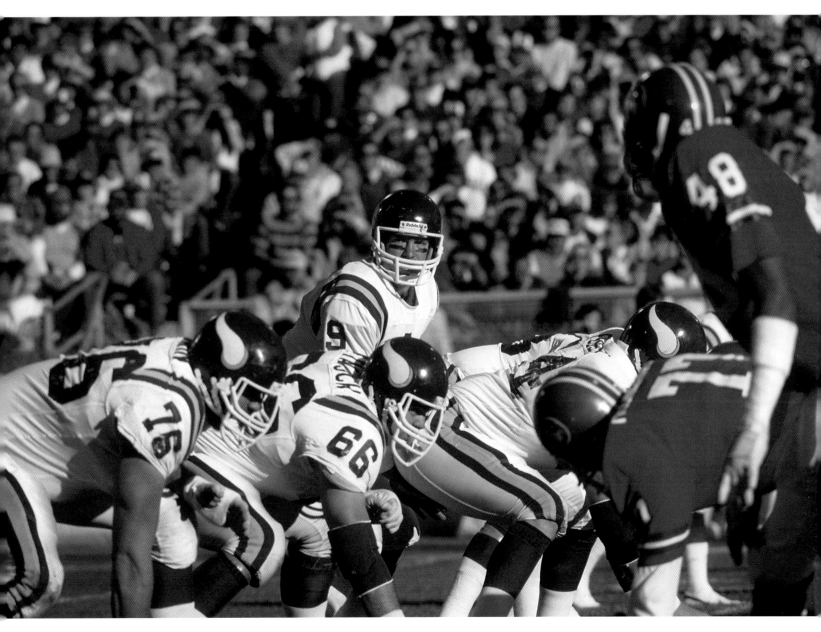

Jerry Burns insisted that the best hands on the Vikings in his years as head coach belonged to Hassan Jones (below). When the ball came down in a crowd, it usually found its way to Hassan. Linebacker Dave Howard (right) didn't have Hassan's hands. He did have bigger shoulders and an ornerier disposition in a crowd.

Millard's to create one of the most powerful pass rushing duos in the league. By then Gary Zimmerman, an all-pro tackle Lynn had wangled from the Giants, joined the offensive line. Millard, Carter and linebacker Dave Howard were other harvests of Lynn's scurrying through the market of former USFL players.

For all of that, the Vikings didn't make the playoffs. Their 9-7 record was their best in six years, which pretty well testified to their descent from the penthouse and to the emergence of the Chicago Bears of Mike Ditka, Walter Payton, Jim McMahon and Richard Dent. And near the end of the next season, 1987, it didn't look much more promising.

Why it didn't was a mystery when you looked at the Vikings' 8-7 regular season finish superficially. The year before, they'd drafted Hassan Jones on the fifth round and linebacker Jesse Solomon on the 12th, low-round choices that constituted acts of piracy by the Vikings in view of their eventual value. The Vikings did bomb on their first choice, defensive end Gerald Robinson from Auburn, but they came back in 1987 by drafting one of the prime-stock lineman of the next decade, Henry Thomas of Louisiana State, on the third round, defensive back Reggie Rutland of Georgia Tech on the fourth, and fullback Rick Fenney of Washington on the eighth.

They put together a team that would send Browner, Doleman, Studwell, Carter, Jordan and Zimmerman to the Pro Bowl. But 1987 was the year of another player strike. This time the league authorized games between non-striking players. The league called them replacements. The striking players called them scabs.

"I wanted to keep our team's solidarity as far as I could," Lynn said. "So I didn't get serious about finding replacement players until it was too late." Whatever the reason, the Vikings' scabs lost the three games they played. The defeats counted in the standings. Coupled with the three out of four the team lost late in the season, they produced an 8-7 record and the Vikings barely squirmed into the playoffs as a wild card.

The playoff schedule looked like the agenda for Death Row. They were going to play every game on the road as long as they lasted. The first was in New Orleans, where the Saints' linebacking stars and their gangway defense were waiting in the Superdome with a 12-3 record, having won nine in a

Making life miserable for the other folks: Jesse Solomon rearranges a Colt runner's head and neck (above) and Henry Thomas assaults a Tampa Bay quarterback (left).

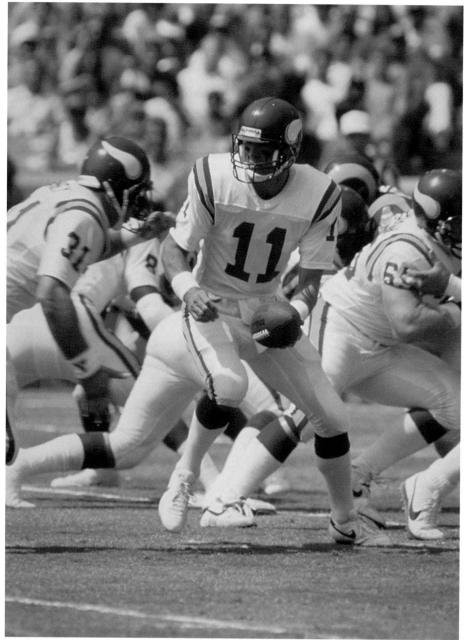

row.

Wade Wilson had quarterbacked most of the season. Kramer was troubled with a pinched nerve and other injuries. Although Wilson legitimately earned his time, Kramer opened against the Saints. He was gone after five minutes with an aggravated neck injury. And the Vikings unloaded. They came with long bombs, punt returns and gadget plays. They came with a little luck and a tidal wave of confidence once they got going. A lot of the time they simply came with A.C. Carter, and the Saints couldn't handle him.

He was the kind of guy who played football with a grin from start to finish. He grinned when he scored and grinned when he got up from an ankle sprain. He was skinny version of Jim Marshall. For A.C., life was a football game. Was there anything better?

There sure wasn't in New Orleans. Carter caught six passes for 79 yards, and one touchdown. He ran back six punts for 143 yards, and one touchdown. He was everywhere, all the time, and the Vikings won 44-10. Wilson, Kramer and a young quarterback named Rich Gannon all directed touchdown drives. It didn't matter much who was playing quarterback. It didn't matter even when the Vikings got stopped. The first half seemed over on an innocuous play into the line by the Vikings. The Saints had 12 men on the field. The Vikings reloaded and Wilson threw the ball into the end zone. "Jump," he yelled as the ball spiraled down field. Hassan Jones jumped. So did everybody else. Jones came down with it.

When the season started, the oracles in Las Vegas designated the Minnesota Vikings a 75 to 1 shot to make it to the Super Bowl. That still looked reasonable when the Vikings arrived at Candlestick in San Francisco. These were the 49ers of Super Bowl bravura, of the Genius and Joe, Bill Walsh and Joe Montana, of Jerry Rice, Dwight Clark, Ronnie Lott, Bubba Paris and people of that stripe. But by now A.C. Carter was sizzling. He didn't exactly say "bring on Jerry Rice, and see who catches more passes," but Wade Wilson got the idea. The Viking pass rush, Millard, Doug Martin, Doleman et al, badgered Montana until Walsh withdrew him in the third quarter. The Viking secondary with

Above: Wade Wilson moves the team on the ground. He preferred the air, of course. Like most quarterbacks, he eventually lost caste with the home crowds. But for three or four seasons he ranked with the finest quarterbacks in the league. He outdueled Joe Montana in a playoff game and once produced four Viking touchdowns in the last eight minutes of a game with Philadelphia, still one of the most astonishing comebacks in NFL history.

Opposite page: If you wanted to light it up in Anthony Carter's best years with the Vikings, you plugged into A.C. He dealt in acrobatics, fingertip catches and ear to ear smiles.

Rutland, Carl Lee, John Harris and the others choked off Rice with shifting coverages, all of them founded on the Viking rush. And Wilson and Carter took off. When it was finished, Wilson had thrown for 298 yards on 20 completions in 34 throws. Among them were touchdown passes from short range to Carl Hilton and Hassan Jones, but the electric charge came via A.C. Carter, who broke an NFL playoff record by grabbing 10 passes for 227 yards, a couple of them definitely bordering on the supernatural. Jerry Rice, in the meantime, caught three for 27 yards. The Vikings won 36-24. In consecutive games they had beaten the two teams with the best records in the NFL, and done it by a combined score of 80-34.

One more on the road, and they were going back to the Super Bowl.

The Hawgs weren't as glamorous as Jerry Rice. Doug Williams wasn't as famous as Joe Montana. The Hawgs and Williams played for the Washington Redskins. And that was the problem of the last game before the Super Bowl. The Redskins were in it, and they were playing it at RFK in Washington.

Nobody ever expected it to be pretty. It wasn't. Nobody expected A.C. Carter and Wade Wilson to duplicate San Francisco. They didn't. What Burns and the Redskins expected is what happened. It was crowbars-and-shovels football, something close to the Neanderthal days of the 1930s. The day was gloomy and it was worse than that for the watchers who wanted artistry.

It might have come down to that most despised of all football bromides: field position. The Vikings were lacking their regular punter, Greg Coleman. He'd been injured but was

available, although not the force he'd once been. The Vikings went instead with his replacement, Bucky Scribner, who didn't kick well that day. Williams threw touchdown passes to Kelvin Bryant and Gary Clark for Washington. Still, the line that mattered wasn't the Redskins Hawgs on offense but the Redskin pass rush on defense. The Redskins sacked Wilson eight times. Yet deep in the fourth quarter the Vikings trailed by only seven points. They reached the Redskins' 6, needing four yards for a first down and six to tie the game. Wilson dropped back and threw to his

left. Darrin Nelson was racing toward the corner. Nelson had to reach below his knees. But it wasn't a bad pass.

"People told me a thousand times that I had plenty of excuse for dropping it," Nelson said later. "I admit I was sick as a dog with flu the night before. I admit the pass might have been a little higher. But did I have an excuse? None. I've made that play a zillion times."

He didn't in January of 1988, and the Redskins won 17-10.

But the Vikings had the look of a rising power-house.

Wilson was developing star quality. Carter, Hassan Jones and Steve Jordan were almost unmatched in the NFL as a versatile receiving corps. Zimmerman, Lowdermilk and Irwin stood among the best in pro

Greg Coleman's skills went far beyond punting the football (above). Opposing coaches insisted that he could have made it at the Guthrie Theater. Coleman was unrivaled in the punter's art of collapsing in agony in the face of an enemy rush. Officials rushed to the scene, flags in hand. Statisticians figured out that Greg's theatrics led directly to a half dozen Viking victories. He was modest. He said that might be a generous estimate – by a game or so. He was also an excellent punter. Bucky Scribner, who followed him, was not nearly as dramatic (right).

Purple Hearts and Golden Memories

football at their offensive line positions. Nelson gave the Vikings a slice of everything as a running back. But in the coaching judgment his size made him vulnerable. So he never became the heavy-duty back all the pro coaches hungered for. The Vikings got increasingly bashful about running the ball. On defense, Millard and Doleman were a constant menace to the skulls and other body parts of opposing quarterbacks. Thomas was already a sound pro. Howard, Studwell and Solomon, backing the line, and Lee, Browner, Rutland, Harris, Ike Holt and Darrell Fullington in the secondary posed additional misery for enemy runners and flankers. Chuck Nelson kicked field goals adequately. No one was surprised when the Vikings won 11 games to finish second in the Central and capped it with a 28-27 victory over the Bears on Walker Lee Ashley's 84-yard interception runback.

When the Vikings' offensive line came at the defenses with Kirk Lowdermilk (above, 63) at center and people like Gary Zimmerman, Tim Irwin, Brian Habib and a young Randall McDaniel, the defenses usually sagged.

A big guy from the hills, Tim Irwin (left). He played offensive tackle for the Vikings for a decade, dependably and massively. Having taken a lot of blows from defensive linemen over the years, he decided to retaliate and became a lawyer.

This was a team, though, of star players and bad actors. It unsettled its followers in ways that weren't associated with Viking football in quieter times. Kramer's erratic conduct in taverns and on the highway put him on the front page. Millard got to be just as notorious. Incidents of rowdy behavior by a half dozen of the others kept the club's public relations department in a constant state of mourning. On the field, egos and stats seemed often to come ahead of the scoreboard. A.C. moaned that he wasn't getting the ball enough. Doleman seemed absorbed with sacks. Some of those personal drives benefited the team. Some didn't. Wilson quarreled on the sidelines with Schnelker, the offensive coordinator. The Vikings, in fact, seemed to be a team with caviar potential and meatball character.

It might not have been much different on the other teams, but it was more visible with the Vikings because the team now had stars by the truckload – Carter, Jordan, Zimmerman, Millard, Doleman, Browner, Lee, Studwell, Wilson, Nelson and more.

They played a rousing first-round playoff game against the Rams at the Metrodome, hounded Jim Everett and won 28-17. Again it was on to San Francisco and Candlestick and there was genuine suspense around the NFL this time. The Vikings had ambushed the 49ers the year before, caught them coasting. The 49ers would be primed this time. But this was a stronger Minnesota than the year before, settled at all positions, mature at most of them, and driving once more for a Super Bowl.

But it didn't drive anywhere past San Francisco. This time, Joe Montana, Jerry Rice and their accomplices were not impostors. The 49ers' offensive line found a solution to the Vikings' pass rush that had disrupted Montana the year before. The solution was a ground game. Roger Craig gutted the Vikings for 135 yards and Montana passed for three touchdowns. It was 34-9 for the 49ers, and putting seven players in the Pro Bowl a few weeks later didn't do much to deaden the Vikings' pain. Yet it had been a season of entertaining and high-level football. When a pro football team falls short of winning the Super Bowl – and all but one of them do each year – the fans and commentators tend to blot out the other four months of achievement. The might-have-beens are juicier.

"That's right," Jerry Burns said. "It ain't fair. What the hell are you going to do? Overhaul human nature?"

It was left to Mike Lynn to undertake a project not quite as monumental as that. But close. Lynn examined the Viking offense early in the 1989 season. The team was awash with Pro Bowlers. It won 11 games in 1988. It was going to lead the NFL in defense from start to finish in 1989. To its offensive line stars the 1988 draft had added Randall McDaniel, who'd be an all-pro for years to come. But the 49ers were the class of professional football and the team the Vikings threw against the 49ers wasn't adequate. It needed punch. It needed high octane. It needed, in short, A Superstar.

He approached Jerry Burns.

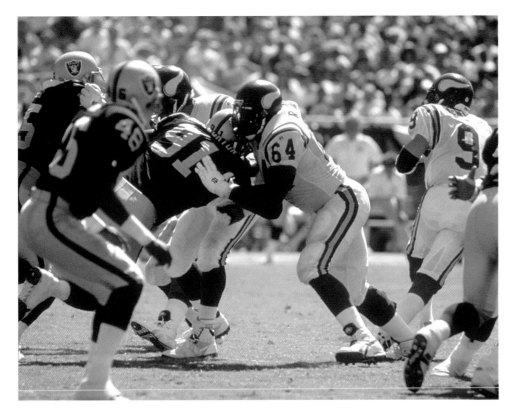

It took Randall McDaniel (64) only a year to establish himself with the strongest offensive linemen in football. By the next year, he was an annual all-pro. By 1994, he was unmatched in his trade.

Nobody move! If you twitch an eyebrow on that offensive line before Kirk Lowdermilk's snap (below), you draw five yards. That didn't mean Lowdermilk was above drawing the other guys offside.

"How about Herschel Walker?"

"What do you mean?"

"Could you find a place for him?"

"Who couldn't?"

In the wake of Walker's eventual disenchantments in Minnesota, which were roundly returned by the fans, a lot of mythology has grown up. He wasn't a has-been when Lynn put down millions of dollars worth of draft choices and five Viking players, to say nothing of cash, to bring Herschel Walker to Minnesota. He'd gained more than 1,000 yards the year before. He'd been a highly productive player for Tom Landry in Dallas, but Jimmy Johnson was the coach when Lynn went shopping and Johnson's boss, Jerry Jones, was the guy who'd chopped up Tom Landry. Herschel wasn't their guy. In fact, he looked vaguely lost in the player upheaval undertaken by Jones and Johnson.

The Louisiana Purchase produced more land, but among the historic transactions of America it never attracted the hindsight of The Herschel Walker Deal. Herschel came to the Vikings in 1989. Mike Lynn's idea was to put the Vikings into the Super Bowl again. Herschel didn't. Some days, though, he ran well. He always ran conscientiously.

Yet nobody but Lynn would have dreamed up the deal. For one thing, the Vikings may not have needed this particular messiah. Although they lacked firepower in their ground game, they could have resolved that without giving away the biggest bonanza in Minnesota since the iron ore strike in Hibbing. But Lynn was a bombastic problem solver. The problem should not only be solved, it should be solved with artillery barrages and Roman candles. It should be a show.

Herschel Walker was the biggest show available. All-America. Star in whatever pro league he played. Individualist. Man of principles. Millionaire. Sprinter speed. Build of a linebacker. Possessor of a very big dog. Herschel was a superman. "Judge this deal," Mike Lynn told open-mouthed media folks, "on whether we get to the Super Bowl with

Herschel Walker on the roster. If we do, the deal was a success. If we don't, it wasn't."

The answer is, it wasn't. But Lynn never apologized for making the trade. In the long run, maybe he shouldn't have. With or without Walker, the Vikings couldn't have beaten the 49ers and the Giants of those years. And regardless of the draft choices they lost in the trade, they were back as a playoff team a year after Herschel left.

They did give up a bundle. Directly to Dallas they sent Jesse Solomon, David Howard, Issiac Holt, Darrin Nelson and Alex Stewart. They gave eight draft choices, including three firsts, three seconds, a third and a sixth. They also acquired Herschel's multi-million dollar salary.

Mike Merriweather (making a tackle) dropped out of football for a year in a contract dispute with Pittsburgh. The Vikings shelled out to sign him. He played competently if somewhat briefly.

Nelson ultimately refused to play in Dallas. "If they were going to get rid of me," he said, "I was going to play in California, where I'd feel comfy and wanted." Both conditions were met by the San Diego Chargers, and Darrin played there for one season before finishing with the Vikings. He had an observation: "You know, no matter how much the Vikings gave up, I'll always look on that as a money deal in which Mike Lynn figured the Vikings were the big money-makers.

"I'll tell you why: First-round draft choices today can be a pain in the butt. They get huge money. Most of them hold out past training season. Most of them are pretty worthless the first season, and some of them are worthless the rest of their careers. Lynn knew that. He wanted to build the team other ways and use the draft only where it made sense. He figured if you're going to throw big money around, do it for guys who already showed they can play."

Old George Allen had plowed that ground, but money wasn't big when George did it. It was harder in the late 1970s, when the competi-

tion drove up salaries for proven players. Still, Lynn was brash and persistent. In addition to Carter, Zimmerman, Millard and Howard, he picked off Mike Merriweather, the linebacker who was stonewalling the Pittsburgh Steelers. And now Herschel.

Walker joined the Vikings a few days before their sixth game in 1989, against the Packers in Minneapolis. The Vikings stood 3-2 at the time. Schnelker introduced Walker to the Viking offense and gave him a few token plays to give the crowd a foretaste. They also assigned him to run back kickoffs. It was supposed to be one of those cameo appearances.

They brought in Herschel relatively early. On his first running play, on second and five, he hit the hole on a slant, broke into the Packer secondary, turned on the burners, and got one of his shoes stripped clean by a Green Bay defensive back. The play went for 47 yards. The crowd of 62,075 shrieked. Mike Lynn closed his eyes and thanked the Lord or Jerry Jones, whichever appeared to be more generous. Ultimately Herschel ran 18 times from scrimmage and gained 148 yards for a monster 8.2 per carry. He caught a pass, ran an audible, carried back two kickoffs and totaled 195 all-purpose yards. The only thing he didn't bring was his big dog.

"Mercy," said Jerry Burns.

"It was the Viking offensive line," Herschel said modestly.

Obviously, he wasn't going to do it every week. And he didn't. The expectations got lopsided. He never did get an offensive formation in which he felt fully comfortable. He was respected by his teammates and the coaches, but over the next 2 1/2 years he seemed to get somewhat detached as the numbers failed to reach the predictions, and as the fans increasingly got restive. He tried, but he was fundamentally a stranger in town.

After a while his running style came under scrutiny. He often seemed to go into a hole sliding, turning his back before he had to. He didn't grouse much. He said he'd do what they asked. He did. But he was not the man to carry the Vikings to the Super Bowl, although he did lead the team in rushing for his three seasons and got up past 700 yards one year. The Vikings went 10-6 for the season and met the 49ers again in the playoffs.

It was a reprise of the previous year. The 49ers took them apart 41-13, and it might have been worse.

So here was a team with great football players, but one that seemed to be living under some dark star in the playoffs, a.k.a. as the San Francisco 49ers. The off-field problems got worse the next season, 1990. The Vikings' management found itself under a takeover attack by a combine of Irwin Jacobs and Carl Pohlad. The record fell to 6-10. It was 8-8 the next season, 1991. Herschel, Lynn and Burns all were going or gone. And the Vikings in 1992 found themselves both with new direction in the front office and on the field.

White knights materialized in the board room and a new sheriff showed up in training camp.

A Sheriff Comes in with Drumrolls

H e came to town with a set of drums, a Super Bowl ring and a silver star.

It struck the locals as an odd collection of hardware, but it shouldn't have. A man who would voluntarily coach for five years at Northwestern has to be driven by rhythms slightly alien to most coaches.

Denny Green. The sheriff's star was strictly symbolic and imaginary. It was something the new Viking coach bestowed on himself in a moment of mock consternation his first day on the job in 1992. He'd just been flown in from Stanford University and was confronted with the usual media grilling about goals and philosophies and quarterbacks.

"The big question of the day seemed to be what was I going to do about problem guys on the team," he remembers. "I'd done my studies about personnel on the team but I didn't know most of these guys personally and I hadn't coached many of them. I wasn't in any position to be talking personalities and laying down laws the first day. But the questions wouldn't go away. It was, 'this guy doesn't like to practice' and 'that guy doesn't think he's getting the ball enough' and the other guy is considered selfish, and that stuff. I finally had to say, 'hey, I'm the new sheriff in town and if people want to play for this team they're pretty much going to have to accept that.'"

It was a statement Green made jocularly. But within a few months it was clear that he wasn't going to be shy about handling his authority. He was also going to make some enemies in the process.

Green took the role without affecting any High Noon glares. Nobody was going to confuse Dennis Green with John Wayne, or Tom Landry for that matter, or Bud Grant. Green was verbal and jazzy, a guy from the asphalt and the baby boom. He was both a coach and part-time musician, identities to which he gave almost equal ardor. He was also black. Not much attention was given to that simple but profound fact when he was named to the job by the Vikings' new CEO, Roger Headrick. The times, after all, are filled with the demands of cultural sensitivity. It was considered sensitive not to dwell on Denny Green's heritage and his trailblazing status. In other words, he was a coach first and an African-American second. That was true. But there was an enormous significance

In the corporate convulsions of the late 1980s and early 1990s (Lynn ousts Winter, Jacobs and Pohlad sue Vikings for control of the team), Roger Headrick emerged as the team's eventual CEO. The controversies started to multiply. Where don't they in the jock business today? Days were quieter for Roger at Pillsbury.

to his appointment, nonetheless. It was a breakout from the historical patterns in the National Football League, or practically any league. Art Shell had been coaching the Raiders for a couple of years. Black assistant coaches were appearing in larger numbers around the NFL as the pressures mounted on NFL teams to widen their opportunities racially. That they hadn't until recently was an embarrassment to the league as well as a social and economic wrong, in view of the dominance of the pro game by black stars.

But here was a head coaching job, available on one of the quality franchises in the NFL.

Headrick was the man to fill it, which represented something of a culture shock in itself. Roger Headrick came out of the mahogany rooms and thick leather chairs of corporate America – Exxon, Pillsbury, organizations like that. Until one day in the late 1980s, his business partners could have looked at all of the jobs which Roger Headrick might be performing in the 1990s. They could have gone through the corporate litany from marketing to investment to product development. None of them would have imagined "CEO and de facto general manager, professional football team."

But one day in the late 1980s, Mike Lynn looked around for comfort and new allies with large pockets. He was the Viking kaiser under siege. He was in charge, running the show, making a lot of money but facing the takeover onslaught of two of the shrewdest millionaires in town, Irwin Jacobs and Carl Pohlad. They were outvoted on the Viking board by the Lynn majority, but they went to court claiming Lynn had put together the trust illegally and that, further, he was running the corporation into the ground.

Jacobs was the pointman. In the days when it was fashionable, he was described as a corporate raider, one of the country's more energetic and imaginative ones. His networks in the Twin Cities' financial and social communities were broad, however, and one of his strategies was to take advantage of Lynn's general unpopularity with the football clientele. For the better part of two years he and Lynn traded accusations in and out of court. Jacobs' partner in the fight couldn't have been more prestigious. Pohlad was the owner of the Twins, a man with deep roots and cash in the banking industry, with net worth in the hundreds of millions.

The Lynn voting trust had the power in the Viking board room, however. Jacobs and Pohlad got into the combat by paying approximately $25 million for Max Winter's stock, which came available after Max got weary of the battle. While Jacobs and Pohlad theoretically controlled a slight majority of the stock, Lynn spoke for two-thirds of the voting shares. Jacobs and Pohlad were nominally joined by a jock-tycoon named Francis Tarkenton, who presumably would have moved in for Lynn as the general manager.

The corporation kept making money despite the divided board and despite the absence of another Super Bowl team. But with no foreseeable end to it and the court costs mounting, Lynn went looking for some prosperous pals. He called them 'white knights,' the usual label for a corporate rescue operation. As new Viking investors and directors he included some of the cream of Twin Cities industry and finance. Eventually each would become a one-tenth owner in the club. When fully invested, the menagerie became Headrick, John Skoglund, Carol Sperry of the Skoglund family, Jaye Dyer, Philip Maas, voting the former Boyer stock, Bud Grossman, Elizabeth MacMillan, Wheelock Whitney, Jim Binger and James Jundt.

Before the final alignment, the incumbents on the Viking board put together an offer Jacobs and Pohlad couldn't refuse. The club gave them approximately $50 million to call off their lawsuits and to leave the board. This they did. With due allowances for Uncle Sam's cut and the lawyers', Jacobs and Pohlad concluded there are worse ways to make $25 million.

The new expanded ownership then bought up loose-end stock so that today each of the ten directors accounts for an equal weight of stock, assets that Lynn estimates to have a current net worth of between $150 and $200 million. But by the turn of the decade, Lynn was getting out and eventually did.

"I told my wife when I signed the last contract that it was going to be my last," he said. "I'm an adventurous type. I'd been with the Vikings since 1974. I think I put a positive stamp on the franchise but it was time to do something else." Lynn had been infatuated with the idea of putting American-style pro football on a global basis. The Vikings had pioneered in that experiment by playing exhibitions in London and Goteburg, Sweden. Lynn formally moved out as the general manager in 1991 and thought Headrick would make a good successor.

Headrick's name was put up and approved by the Viking board. Lynn's equity in the club eventually got to be an issue. It was resolved for something close to $10 million.

Headrick spent the better part of his first year in 1991 learning about pro football, how it runs, how it's marketed, where it's going. What he found was that for years the Vikings' success enabled the club to run in the relaxed style of an exclusive businessman's lodge. Before Bud Grant retired, his teams won year-in and year-out. The team sold itself, without needing high-powered marketing stunts. The players had no mobility or bargaining power comparable to that of baseball players', and the payrolls reflected the owners' tight control.

Mike Lynn could practically run the franchise out of his back pocket.

But the new ownership wasn't a football family. It was a consortium. And it took over behind Headrick at a time when players' salaries were escalating. Free agency had come to pro football. So had the salary cap. Everybody was going to lose blue chip players sooner or later. The free agency market got to be a multi-million dollar rummage sale. The swashbuckling Lynns were giving way to the accountants.

"We first had to start setting out an actual budget," Headrick said. "The days when you could pull big profits out of pro football were pretty much over. Competition for the buck was tighter. We had to organize marketing plans, sell side products and bring in new fans."

Denny Green came to the Vikings from Stanford via the 49ers. He said his goal was to build a team with the 49ers winning aura, its offensive firepower and its steadiness. That is a load. Heading into 1995, he said, the goal was still there, and attainable.

But first they had to bring in a new coach. Jerry Burns left voluntarily, widely liked by players and associates but pretty well burned out with the fans. About the same time the Vikings put the official epitaph to the Herschel Walker trade. He'd played for 2 1/2 years but he was looking elsewhere, a search the Vikings cheerfully encouraged in view of his salary and the absence of any blockbuster performance by Herschel after his first game.

So at the end of the 1991 season, Headrick was the CEO, Burns was about to retire and Walker was about to find a new kennel for his big dog in Philadelphia. Setting out to hire a coach, Headrick walked down the hall in the Vikings' Winter Park and consulted the coaching emeritus, Bud Grant.

"I asked Bud what qualities it took to make a great coach," Headrick said. Whether he was the head coach or later as the live-in legend, Grant never burned up the vocabulary. "He told me he'd be brief," Headrick said. "I said that's OK by me."

"What it takes," Grant said, "is great players."

The interview ended amiably but quickly. Headrick didn't argue much. He did re-examine the Viking roster, found some substantial names and talents there, and began making phone calls. Eventually he got advice from people like Bill Walsh, Tom Landry, Dick Vermeil, Bill Parcells and his own staff. He talked to some college coaches, and to prospects in the NFL. It got down to Pete Carroll, the popular assistant on Burns' staff, and Denny Green.

Walsh's recommendation of Green was almost exuberant. It could be argued that having left the 49er coaching job for broadcasting, but pining for a return to the college game, Walsh found his goals enhanced if the Vikings hired Green. Walsh found something idyllic about the Stanford head coaching job. It was occupied then, of course, by Denny Green, and occupied successfully. Among his other achievements, Green had beaten Notre Dame at South Bend at a time when the Irish were ranked No. 1, and he'd taken Stanford to a bowl game at the end of his third season there in 1991. But Walsh had legitimate reasons for recommending Green, who had been a key assistant for the 49ers at the time of Walsh's last Super Bowl champion. Green's record as a college assistant, college head coach for eight years at Northwestern and Stanford and his performance as a pro coaching assistant all attracted flattering reviews. He won as many games at Northwestern as anybody short of Houdini could be expected to win. He won at Stanford and he knew the National Football League.

"What I liked best about him," Headrick said, "was that he did his homework. When we got around to talking about Viking personnel, he knew who and what he was talking about. If he hadn't had any direct contact with the players, he'd talked with people who did. He wanted football that was not only winning football but entertaining football."

Cris Carter sprints downfield. He cost the Vikings $100 in a waiver deal with Philadelphia. Five years later, he's worth millions. He isn't just record statistics and touchdowns. Carter bangs and gives his body on every play. He deserves the millions.

In short, he was a 49er man. Move the ball around. Never forget that defense wins. But it won't win as often if it doesn't have an aggressive, creative partner on offense. Green called it a high-flying offense and said he wanted that for the Vikings.

It was not immediately available. What was available to Green was a respectable talent pool that invited some engineering and re-tooling. So the man with the sheriff's badge, Super Bowl ring and drums also came on as a juggler. "The team was 8-8 the year before," he said. "Before that, it was 6-10. It came close in 1987. The next two years it fell off from that, and the two years after that it skidded faster. Looking at it that way, I saw it as a turnaround job. If we went into the 1992 season the way the team was set up in 1991, we were inviting an even deeper skid. We had to move some people around and get new ones in there where they were needed."

The process was sped by some random acts of clairvoyance by the Viking talent sleuths. One involved a discontented pass-catcher in Philadelphia, Cris Carter. The other brought in a linebacker whose card read, Have Helmet, Will Travel, Jack Del Rio.

John Randle (above) arrived without a band. He was nobody, or at least the pro ball version of it. He was utterly ignored in the draft because of injuries in college. The Vikings gave him a contract as free agent in 1990. By 1994 he was an all-pro defensive linemen. Strike up that band.

Jack Del Rio (right) heads for the ball and somebody's ribs. The Cowboys didn't expect to lose him to free agency. A year later they'd have given a million to get him back.

In early September of 1990, the Philadelphia Eagles' Buddy Ryan decided that Cris Carter was not a NFL-type wide receiver. He reached this conclusion despite the somewhat convincing evidence of the 1989 season, in which Carter caught 11 touchdown passes. Buddy was unimpressed. Carter's skills were limited, he said. He can go up and catch a ball in the end zone, but what else?

Buddy dumped Cris Carter on waivers.

To the distant Carter-watchers in Minneapolis (Frank Gilliam, Jerry Reichow, Jeff Diamond, who handled signings, and Jerry Burns), 11 touchdowns and an obvious ability to outjump defensive backs in the end zone looked like a fair start on NFL credentials for a receiver. Ryan obviously was fed up with Carter. Why? Well, Buddy Ryan's appetite for getting fed up with football players is probably larger than most. There were stories that Carter was a problem, about work ethic and about animosities that boiled in him. And more stories.

On the waiver wire at the time, the Vikings had priority over anybody else interested. So they bid for Carter and paid the requisite $100.

Four years later, this man set the National Football League record for pass receptions in one season, 122.

He was an All-Pro, a Pro-Bowler, and a player recognized for his refusal to accept any yardage less than enough. He would lunge with the ball, smash into linebackers and defensive backs after catches, look for daylight after a catch or hit somebody in the gut. When Carter caught the ball, he, not the defensive back or linebacker, was the attacker.

By 1992, Green's first year, Carter was ready for star status with the Viking receiving corps. Ready, also, was John Randle, the defensive tackle, another All-Pro who in 1990 was signed by the Vikings as an undrafted free agent out of Texas A&I. So was halfback Terry Allen, chosen on

the 9th round in the 1990 draft, passed over in earlier rounds because of surgery late in his college career at Clemson. A year before Green arrived, the Vikings had drafted Carlos Jenkins, an undersized but trigger-quick linebacker from Michigan State, Jake Reed, a big wide receiver from Grambling (a choice the Vikings got, incidentally, from Dallas in the Herschel Walker trade) and Todd Scott, a defensive back from Southwest Louisiana.

And also from Dallas, remarkably, they got Jack Del Rio. In 1992 the NFL was still operating under a Plan B arrangement that gave certain players free agency. Del Rio was one. He was a quality middle backer, a team leader. Dallas, running into salary problems, assumed it could keep Del Rio for less than somebody else would pay because he was entrenched with the Cowboys and lived in Dallas.

Jack Del Rio said "adios" to Dallas in his most cultured Southern California accent. When he joined the Vikings in 1992, he was handed the No. 55 worn for so many distin-

Remember that awful Herschel Walker trade? Reconsider it with some charity. As part of it, the Vikings got a third-round draft choice in 1991. It turned out to be a big receiver named Jake Reed from Grambling (leaping to pull down a pass, below). In 1994, Cris Carter and Jake gave the Vikings the most successful receiving partnership in the NFL.

Rich Gannon throws against the Packers. He came into pro football as a runner who happened to be a quarterback. He upgraded his passing in the years that followed, but lost out in the Viking quarterback shuffling in the early 1990s.

guished years by middle linebacker Scott Studwell, he of the brick-piercing x-ray eyes the TV cameras loved. Studwell had no objection to Del Rio's acquisition of his old number. He stayed in the Viking organization doing player relations and later became the player personnel coordinator.

The team worked the Plan B market ambitiously. Veterans Vencie Glenn and Anthony Parker reinforced the secondary put together by Tony Dungy, the defensive coordinator. While this was happening Green decided to install Rich Gannon at quarterback with Sean Salisbury No. 2. It meant the departure of Wade Wilson, one of the heroes of the 1987 playoff victories and the No. 1 quarterback for most of the prior five seasons. Wilson left with some bitterness, contending he'd been dangled on a string by Green and the Viking management during the summer of that year. He was angered by the way he finally got the news, not from the coach but from vice president of administration Jeff Diamond. Green explained it this way: "In 95 percent of the cases, I'm the one who informs the player. I'm one of hundreds of coaches who'll tell you it's the worst part of coaching. But I didn't in Wade's case (there were a few others) because his dealings had either been with Jeff on contract matters or Jerry Burns as his coach. I'd never coached Wade. We had no relationship. It seemed the right thing to have Jeff talk to him."

Relationships. Sometimes they're as hard in the world of tough-gut football players as they are in love. The decision on Wade Wilson didn't finish Wilson's career. He stayed on in the NFL. It was not the last time Denny Green would face the accusation of being insensitive towards the feelings of veteran football players cut loose. Carl Lee was also critical. Green's answer: "You'd love to give an extra year to veteran football players who contributed to a team's success and continuity. A year past their prime. That was possible years ago. With today's salaries, it isn't."

Should a head coach in today's era of capitalist football players have the time and disposition to be thoughtful about those things?

"I think so, yes," Darrin Nelson said after his retirement. "I think Denny did a great job his first three years. But when a veteran player has to leave (in the frame of mind in which Wilson left) you can say it could have been handled better."

Neither Gannon nor Salisbury, who survived Wilson, were among the upper echelons of NFL quarterbacks. But the team had a veteran offensive line in 1992, one of the better ones in football. It got more than 1,200 yards running from Terry Allen. It had Cris Carter and A.C.

Carter and Steve Jordan as receivers. Salisbury was an itinerant quarterback who'd played in Canada, had a strong arm and gift – some folks said almost a mania – for public relations. Gannon was the athlete, sometimes more productive running than throwing, although his passing skills were generally underrated. For most of the season he ran the offense put together by Jack Burns, the offensive coordinator. Burns had come to the Vikings from the Washington Redskins with ideas that seemed at least from the outset to mesh with Green's. But 1992 was his only full season with the Vikings.

Their names were at the top of the charts: Despite two surgeries that would have ended most careers, Terry Allen (upper right) gained nearly 2,800 yards in four years with the Vikings and holds the highest rushing average of all Viking backs, 4.4 yards a carry. A.C. Carter, airborne once more (above) leads all Viking receivers with 52 touchdowns and Steve Jordan, packing it downfield (right), leads in total receptions with 498 in 13 seasons.

Green removed him as offensive coordinator the next season and replaced him with Brian Billick. It was one of the earlier spins of a revolving door of coaching changes on the Vikings' staff in the next three years.

"Some of those changes simply meant other teams were impressed by the quality of our coaches," Green said. "The others were things I thought I had to do to get us to the Super Bowl. That's the goal. It was the goal when I coached with the 49ers and it's my goal with the Vikings. Every season."

The player departures included those of Keith Millard, whose career had declined because of injuries, and Joey Browner as well as Walker. The list was lengthy. In his first season, Green put 17 new players on the Viking roster from the 8-8 team of the year before. Among the additions was a fellow Green recruited for Stanford years before, Darrin Nelson, revived as a Viking after a season in San Diego. Another was Roger Craig, the high-kicking battlehorse out of the 49er backfield.

The honorable retreads, Darrin Nelson (20, above) and Roger Craig (below), helped the Vikings to a division title in 1992.

With all this renovation and strenuous fine-tuning, the Vikings finished 11-5 and won the division title. It was generated mainly by a ball-hawking, quarterback-pressuring performance by Dungy's defense that harvested eight defensive touchdowns. The mark of the season was a flair for comeback victories, including a memorable one in the Metrodome against the Chicago Bears. With the Bears leading 20-0 in the second half, quarterback Jim Harbaugh inexplicably called an audible near the Bears' 20 and threw into the flat at a time when it was almost impossible for the Bears to lose. Todd Scott read it and picked off Harbaugh's pass to open the gates to a late-game outpouring that beat an apoplectic Mike Ditka. It nearly drove Mike back into the hospital and put him on the road to retirement.

Symbolically, it was a victory engineered by a defense that was fraught with play-makers and imbued with the idea of winning-by-turnover. Thomas, Randle, Doleman and Al Noga formed the defensive front with Del Rio, Jenkins and Mike Merriweather as the linebackers and the reconstituted secondary of Scott, Audray McMillian, Carl Lee, Glenn, et al working the passing lanes. When the team hit a lull and lost two in a row in November, Green replaced Gannon with Salisbury for the last four games. It was all pretty heady stuff for the Viking crowds, but it ended abruptly. The Redskins, Super Bowl champions the previous year, came to the Metrodome in the first round of the playoffs, hit harder, hit more often and beat the Vikings 24-7.

What the Vikings needed, Green concluded, was something more dynamic at quarterback. They scanned the free agency catalogues, the waiver lists and the propositions from player agents. Dynamic quarter-

Strong safety and 1992 pro-bowler, Todd Scott, was the defensive backfield's inspirational leader in the early 1990s.

backs looking for a job were in short supply. One appeared to qualify.

Jim McMahon was looking for a job. This was the same McMahon who once hassled the Vikings in the Chicago Bears' championship seasons, James the Eccentric, James the Iconoclast but, above all, James the guy who won practically all of the Central Division games he started. McMahon had been out of the division for several seasons, first with San Diego and then with the Philadelphia Eagles as a backup to Randall Cunningham. By then he had a well-deserved reputation for being injury-prone. He got hurt often and wherever he played, but he also played through a lot of the injuries and he never lost his reputation for being a winner.

So the Vikings signed him to quarterback the 1993 season. "He was an interim guy," Green said. "We thought we had a potential playoff winner with the kind of defense we had. We needed somebody like

McMahon on offense. A veteran quarterback who could get the team's attention, a scrapper and a winner."

They got most of that. They also got McMahon a year older and a little more fragile. It didn't help him to work with a rebuilt offensive line. Gone were Gary Zimmerman, Kirk Lowdermilk and Brian Habib: Zimmerman one of the best offensive tackles in football, Lowdermilk an established center and Habib a veteran guard. This was the era of player mobility and of understandable resentment by veteran players when unproved young players got hundreds of thousands of dollars more. This was the full flowering of the era of escalating salaries and unsentimental decisions by management on who was expendable under the salary cap. Zimmerman announced his retirement. Eventually he was dealt to Denver for first, second and sixth round draft choices. Two of these materialized in the 1994 draft, defensive back DeWayne Washington on the first round and tight end Andrew Jordan on the sixth. Lowdermilk and Habib both went via free agency. This meant patching the offensive line with such folks as Adam Schreiber, Bernard Dafney and Todd Kalis. The patching extended into the next season with the emergence of Jeff Christy and John Gerak and rookie Todd Steussie and the addition of Chris Hinton at tackle to replace Tim Irwin.

McMahon didn't bellyache much about the disap-

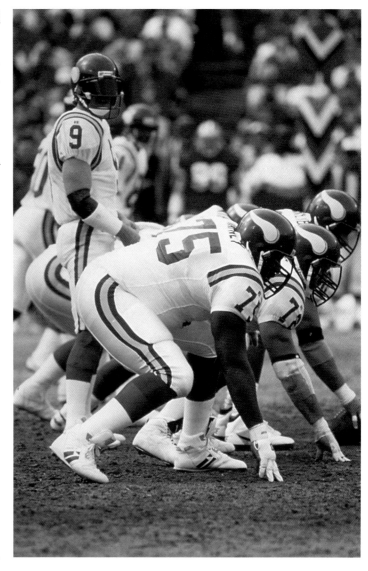

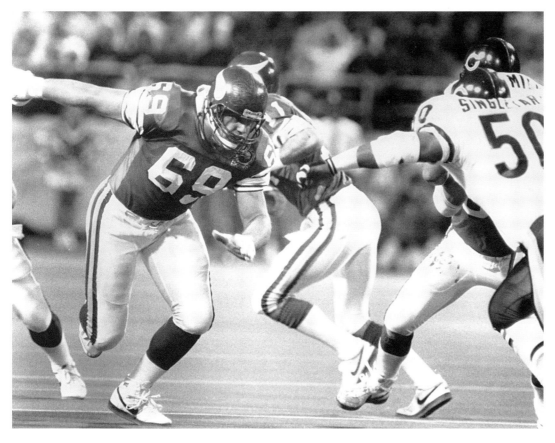

When Jim McMahon looked out on the landscape as the Viking quarterback in 1993, he saw an offensive line scarcely recognizable from the Viking lines he remembered. Zimmerman, Lowdermilk and Habib were gone. Todd Kalis (left) was a veteran along with Randall McDaniel and Tim Irwin. They were enough to help get the team back into the playoffs.

Fuad Reveiz will tell you it's all in technique. Get the routine down, believe in it and the field goals will follow. For Reveiz, they almost always do. When the 1994 season ended, Fuad was working on a record streak of 28 consecutive field goals, under domes, in wind, in cold and with playoffs hanging in the balance. Nothing shook him. In five years he averaged nearly 80 percent success in his field goals. If you watch Fuad, it's easy. Loosen your shoulders. Pull at your face bar. Take a step, and kick. Twenty-eight in a row. Try it sometime, with a half dozen maneaters roaring in from seven yards away.

pearance of the veterans from his offensive line in 1993. Randall McDaniel was still there; and after all, Irwin could play and the others weren't ornaments. McMahon put up no sensational numbers. He was hurt off and on and Salisbury had to throw nearly 200 passes. McMahon hit 60 percent of his own, threw for a modest nine touchdowns but still won 8 of the 11 games he started. Those included a McMahon special, a wild, God-is-our-witness play in the final minute of an early season game against Green Bay at the Metrodome. The Vikings trailed 13-12 when McMahon threw deep toward the goal line. Eric Guliford, a kid free agent who hadn't caught a pass in the NFL, found himself floating free near the end zone after the Packers' butchered their coverage. Guliford caught the ball with six seconds left and was nailed before getting in. Fuad Reveiz, en route to becoming one of the finest of all Viking field goal kickers, hit a 22-yarder and the Vikings won, 15-13.

New people in the backfield helped. They had to because Terry Allen never got out of the blocks in 1993 after his knee surgery. The Vikings acquired the protypical big back from Kansas City, Barry Word, who worked well for a few games. Robert Smith, the thinking man's speedster drafted on the first round from Ohio State, broke in with impressive numbers and versatility. The discovery, though, was Scottie Graham, a fullback from Ohio State who had been released by a couple of pro teams and was selling tranquilizers in a Columbus, Ohio, pharmacy when the Vikings hired him in early fall. He graduated from the practice squad after a few weeks and became the plugging line-hacker the Vikings needed to salvage their season in December when it almost got away. Graham kept rolling up the first downs. On defense, the unheralded Hawaiian, Esera Tuaolo, replaced the injured Henry Thomas late in the season, and John Randle was worth two of the other guys on most plays. McMahon came back to play hurt. And the Vikings finished by beating Detroit and Green Bay on the road and Joe Montana's Chiefs at the Metrodome for a

The Vikings found Scottie Graham in a pharmacy in Ohio. If the Green Bay Packer defensive line had any voice in it, he should have brought all the aspirin in the store (below).

Save some of that aspirin for the Packer backfield. Doleman (lower right) penetrates to make a tackle behind the line.

9-7 season record and a game in the Meadowlands in New York in the playoffs.

It was football out of the deep mists of the medieval NFL. It was played in a cold wind, with muscle and curses. The Vikings might have won it. They might have won it if Rodney Hampton didn't run 51 yards on toughness and against some atrocious tackling. They might have won it if Chris Doleman and John Randle didn't jump offsides to keep Giant drives going. Above all, they might have won it if Cris Carter didn't fumble grasping for extra yardage near the Giant goal line on the end of a long pass play. New York won 17-10, inflicting the second consecutive first-round playoff loss on a Denny Green Viking team. Green: "Again, we

were close. We had more retooling to do for 1994. Again, you can't keep all the players you want to keep in today's football economics. But what we needed in the worst way was a quarterback to get us to the Super Bowl."

The one they eventually found had never been to the Super Bowl, but he was clearly capable of it in any season, then or now. The revolving door on quarterbacks was activated again. The Vikings weren't interested in re-signing Jim McMahon. As it turned out, they weren't interested in keeping people like Gino Toretta and Andre Ware. Rich Gannon was gone. The Vikings also got rid of and then re-acquired Sean Salisbury and nominally installed Brad Johnson as No. 2. The search for No. 1 began early in the year. The Vikings were going to make a deal with Atlanta for Chris Doleman, whose verve and sacks had dwindled. McMahon's salary was removed from the cap. They had bucks to spend. The intended destination of that money was the bank account of young Scott Mitchell, the powerful left-handed quarterback who had all of the NFL slavering after his performance as the replacement for injured Dan Marino in Miami.

Warren Moon came from Houston, the site of the space program. It meant some form of rocketry was assured for the Vikings offense in 1994. It materialized in a passing performance that was unprecedented in Viking history. Moon threw for 4,264 yards on 371 completions in 601 attempts, a success rate of 61.7 percent. The Vikings won the Central Division. But a journeyman pro from St. Paul, Steve Walsh, threw better in the playoffs and the Bears won at the Metrodome.

"We wanted him pretty badly," Green said. "We went after him hard, with a lot of money. So did Detroit. We figured the worst thing we could do was lose him to a team in our own division."

Green was wrong. The worst thing the Vikings could have done, quite likely, was to finish first in the bidding. Detroit signed Mitchell to a huge contract. He flopped before getting hurt in midseason. He might not have flopped in Minnesota. He may eventually make it big in Detroit. But losing Mitchell meant that the Vikings had to go with all arms outstretched and money-in-hand when Houston decided it could live and prosper in the NFL without Warren Moon.

Nobody has fully explained what provoked Houston into this odd logic. Moon had been one of the great quarterbacks in football for years. Playing in the run-and-shoot offense, he'd rolled up numbers that were vast and victories that happened week in and out. He was hugely popular with the Houston players and in the community. His character and performance made him one of the exemplary figures in all of football. He was into his late 30s, true, but he was well-conditioned and still capable of

playing championship football for several years to come.

The Oilers had been frustrated. They'd come so close to the Super Bowl, but hadn't reached it. There had also been the hideous afternoon in Buffalo when the Oilers blew an enormous lead and lost a playoff game in the face of odds that were almost beyond calculating. There was also Moon's salary, but on the scale of pro quarterback salaries, it shouldn't have fazed a successful franchise. The Oilers decided their Moonglow had ebbed. Green and Headrick and anybody else they could recruit surrounded Warren Moon. They gave him attention, respect and as much cash as they could scrounge. The deal was made. Moon came to Minnesota under a two-year contract with an option on a third. He cost the Vikings two insignificant draft choices and, of course, the $2.7 million or thereabouts in his contract.

"I don't know how we could have made a better deal," Green said. "Of all the quarterbacks in football you want to lead your team for two or three years when you think you've got a shot at the Super Bowl, you would put Warren Moon right at the top of the list, and there he was on our team."

Doleman, though, was gone. Steve Jordan did not sign a contract until the season was almost over. But as his successors at tight end the Vikings acquired Adrian Cooper in a trade with Pittsburgh and found that Andrew Jordan, the rookie, could also play. Their problems were at defensive end on either side of the John Randle-Henry Thomas meat-

Moon kept the Viking offense moving. Terry Allen, Robert Smith, Scottie Graham and Amp Lee juiced up the running game, but Moon's arm and experience meant the Vikings passed often. Call it incessantly.

grinder that was called the best tackle combination in the league. Roy Barker, James Harris and Robert Harris worked at defensive end with something less than pulverizing effect, although it was early in their careers. Jenkins, Del Rio and Ed McDaniel represented a highly mobile linebacking group and Parker, Scott, Glenn and the rookie Washington were the regular defensive backs in a secondary thinned by the departure of Carl Lee and Audray McMillian.

Although they went into the season with one of the great passers of the era, the Vikings wanted to run as well. Flying circuses don't often get to the Super Bowl. They were stocked with runners who gave them one of the deepest backfields in football – Allen as the all-purpose regular, Graham for short yardage, Robert Smith as a kind of No. 2 Allen and Amp Lee, acquired from San Francisco, as a 3rd down back in passing situations. All of them could catch as well as run. A minor problem, long ago discovered by Bud Grant, was the basic arithmetic presented by four good backs. There's only one ball. Keeping them productive and content might have been sticky, except that all of them were pretty well-adjusted guys as pros. At least for the time being, they seemed to understand pro ball's

Henry Thomas (above) usually figured out a way to be near the ball. When he grabbed it, nobody was going to pry it loose.

Thomas' confederate in assault, John Randle (right), was invariably double-teamed. Some days, though, opponents found John impossible. Make that most days.

PURPLE HEARTS AND GOLDEN MEMORIES

son at the dome, and despite Steve Walsh's calm and plucky quarterbacking from mid-season on, it looked to be a Viking stroll. They'd beaten the Bears six straight games. Chicago had lost a critical game at home to New England the previous week and scored only three points. Moon had led the NFC by throwing for 4,264 yards and 371 completions. Carter broke the NFL record by catching 122 of those and Jake Reed caught 85 more. Qadry Ismail, the young speedster with unpredictable hands, made some critical catches. John Randle made 13 1/2 sacks. The defense held opponents to only 68 rushing yards a game, the fourth lowest in NFL history and the defense logged seven touchdowns, making it 17 in Dungy's three years as the defensive coordinator.

But against Chicago, the Vikings found themselves in Bear territory 10 times – and scored 18 points. They produced just three points out of two turnovers. The running game was smothered by the Bear defensive line and the Vikings' own defensive line found itself outgunned. Steve

When the Vikings went deep in 1994, Qadry Ismail (above) worried the defense with his speed and impetuosity. But when the Vikings got into the end zone, Cris Carter (right, 80) usually was in the middle of the scene.

Walsh threw ably. Moon threw well most of the time, but too often (52 times). The Bears made practically no mistakes en route to the scoring red zone, and plastered the Vikings 35-18.

And what did the post-game morticians have to say?

Vikings fold again in the playoffs. Was that correct? Well, yes. This was a team, after all, that looked as strong as Dallas and San Francisco in midseason. Was there anything to explain it? "This sounds lame," Green said. "We'd played the 49ers on a Monday night. This game was Sunday. We had a day less to get ready. Those things count, but not as much as the fact that we didn't play well. We'd played about average. The Bears were better than that."

Which means the quest continues.

But, if you hired a football prophet to look at the Vikings' future in 1961 and asked what could this football team be reasonably expected to give its audiences and its proprietors in the next 35 years, the prophet would probably have said this:

Thrills and pratfalls by the bunches, characters and stars and some oversold deadbeats, some championships, and maybe The Big One.

The prophet was conservative. The Big One is still out there. But the prophet could not have predicted four NFL or NFC championships, 14 division championships and 18 playoff appearances, profitable seasons practically every year, a midstream change from the dumpy little stadium in Bloomington to a kookie, inflated cream jar of an arena in downtown Minneapolis, and an increase in the team's value from $1 million to more than $150 million.

Yet those would not have been the biggest dividends.

The biggest dividends would have been the mixed and sometimes maddening cast of thousands, and from that cast the unforgettable ones: Dutch Van Brocklin, Fran Tarkenton, Bud Grant, Alan Page, Carl Eller, Jim Marshall, Bill Brown, Hugh McElhenny, Mick Tingelhoff, Ron Yary, Ed White, Paul Krause, Fred Cox, Karl Kassulke, Jeff Siemon, Matt Blair, Tommy Kramer, Ahmad Rashad, Keith Millard, Steve Jordan, Chris Doleman, A.C. Carter, Cris Carter, Randall McDaniel, Warren Moon, Jerry Burns, Denny Green, Floyd Peters, Jim Finks, Mike Lynn and the others, great or comical, or simply pro football people, who moved in the processional with them.

If you had the foresight to buy a season ticket in 1961 and to keep it, it would have been worth it.

If you watched all of it in front of the TV screen, you probably would not have second-guessed yourself for doing it.

But second-guessing the Van Brocklins, Tarkentons, Grants, Kramers and the Greens, that's another matter. That is the birthright of the fan. That and the most tantalizing of all of the football fans' visions:

Maybe this will be the year.

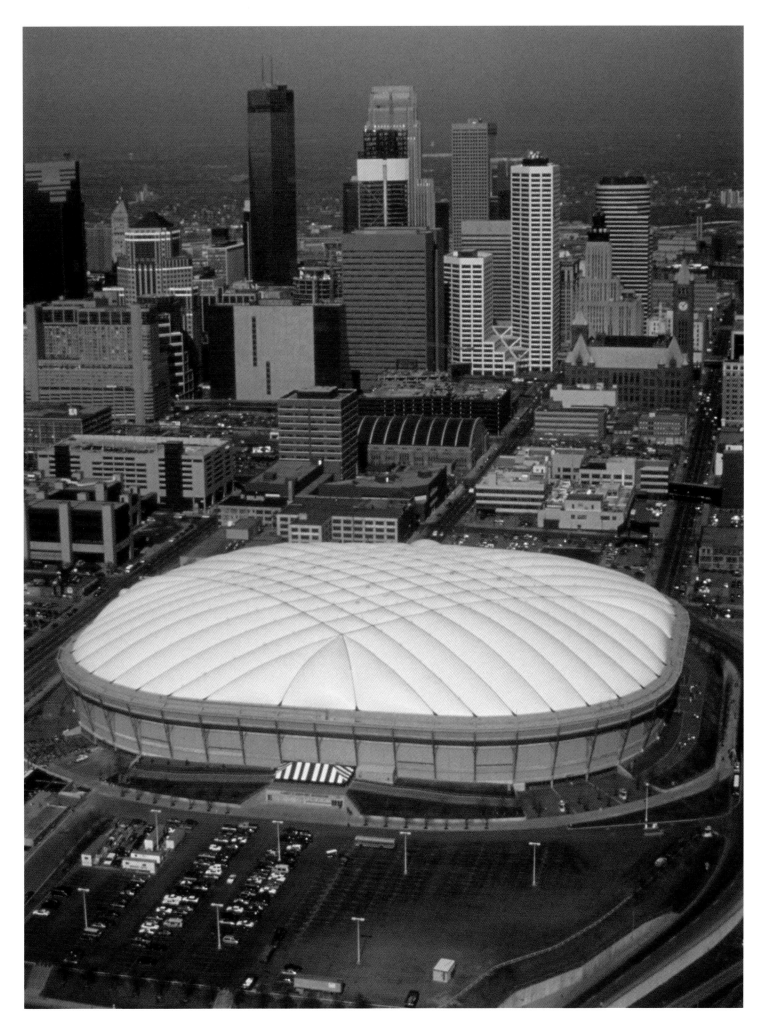

Where Did They Go? The World After Football

Some people who play pro football look on the last trip to the locker room as a liberation. For them, the stress and hazard of big time football finally eroded the old-boys fraternity in it, and even dampened the allure of the big money.

But most pro football players dread the last year. It means that the fantasy world, the money and the camaraderie dissolve or recede.

From there it's a kind of blind leap into another cosmos. Most of the ballplayers of today have negotiated that suspenseful jump with some level of fulfillment. Today in any grand reunion of the Vikings of the last 35 years, you would mingle business execs and marketers with professional people, miscellaneous salesmen, self-promoters, administrators, middle-aged men still in football and some who never quite crossed the divide from athletic success to comfort after football.

But consider the remarkable life of Freddie Cox.

When Freddie Cox joined the Minnesota Vikings in 1963, they were paying field goal kickers on the order of ten grand. Not per game. Per season. Trash haulers, necktie salesmen and even a few journalists got more. When he finished in 1977, the pros were paying field goal kickers a living wage. But they never accorded field goal kickers much security or any noticeable dignity.

Yet today Fred Cox lives the country gentleman's retirement in a lovely home above a bend in the Mississippi River in the town of Monticello, Minnesota, northwest of the Twin Cities. He prospered in three careers – football, chiropractic and the multi-million dollar marketing of a toy football. Of those three enterprises, pro football was the least lucrative.

"But tell me where I'd be without it?" he asked.

In the era in which Fred Cox played, the thought – or threat – of The World After Football was an elusive and gnawing unknown in the lives of those who played the game. It was hazard or opportunity. Pro football became a dependency for a lot of players, emotionally as well as financially. The huge salaries available to the best players today, and the quarter-million dollar salaries available to its mediocrities, make life after football less worrisome to the jocks of the 1990s. But even today the presumption of security can be full of air. A rookie's half-million dollar bonus isn't going outlast his creditors if he flops or blows a knee.

In the time of Freddie Cox, some players planned seriously for the day the mythical Turk arrived with a message that couldn't be mistaken: "Coach wants to see you. Bring your playbook." Others drifted from scheme to scheme or pretended to plan. A lot of them simply practiced the pro athlete's version of denial. There was always going to be another season, always another ball game. Some of those are hurting today. The attention they got from football, the temporary advantage in the pursuit of new work, often failed to balance another reality. In their late '20s to mid '30s, they were competing with men and women with a 10-year head start in the business.

But in one form or other, most professional football players of the last 30 years – the age in which the game graduated from a fuzzy black and white novelty on TV to a national passion – have been able to capitalize on their visibility. That hasn't guaranteed them success or ease in life after football. It does open the door, a door vastly wider than the one available to the working stiffs who didn't have coast-to-coast audiences when they came out of school. The star players of today don't much have to fret about a career change. If you draw close to a million dollars a year for six or seven years, your next career may come down to figuring out ways to spend it.

But...

"But most of the marginal players still have to look at the future and ask themselves if they're serious about what it's going to be," Fred Cox said. "Some of the people I played with decided pretty early that they weren't going to be able to soak in the sun the rest of their lives. Some of them didn't really want to think about crossing the bridge from football into the other world, where you weren't a star and were you weren't catered to. One thing that makes me feel good about playing with the Vikings for 15 years is that a big percentage of them have been able to lead satisfying lives afterward. Some of them have gotten rich. Most of them are comfortable and like what they're doing. We've even got a few millionaires."

They've also got lawyers, doctors, ministers, counselors, at least one judge and platoons of businessmen. Fred Cox' transition wasn't typical, which is probably fitting, because kickers in pro ball are usually derided as odd characters from distant galaxies. Cox, though, was an athlete who happened to kick. At the University of Pittsburgh he was fullback first and then a kicker. Van Brocklin brought him in for a trial in 1962. He kicked well through the whole exhibition season. The final pre-season game in Atlanta was advertised as Fred's trial by combat. He was spectacular. He kicked off seven straight times through the end zone. He made all of his conversions and the one field goal he tried, from 43 yards. And two days later Van Brocklin cut him. The coach apologized. "You can kick in this league," he said. "But I have to save a spot on the roster. We have a guy who can kick field goals and punt. I hate like hell that this is happening to you."

It was a regret richly shared by Fred Cox. But he won the job the next year and held it through 1977. It occurred to him early in his career that he might not be kicking field goals as a golden ager. So he went to chiropractic school. And he was a chiropractor before he finished kicking field goals. He also met an associate who developed a foam-filled toy football that since has sold millions. And today he has sold his three chiropractic clinics, receives revenues from the foamy football and lives the life of a prairie squire in Monticello.

"A lot of people don't know one other side to Bud Grant," he said. "There was a time when we had guys seriously involved in studies or work for their lives after football. Alan Page was studying law. I was in chiropractic school. Grady Alderman was becoming a certified public accountant. Gary Cuozza was either going to be a dentist or already was. And Bud gave us time off, let us miss some practices to do it. The other players understood that. I never heard a complaint about it."

It's a matter of record that today Fred Cox has made it and retired from business, that Alan Page sits on the bench of the Minnesota Supreme Court, that Gary Cuozzo has been an orthodontist for years in Lincroft, New Jersey and that Grady Alderman is in business in Colorado after a career in football administration that took him to the general manager's job with the Denver Broncos.

Nostalgia doesn't flourish as thickly in the atmospherics of pro football as it does in baseball. Not much poetry is written about the boys of autumn. But a Minnesota Viking fan still is intrigued by "what happened to...?"

All right, what did?

More than 500 players have worn the Viking colors for at least a season. For every Alan Page who reached the Minnesota state Supreme Court or Fred Cox who made it in three different careers, there are dozens who disappeared from the view of all but their closest friends in football. The big majority left football years ago and now watch the game simply as fans. To locate them, you'll have to roam the full spectrum of American industry and community life, from the big city asphalt to the country hamlets.

You're not going to find all of them. The Viking and NFL researchers are aggressive about trying to keep in touch with their alumni, but have lost thread with a lot of them. What follows here should bring the Viking fan up to date with enough of them to link the years and to renew some old affections.

A sizable number of them have never left athletics, or haven't left it far behind. When you talk about affections, layers of it still linger for Joe Kapp among the riper Viking fans. Joe acted on television and film for a few years after leaving pro football, roamed around in a variety of business adventures and then coached his alma mater California Golden Bears for five years before settling back into the restaurant business and three or four other enterprises in northern California. Ed White has been

coaching the offensive line at San Diego State for several years and Jim Christopherson, a linebacker and field goal kicker in the early years, became one of the Minnesota college coaching deans at Concordia in Moorhead. Bobby Lee, who nearly made it to the Super Bowl as one of the Viking quarterbacks in the early 1970s, is the athletic director at the University of Pacific. Bob Lurtsema, reincarnated by TV as "Benchwarmer Bob," defines his after-football career in a half dozen ways. But it comes to merchandising the mush-mouthed benchrider and folk hero as a sports bar operator, speaker, media personality and publisher of a Viking fan newspaper. Charlie West went into coaching and is now on the staff at Syracuse. Mike Mularky is coaching with the pros.

Jerry Reichow, who played for Van Brocklin's first teams, has worked for years as the Viking player personnel director and head of scouting. Bob Schnelker, one of his teammates on the first Viking team, got into the dicey business of professional coaching and ran the Green Bay and Viking offenses in the 1980s and early 1990s. A third member of the first Viking team, defensive back Charlie Sumner, has coached for years in the NFL. Scott Studwell, the Vikings' middle linebacker for years, remained with the team in administration. Jerry Shay, a defensive tackle in the late 1970s, became a director of college scouting for the New York Giants. Don Joyce and Bill Jobko, whose round and florid face earned him the title of The Red Owl in his playing years, went into pro scouting. Tom Adams, a northern Minnesota kid who played a season for Van Brocklin as a wide receiver, became the athletic director at Greenway high school in Coleraine. Joey Browner, the crunching defensive back, is marketing his karate expertise, versions of which he practiced on NFL halfbacks. Milt Sunde, an offensive linemen for nearly a decade, went from football to the operation of a fitness enterprise in Bloomington. Eddie Payton, the popular runback specialist of the 1980s, teaches golf at Jackson State in Mississippi and predictably runs a public relations business.

Bob Stein was one of those pro football rarities who acquired higher visibility after he left the game. Stein played a couple of seasons as a linebacker and on the special teams with the Los Angeles Rams in the 1970s after graduating from the University of Minnesota. He played for the Vikings in 1975, became a lawyer, a player agent and then the general manager of the Minnesota Timberwolves until their sale in 1995 to the current owners.

The law attracted more than Stein and Alan Page. Fred McNeill, a linebacker who played in the Super Bowl, is a practicing attorney in Minneapolis. Doug Dumler, and an offensive lineman of the 1970s, went into law. Tommy Mason, the Vikings' first draft choice in their first draft in 1961, earned a law degree but settled into a lucrative beverage distributorship in California, which he sold in 1994 to get into the automotive business. Tim Irwin, still an active player in the NFL in 1994, also has a law degree. Rip Hawkins practiced law for years.

What became of the highest magnitude stars? Francis Tarkenton, of course, was a business conglomerate while he was still quarterbacking.

From football he went into national television as a prime time host of a series called "That's Incredible," and extended his motivational company in Atlanta to computer software combined with TV infomercials. Page progressed from corporate law to the state attorney general's staff, the University of Minnesota board of regents and then the state Supreme Court. En route he did commentary on athletics on public broadcasting and organized a foundation to deepen educational opportunities for minority youth. Two of his teammates on the great Viking defensive line of the team's prime years, Carl Eller and Jim Marshall, both experienced drug problems in the years immediately after football but righted themselves in a way that earned the respect of the Twin Cities and football community. Eller became a drug awareness consultant and speaker, and Marshall a leader – along with the former running back, Oscar Reed – in community work to uplift city kids and to expand their goals. The fourth member of the Purple Gang defense, Gary Larsen, moved to Seattle, Washington, where he's a sales manager for an automobile company.

There, he's practically a neighbor of Hugh McElhenny, the Hall of Fame running back who played two of his last seasons with the Vikings. Hugh spent almost all of his post-football business life in Seattle and now lives there in retirement. Tommy Kramer operates a chain of restaurant out of San Antonio, Texas, his home town. Jim Langer, who played only one year for the Vikings but was one of the most prestigious centers in pro football history in his years in Miami, is a manager of truck parts distribution firm in Brainerd, Minnesota. Chuck Foreman is an account executive for an office copier company out of Richfield, directs a youth program and is the father of Jay Foreman, now playing for the University of Nebraska. Paul Krause, the NFL's all-time leader in pass interceptions, operates a real estate company in Lakeville, Minnesota, owns a golf course in Elk River and – being a former defensive back accustomed to high risk – is getting into Dakota County politics. Ron Yary, the great offensive tackle, returned to his photo business in Anaheim, California, in partnership with his brother.

Somebody once asked Jeff Siemon if there was room for God in the pro football huddle, and in the player's life afterwards. Clearly, there was and is. After working in insurance for several years and remaining active in the Fellowship of Christian Athletes, Siemon has entered the ministry in a role that brings the Christian message across denominational lines. He and his family live in Edina. His spiritual involvement as a player led to a network of Viking players who joined the Christian fellowship and remained active in their witness after football. They include Wally Hilgenberg, who is the vice president of a benefits consulting group in his business life; John Campbell, who operates an office supply business; Wes Hamilton, the owner of a printing business; and Karl Kassulke, who coached football from his wheelchair at Bethel College in the Twin Cities for a time and has stayed active in a variety of businesses and humanitarian causes. All live in the Twin Cities. Another member of the fellowship, Allen Rice, directs a ministry called "Together We Stand" in Texas, and

another, Robert Miller, a halfback in the 1970s, works in community relations for a power company in Florida.

There were special players who one way or another won the fans' endearment for their blast-their-eyeballs style or for other reasons best understood by the fans. Bill Brown was one. He's now is a sales rep for a Twin Cities printing company. The incorrigible roughneck of that Viking crew of that era was defensive back Dale Hackbart, who is the regional products manager for a truck tire producer in Boulder, Colorado. The silky pass receiver on that team, Gene Washington, is the staffing manager and college relations director for 3M in St. Paul. Another wide receiver of those years, John Henderson, is the director of operations quality for Honeywell in Minneapolis. Mick Tingelhoff, the all-pro center who was one of the few players Bud Grant tried to discourage from retiring, is an investment consultant and stockbroker living in Prior Lake. Dave Osborn, the hard-grinding halfback, manages a copying machines company in the Twin Cities and Ed Sharockman, the tough defensive back of the 1960s and '70s, works in real estate out of Bloomington. Dave Roller, the bulbous defensive tackle, went into real estate investments in Georgia. Lonnie Warwick, the brick-jawed linebacker from the country, partnered with Roy Winston for a time in a fishing operation before retiring to West Virginia to fish and to marvel at the going price of linebackers today. Winston lives in Louisiana and works as a sales representative in a tube testing business. A fellow Louisianan is Sammy White, the skittering wide receiver of the 1970s and '80s, who now is the executive of a vending machine company. The other White, defensive tackle James (Duck) White, sells real estate in Houston, Texas.

Some of them held onto sizable audiences, including national TV audiences. Tarkenton was one. Ahmad Rashad became a network sports interviewer and TV personality. Ed Marinaro, the Ivy League running back who played with the Vikings in the 1970s, became an actor known to millions from his role in "Hill Street Blues" and other series.

The plugging and popular tight end on the winning Viking teams of the '70s and '80s, Chainsaw Stu Voigt, was one of several of the Vikings who stayed connected with the game in radio and TV, at least part-time. Voigt did analysis for several years on the Viking radio broadcasts before entering the real estate development business full time. Paul Flatley, one of the most successful of the post-football entrepreneurs, runs a large employment service in the Twin Cities and does college and pro football commentary. Greg Coleman, the durable and occasionally theatric punter, did sports commentary on the Twin Cities television before becoming the full time director of marketing and vice president of an estate planning business in Minneapolis. Darrin Nelson trades barbs with colleagues as a football analyst on a Twin Cities sports talk station but spends the bulk of his time as a marketing specialist. Dave Huffman, the glib and comedic offensive lineman, also does football commentary and other broadcasting in addition to following calmer business pursuits. Palmer Pyle, the wandering lineman of the Van Brocklin years, is associ-

Somebody call 911. It's Greg Coleman, clawing the ground for relief after going down trying to punt. Greg may have been hit. He may not. It didn't matter. Nobody did excruciating pain the way Greg did. He drew a flag, the Vikings kept the ball, and scored. And Greg came back from the dead immediately.

ated with a radio station in Florida.

Some of the less-than-famous of the Vikings achieved high levels of business success. Kurt Knoff, a defensive back, became a senior vice president for a commercial real estate operation in the Twin Cities. Dave O'Brien, an offensive lineman on the Van Brocklin teams, is the president of a commercial real estate holding company in Boston. George Shaw, the starting quarterback in the Vikings' first game, is vice president of a stock brokerage in Portland, Oregon. Mike Reilly, the linebacker, is senior vice president of marketing for a bank in Dubuque, Iowa. Charlie Ferguson, a lanky receiver who once caught three touchdown passes from Tarkenton against the Bears, is successful in business in upper New York. Bobby Reed, another receiver from the Van Brocklin era, works in sales and marketing for a Canadian telecommunication company and is practically a neighbor of Charlie's in New York state. Lee Calland, a linebacker in the mid 1960s, is president of an international trading company in Douglasville, Georgia, and Ken Byers runs an insurance and estate plan-

PURPLE HEARTS AND GOLDEN MEMORIES

ning company in Cincinnati. Dean Derby, a defensive back of the 1960s, operates a pension fund consulting group.

Only the Viking fans of long tooth will remember a wide receiver named Dave Middleton, a starter on Van Brocklin's first team. He became a full time OB-GYN physician after football. Chuck Arrobio, a lineman of the middle 1960s, is also a doctor in Pasadena, California.

The kickers and punters, allegedly the creatures from another planet in football, have managed to accommodate to a world without goalposts or hangtime. There are Cox and Coleman. Jan Stenerud, the Hall of Fame field goal kicker from Norway who played most of his football with Kansas City, is the director of business development for Kansas City company that designs sports facilities. Bobby Walden manages an oil company in Bainbridge, Georgia. Rick Danmeier is a sporting goods distributor out of Edina. Mike Eischeid works in food distribution in East Grand Forks, Minnesota.

Scores of the Viking alumni settled in Minnesota. That was no trivial culture switch for the ones who arrived petrified at the thought of Siberian weather for six months. Others scattered to places as predictable as the citrus belt and as improbable as St. Thomas in the Virgin Islands, where quarterback Bob Berry moved into the boat rental business. John Gilliam, the debonair pass receiver, went back south to a run and office maintenance business in Georgia. Dick Pesonen, a northern Minnesotan who played with the first Viking team in 1961, became a terminal manager for a transport company in Florida, and a teammate, linebacker Clancy Osborne, returned to his home town of Blythe, California, as a real estate dealer. Cliff Livingston, a swinging Californian on the early Viking teams, went from linebacker to advertising model, and became the operator of patio supply company in Newport Beach, California. Nate Wright, the likable defensive back who was victimized on the unforgettable Hail Mary play of the Viking-Dallas playoff, returned to California as a school teacher in Lake Elsinore.

You'll find an impressive colony of former Vikings in the southwest. In addition to Kramer, Alfred Anderson, the running back, went back to Texas as the owner of a nutrition center in Arlington. A running back of a decade before, Jim Lindsay, is president of a real estate company in Fayetteville, Arkansas. Terry Brown, a defensive back who produced a safety for the Vikings in one of the Super Bowls, became an insurance agent in Marlow, Oklahoma. Dennis Swilley, an offensive lineman of the 1980s, is the president of a furniture design company in Martindale, Texas, and a teammate on the offensive line, Terry Tausch, is a manager of a medical sales company in Garland, Texas. John Ward, who played on the offensive line in the 1970s, became the executive director of lobbying and research for a county commissioners' association in Oklahoma City, Oklahoma. Willie Teal, a defensive back of the 1980s, runs a retail sales company in Baton Rouge, Louisiana.

Chuck Lamson, a charter player as a defensive back in the 1960s, went back to the western mountains to run a ranch near Dillon,

Colorado. Fullback Rick Fenney returned to Washington state as an officer in an investment service in Kirkland. Sam McCullum, the receiver, is sales manager for a novelty products firm in Bellevue, Washington, and Bob Grim, who played two hitches with the Vikings in the '60s and '70s as a wide receiver, runs a beverage distribution in Bend, Oregon.

Another one of the Viking originals was lineman Bill Bishop, who threatened to throw Norm Van Brocklin off an airplane on the way home from Chicago. Bill may have been driven by simple homesickness. He played most of his football in Chicago and returned there to become a manufacturing rep for a metals company and to run his own sales company. Billy Butler, a defensive back on the early Viking teams, returned to his hometown of Berlin, Wisconsin, and the garden tractor business.

But Paul Dickson, a Super Bowl veteran and another charter Viking player, stayed in town to work in the computer business. He expends hundreds of hours of volunteer work annually to help disadvantaged kids. A teammate, lineman Frank Youso, ran a motel and resort business in his native International Falls, Minnesota, for years before retiring. Windlan Hall, Leo Lewis, John Turner, Matt Blair, Jeff Wright and Rickey Young all stayed in the Twin Cities to prosper in business.

But 35 years in the life of a professional football team exacts a toll. At least ten players and one head coach, Norm Van Brocklin, have died since Dutch assembled that first picturesque group in Bemidji in 1961. Mike Rabold, a popular guard on the first team, was killed in a freeway accident not long after he retired. Terry Dillon, a defensive back from the Twin Cities who had started in his rookie season in 1963, drowned the following summer in the Yellowstone River while working on a construction job. Jim Vellone died of Hodgkin's disease, diagnosed while he was still playing. Steve Stonebreaker, who played tight end on the 1962 team and moved to linebacker in 1963 before going on to Baltimore and New Orleans, died in 1995. A.D. Williams and Errol Linden of the 1961 team, Phil King, Pat Russ, Wayne Meylan and John Powers all are gone.

You don't have to be a charter fan to bridge the years. Paul Flatley, the Viking alumni's volunteer historian, calls the collection "a pretty amazing bunch, when you think about it. Old Dutch used to say, 'they were nothing until I got there.' That wasn't bragadaccio. He was pretty much right. But there definitely was something afterwards, what you discover when you sift through all of those marvelous characters and the team's performance over the years. It's not just another football team. It belongs right up near the top – not only in the records but in the personalities."

Nobody ever found out what became of the truck driver who tried to make the team.

He could have become a college president. Spending a few weeks with the Vikings in their beginnings may have terrified him into the contemplative life.

88	Hasselbeck, Don, TE, Colorado	1984	69	Kalis, Todd, G, Arizona State	1988-93
58	Hawkins, Rip, LB, North Carolina	1961-65	11	Kapp, Joe, QB, California	1967-69
44	Hayden, Leo, RB, Ohio State	1971	3	Karlis, Rich, K, Cincinnati	1989
32	Hayes, Ray, RB, Central Oklahoma	1961	29	Kassulke, Karl, DB, Drake	1963-72
80	Henderson, John, WR, Michigan	1968-72	39	Kellar, Mark, RB, Northern Illinois	1976-78
30	Henderson, Keith, RB, Georgia	1992	43	Key, Brady, DB, Colorado State	1967
24	Henderson, Wyman, DB, UNLV	1987-88	44	Kidd, Keith, WR, Arkansas	1984-85;87
60	Hernandez, Matt, T, Purdue	1984	24	King, Phil, RB, Vanderbilt	1965-66
58	Hilgenberg, Wally, LB, Iowa	1968-79	89	Kingsriter, Doug, TE, Minnesota	1973-75
43	Hill, Gary, DB, USC	1965	36	Kirby, John, LB, Nebraska	1964-68
10	Hill, King, P-QB, Rice	1968	52	Kirksey, William, LB, So. Mississippi	1990
89	Hillary, Ira, WR, South Carolina	1990	25	Knoff, Kurt, S, Kansas	1979-82
82	Hilton, Carl, TE, Houston	1986-89	68	Koch, Greg, G, Arkansas	1987
85	Hilton, John, TE, Richmond	1970	26	Kosens, Terry, DB, Hofstra	1963
98	Hinkle, George, DT, Arizona	1992	89	Kramer, Kent, TE, Minnesota	1969-70
78	Hinton, Chris, T, Northwestern	1994	9	Kramer, Tommy, QB, Rice	1977-89
85	Holland, John, WR, Tennessee State	1974	22	Krause, Paul, S, Iowa	1968-79
75	Holloway, Randy, DT, Pittsburgh	1978-84	59	Lacey, Bob, C, North Carolina	1964
54	Holmes, Bruce, LB, Minnesota	1993	21	Lamson, Chuck, DB, Wyoming	1962-63
30	Holt, Issiac, CB, Alcorn State	1985-89	58	Langer, Jim, C, South Dakota State	1980-81
51	Hough, Jim, OL, Utah State	1978-86	52	Lapham, Bill, C, Iowa	1961
24	Howard, Bryan, S, Tennessee State	1982	77	Larsen, Gary, DT, Concordia	1965-74
51/99	Howard, David, LB, Long Beach State	1985-89	82	Lash, Jim, WR, Northwestern	1973-76
56/72	Huffman, David, OL, Notre Dame	1979-83; 85-90	65	Lawson, Steve, G, Kansas	1973-75
83	Hultz, Don, DE, Southern Mississippi	1963	80	LeCount, Terry, WR, Florida	1979-83; 1987
65	Huth, Gary, G, Wake Forest	1961-63	32	Lee, Amp, RB, Florida State	1994
4	Igwebuike, Donald, K, Clemson	1990	19	Lee, Bob, QB, Pacific	1969-72;1975-78
86	Ingram, Darryl, TE, California	1989	39	Lee, Carl, CB, Marshall	1983-93
76	Irwin, Tim, T, Tennessee	1981-93	59	Leo, Jim, DE, Cincinnati	1961-62
82	Ismail, Qadry, WR, Syracuse	1993-94	31	Lester, Darrell, RB, McNeese	1964
89	Jackson, Harold, WR, Colorado	1983	87	Lewis, Leo, WR, Missouri	1981-91
76	Jackson, Joe, DT, New Mexico State	1977	73	Linden, Errol, T, Houston	1962-65
52	Jenke, Noel, LB, Minnesota	1971	61	Lindsay, Everett, G/T, Mississippi	1993
51	Jenkins, Carlos, LB, Michigan State	1991-94	21	Lindsey, Jim, RB, Arkansas	1966-72
28	Jenkins, Izel, CB,North Carolina State	1993	76	Lingenfelter, Bob, T, Nebraska	1978
57	Jobko, Bill, LB, Ohio State	1963-65	55	Livingston, Cliff, LB, UCLA	1962
14	Johnson, Brad, QB, Florida State	1992-94	13	Livingston, Mike, QB, Southern Methodist	1980
65	Johnson, Charlie, NT, Colorado	1982-84	38	Louallen, Fletcher, S, Livingston	1987
52	Johnson, Dennis, LB, USC	1980-85	63	Lowdermilk, Kirk, C, Ohio State	1985-92
41	Johnson, Gene, DB, Cincinnati	1961	57	Luce, Derrel, LB, Baylor	1979-80
53	Johnson, Henry, LB, Georgia Tech	1980-82	75	Lurtsema, Bob, DE, Western Michigan	1972-76
89	Johnson, Joe, WR, Notre Dame	1992	27	Lush, Mike, S, East Stroudsburg	1986
22	Johnson, Ken, S, Florida A&M	1989-90	71	MacDonald, Mark, G, Boston College	1985-88
48	Johnson, Sammy, RB, North Carolina	1976-78	46	Mackbee, Earsell, DB, Utah State	1965-69
26	Jones, Clinton, RB, Michigan State	1967-72	4	Manning, Archie, QB, Mississippi	1983-84
84	Jones, Hassan, WR, Florida St.	1986-92	91	Manusky, Greg, LB, Colgate	1991-93
82	Jones, Mike Anthony, WR, Tennessee State	1983-85	49	Marinaro, Ed, RB, Cornell	1972-75
89	Jones, Mike Alonzo, TE, Texas A&M	1990-91	70	Marshall, Jim, DE, Ohio State	1961-79
32	Jones, Shawn, DB, Georgia Tech	1993	48	Marshall, Larry, RS, Maryland	1974
69	Jones, Wayne, OL, Utah	1987	55	Martin, Amos, LB, Louisville	1972-76
83/89	Jordan, Andrew, TE, West Carolina	1994	89	Martin, Billy, TE, Georgia Tech	1968
22	Jordan, Jeff, DB, Tulsa	1965-67	56/94/98/57	Martin, Chris, LB, Auburn	1983-88
83	Jordan, Steve, TE, Brown	1982-94	79	Martin, Doug, DE, Washington	1980-89
83	Joyce, Don, DE, Tulane	1961	20	Mason, Tommy, RB, Tulane	1961-66

66	Maurer, Andy, G, Oregon	1974-75
88	May, Marc, TE, Purdue	1987
35	Mayberry, Doug, RB, Utah State	1961-62
23	Mayes, Mike, CB, LSU	1991
73	Mays, Stafford, DT, Washington	1987-88
33	McClanahan, Brent, RB, Arizona State	1973-80
96	McClendon, Skip, DE, Arizona State	1992
15	McCormick, John, QB, Massachusetts	1962
84/80	McCullum, Sam, WR, Montana State	1974-75;82-83
74	McCurry, Mike, G, Indiana	1987
58	McDaniel, Ed, LB, Clemson	1992-94
64	McDaniel, Randall, G, Arizona State	1988-94
88	McDole, Mardye, WR, Mississippi State	1981-83
39	McElhenny, Hugh, RB, Washington	1961-62
60	McElroy, Reggie, T, West Texas State	1994
55	McGill, Mike, LB, Notre Dame	1968-70
37	McGriggs, Lamar, S, Western Illinois	1993-94
86	McKeever, Marlin, TE, USC	1967
9	McMahon, Jim, QB, Brigham Young	1993
26	McMillian, Audray, CB, Houston	1989-93

12	McNeil, Tom, P, Stephen F. Austin	1970
54	McNeill, Fred, LB, UCLA	1974-85
60	McQuaid, Dan, T, UNLV	1988
32	McWatters, Bill, RB, North Texas	1964
53	Meamber, Tim, LB, Washington	1985
18	Mercer, Mike, K, Arizona State	1961-62
57	Merriweather, Mike, LB, Pacific	1989-92
56	Meylan, Wayne, LB, Nebraska	1970
98	Micech, Phil, DE, Wisconsin-Platteville	1987
21	Michel, Tom, RB, East Carolina	1964
84	Middleton, Dave, E, Auburn	1961
75	Millard, Keith, DT, Washington State	1985-91
87	Miller, Kevin, WR, Louisville	1978-80
35	Miller, Robert, RB, Kansas	1975-80
68	Mitchell, Mel, G, Tennessee State	1980
90	Molden, Fred, DT, Jackson State	1987
1	Moon, Warren, QB, Washington	1994
36	Moore, Manfred, RB, USC	1977
35	Morrell, Kyle, S, BYU	1985-86
40	Morris, Jack, DB, Oregon	1961

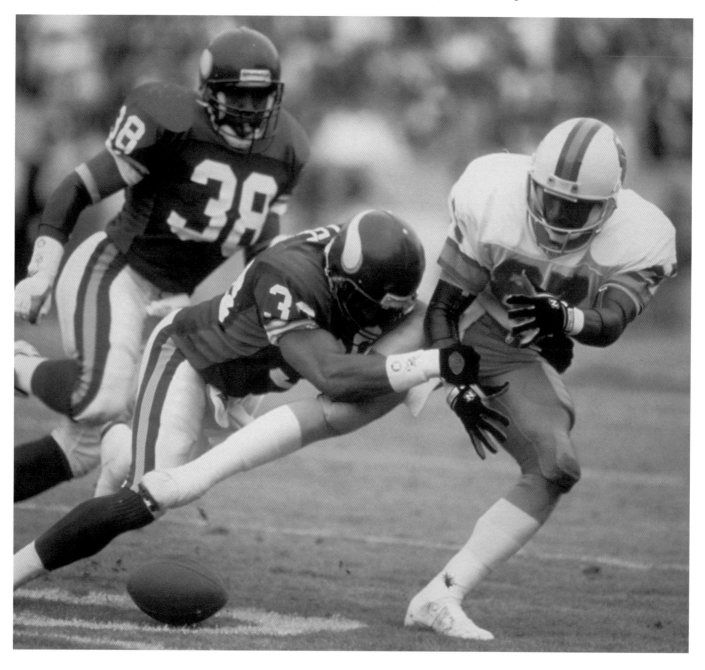

68	Morris, Mike, C, N.E. Missouri State	1991-94		22	Redwine, Jarvis, RB, Nebraska	1981-83
24	Mostardi, Rich, DB, Kent State	1961		27	Reed, Bob, RB, Pacific	1962-63
86	Mularky, Mike, TE, Florida	1983-88		86	Reed, Jake, WR, Grambling	1991-94
77	Mullaney, Mark, DE, Colorado State	1975-87		32	Reed, Oscar, RB, Colorado State	1968-74
31	Munsey, Nelson, CB, Wyoming	1978		89	Reichow, Jerry, E, Iowa	1961-64
88	Murphy, Fred, E, Georgia Tech	1961		56	Reilly, Mike, LB, Iowa	1969
48	Mustafaa, Najee, CB, Georgia Tech	1987-92		14	Renfroe, Gilbert, QB, Tennesse State	1990
74	Myers, Frank, T, Texas A&M	1978-80		19	Rentzel, Lance, E, Oklahoma	1965-66
51/59	Najarian, Pete, LB, Minnesota	1987		7	Reveiz, Fuad, K, Tennessee	1990-94
1	Nelson, Chuck, K, Washington	1986-88		88	Rhymes, Buster, WR, Oklahoma	1985-87
20	Nelson, Darrin, RB, Stanford 1982-89,	1991-92		1	Ricardo, Benny, K, San Diego State	1983
53	Newbill, Richard, LB, Miami	1990		36	Rice, Allen, RB, Baylor	1984-90
86	Newman, Pat, WR	1990		89	Richardson, Greg, WR, Alabama	1987-88
18	Newsome, Harry, P, Wake Forest	1990-93		78	Riley, Steve, T, USC	1974-84
96	Newton, Tim, DT, Florida	1985-89		95	Robinson, Gerald, DE, Auburn	1986-87
71	Niehaus, Steve, DT, Notre Dame	1979		60	Rodenhauser, Mark, C, Illinois State	1989
79	Nix, Roosevelt, DT, Cental St. (Ohio)	1994		76	Roller, Dave, DT, Kentucky	1979-80
99	Noga, Al, DE, Hawaii	1988-92		47	Rose, George, DB, Auburn	1964-66
49	Nord, Keith, S, St. Cloud State	1979-85		28	Rosnagle, Ted, S, Portland State	1985, 87
97	Norman, Tony, DE, Iowa State	1987		68	Rouse, Curtis, OL, Tennessee-Chattanooga	1982-86
85	Novoselsky, Brent, TE, Pennsylvania	1989-94		89	Rowe, Ray, TE, San Diego State	1994
74	O'Brien, Dave, G, Boston College	1963-64		47	Rowland, Justin, DB, Texas Christian	1961
69	Ori, Frank, G, Northern Iowa	1987		54	Rubke, Karl, LB, USC	1961
31	Osborne, Clancy, LB, Arizona State	1961-62		65	Ruether, Mike, OL, Texas	1994
41	Osborn, Dave, RB, North Dakota	1965-75		75	Russ, Pat, DT, Purdue	1963
88	Page, Alan, DT, Notre Dame	1967-78		12	Salisbury, Sean, QB, USC	1990-94
22	Palmer, David, WR, Alabama	1994		72	Sams, Ron, C, Pittsburgh	1984
27	Parker, Anthony, CB, Arizona State	1992-94		89	Sanders, Ken, DE, Howard Payne	1980-81
81	Parks, Rickey, WR, Arkansas-Pine Bluff	1987		4	Saxon, Mike, P, San Diego State	1994
40	Paschal, Doug, RB, North Carolina	1980-81		78	Scardina, John, T, Lincoln	1987
79	Patton, Jerry, DT, Nebraska	1971		89	Schenk, Ed, TE, Central Florida	1987
31	Payton, Eddie, KR, Jackson State	1980-82		68	Schmidt, Roy, G, Long Beach State	1970
24	Pearson, Jayice, S, Washington	1993		54	Schmitz, Bob, LB, Montana	1966
66	Pentecost, John, G, UCLA	1967		80	Schnelker, Bob, E, Bowling Green	1961
68	Perreault, Pete, G, Long Beach State	1971		60	Schreiber, Adam, C, Texas	1990-93
22	Pesonen, Dick, DB, Minnesota-Duluth	1961		53	Schuh, Jeff, LB, Minnesota	1986
66	Peterson, Ken, C, Utah	1961		38	Scott, Todd, S, S.W. Louisiana	1991-94
82	Phillips, Jim, E, Auburn	1965-67		13	Scribner, Bucky, P, Kansas	1987-89
91	Phillips, Joe, DT, SMU	1986		60	Selesky, Ron, C, North Central College	1987
63	Ploeger, Kurt, DT, Gustavus Adolphus	1987		57	Sendlein, Robin, LB, Texas	1981-84
86	Poage, Ray, E, Texas	1973		81	Senser, Joe, TE, West Chester	1979-84
29	Poltl, Randy, S, Stanford	1974		45	Sharockman, Ed, DB, Pittsburgh	1962-72
52	Porter, Ron, LB, Idaho	1973		14	Shaw, George, QB, Oregon	1961
83	Powers, John, TE, Notre Dame	1966		21	Shaw, Glenn, RB, Kentucky	1961
79	Prestel, Jim, DT, Idaho	1961-65		73	Shay, Jerry, DT, Purdue	1966-67
28	Provost, Ted, DB, Ohio State	1970		59	Sheppard, Ashley, LB, Clemson	1993-94
66	Pyle, Palmer, G, Michigan State	1964		43	Sherman, Will, E, St. Mary's	1961
92	Quinn, Kelly, LB, Michigan State	1987		77	Shields, Lebron, DE, Tennessee	1961
64	Rabold, Mike, G, Indiana	1961-62		50	Siemon, Jeff, LB, Stanford	1972-82
93	Randle, John, DT, Texas A&I	1990-94		69	Simkus, Arnold, DT, Michigan	1967
34	Randolph, Al, DB, Iowa	1973		57	Sims, William, LB, SW Louisiana	1994
28	Rashad, Ahmad, WR, Oregon	1976-82		75	Simpson, Howard, T, Auburn	1964
52	Rasmussen, Randy, G, Minnesota	1987-89		30	Smith, Cedric, RB, Florida	1990
11	Reaves, John, QB, Florida	1979		25	Smith, Daryl, CB, North Alabama	1989

95	Smith, Fernando, DE, Jackson State	1994
87	Smith, Gordon, TE, Missouri	1961-65
91	Smith, Greg, DT, Kansas	1984
79	Smith, Lyman, DT, Duke	1978
26/20	Smith, Robert, RB, Ohio State	1993-94
74	Smith, Robert, DE, Grambling	1985
74	Smith, Steve, DE, Michigan	1968-70
40	Smith, Wayne, CB, Purdue	1987
16	Snead, Norm, QB, Wake Forest	1971
54	Solomon, Jesse, LB, Florida State	1986-89
31	Spencer, Willie, RB, no college	1976
34	Starks, Tim, DB, Kent State	1987
82	Steele, Robert, WR, North Alabama	1979
52	Stein, Bob, LB, Minnesota	1975
3	Stenerud, Jan, K, Montana State	1984-85
74	Stensrud, Mike, DT, Iowa State	1986
71	Stephanos, Bill, T, Boston College	1982
95	Stephens, Mac, LB, Minnesota	1991
73	Steussie, Todd, OL, California	1994
95	Stewart, Mark, LB, Washington	1983-84
27	Stills, Ken, S, Wisconsin	1990
82	Stonebreaker, Steve, LB, Detroit	1962-63
94	Strauthers, Thomas, DE, Jackson State	1989-91
53	Strickland, Fred, LB, Purdue	1993
55	Studwell, Scott, LB, Illinois	1977-90
26	Sumner, Charley, DB, William & Mary	1961-62
64	Sunde, Milt, G, Minnesota	1964-74
69	Sutherland, Doug, DT, Superior State	1971-81
72	Sutton, Archie, T, Illinois	1965-67
94	Sverchek, Paul, DT, Cal-Poly SLO	1984
52	Swain, Bill, LB, Oregon	1964
29	Swain, John, CB, Miami	1981-84
67	Swilley, Dennis, C, Texas A&M	1977-83; 85-87
10	Tarkenton, Fran, QB, Georgia	1961-66; 72-78
33	Tatman, Pete, RB, Nebraska	1967
66	Tausch, Terry, G, Texas	1981-88
37	Teal, Willie, CB, LSU	1980-86
46	Tennell, Derek, TE, UCLA	1992-93
97	Thomas, Henry, DT, LSU	1987-94
94	Thornton, John, DT, Cincinnati	1993
87	Tice, Mike, TE, Maryland	1992-93
74	Tilleman, Mike, DT, Montana	1966
53	Tingelhoff, Mick, C, Nebraska	1962-78
51	Tobey, Dave, LB, Oregon	1966
13	Torretta, Gino, QB, Miami	1993
33	Triplett, Mel, RB, Toledo	1961-62
89	Truitt, Olanda, WR, Mississippi State	1993
98/95	Tuaolo, Esera, DT, Oregon State	1992-94
38	Tucker, Bob, TE, Bloomsburg State	1977-80
27	Turner, John, S, Miami	1978-83;85;87
24	Turner, Maurice, RB, Utah State	1984-85
15	VanderKelen, Ron, QB, Wisconsin	1963-67
25	Vargo, Larry, DB, Detroit	1964-65
69	Vaughan, Ruben, DT, Colorado	1984

71	Vella, John, T, USC	1980
63	Vellone, Jim, G, USC	1966-70
83	Voigt, Stu, TE, Wisconsin	1970-80
88	Waddy, Bill, WR, Colorado	1984
31	Wagoner, Don, DB, Kansas	1984
54	Waiters, Van, LB, Indiana	1992
39	Walden, Bobby, P, Georgia	1964-67
34	Walker, Herschel, RB, Georgia	1989-91
93	Walker, Jimmy, DT, Arkansas	1987
25	Wallace, Jackie, CB, Arizona	1973-74
81	Walsh, Chris, WR, Stanford	1994
72	Ward, John, G-C, Oklahoma State	1970-75
59	Warwick, Lonnie, LB, Tennessee Tech	1965-72
20	Washington, Dewayne, CB, North Carolina State	1994
84	Washington, Gene, WR, Michigan State	1967-72
80	Washington, Harry, WR, Colorado State	1978
68	Webster, Kevin, C, Northern Iowa	1987
32	Welborne, Tripp, S, Michigan	1992
15	Wells, Mike, QB, Illinois	1973-74
40	West, Charlie, DB, Texas-El Paso	1968-73
35	West, Ronnie, wr/rb, Pittsburgh State	1992-93
92	Westbrooks, David, DE	1990
82	Whitaker, Danta, TE, Mississippi Valley St.	1992
62	White, Ed, G, California	1969-77
72	White, James, DT, Oklahoma State	1976-83
85	White, Sammy, WR, Grambling	1976-86
41	Wilcots, Solomon, S, Colorado	1991
82	Williams, A.D., E, Pacific	1961
23	Williams, Jeff, RB, Oklahoma State	1966
58	Williams, Jimmy, LB, Nebraska	1990-91
44	Williams, Walt, CB, New Mexico State	1981-82
80	Willis, Leonard, WR, Ohio State	1976
27	Wilson, Brett, RB, Illinois	1987
24	Wilson, David, S, California	1992
24	Wilson, Tom, RB, no college	1963
11	Wilson, Wade, QB, East Texas State	1981-91
45	Wilson, Wayne, RB, Sheperd	1986
36	Winfrey, Carl, LB, Wisconsin	1971
60	Winston, Roy, LB, LSU	1962-76
29	Wise, Phil, S, Nebraska-Omaha	1977-79
73	Wolfley, Craig, G, Syracuse	1990-91
33	Womack, Jeff, DB, Memphis State	1987
5	Wood, Mike, P, Missouri State	1978
23	Word, Barry, RB, Virginia	1993
22	Wright, Felix, S, Drake	1991-92
23	Wright, Jeff, DB, Minnesota	1971-77
43	Wright, Nate, CB, San Diego State	1971-80
91	Yakavonis, Ray, DT, East Stroudsburg	1980-83
73	Yary, Ron, T, USC	1968-82
34	Young, Jim, RB, Queens Ontario	1965-66
34	Young, Rickey, RB, Jackson State	1978-83
72	Youso, Frank, T, Minnesota	1961-62
51	Zaunbrecher, Godfrey, C, LSU	1971-73
65	Zimmerman, Gary, T, Oregon	1986-92

Armstrong, Neill	1969-77	Faulkner, Jack	1965	Rhome, Jerry	1994
Batta, Tom	1984-93	Fichtner, Ross	1984	Rowen, Keith	1994
Baughan, Maxie	1989-91	Foerster, Chris	1993-94	Ryan, Buddy	1976-77
Berry, Raymond	1984	Gilmer, Harry	1961-64	Schnelker, Bob	1986-90
Billick, Brian	1992-94	Hargrave, Carl	1994	Shaw, Willie	1992-93
Bjornaraa, Bud	1984	Hollway, Bob	1967-70; 1978-86	Solomon, Richard	1992-94
Brewster, Darrel	1961-63	Hughes, Jed	1982-83	Steckel, Les	1979-83
Brittenham, Dean	1984	Kiffin, Monte	1986-89; 1991-94	Sweatman, Mike	1984
Brown, Jerry	1988-91	Leahy, Bob	1984	Teerlinck, John	1992-94
Brunner, John	1987-91	McCormick, Tom	1963-66	Trestman, Marc	1985-86; 1989-91
Burns, Jerry	1968-85	Mertes, Buster	1967-84	Walters, Trent	1994
Burns, Jack	1992-93	Michels, John	1967-93	Warmath, Murray	1978-79
Campbell, Marion	1964-66	Moore, Tom	1989-93	West, Stan	1961-63
Carpenter, Lew	1964-66	Nelson, Jocko	1971-78	Wetzel, Steve	1992-94
Carr, Jim	1966-68; 1978-81	Patera, Jack	1969-75	Wiggin, Paul	1985-91
Carroll, Pete	1985-89	Peters, Floyd	1986-90	Willingham, Tyrone	1992-94
Cecchini, Tom	1980-83	Radakovich, Dan	1984	Wolf, Mike	1992-94
Dotsch, Rollie	1987	Reese, Floyd	1979-85	Yowarsky, Walt	1961-66
Dungy, Tony	1992-94	Rehbein, Dick	1984-91	Zauner, Gary	1994

All-Time Records & Statistics
1961-1994

ALL-TIME GAMES PLAYED
(TOP 20)

270	Jim Marshall, DE
240	Mick Tingelhoff, C
210	Fred Cox, K
209	Carl Eller, DE
202	Scott Studwell, LB
199	Ron Yary, T
194	Grady Alderman,
190	Roy Winston, LB
188	Tim Irwin, T
182	Bill Brown, RB
177	Fran Tarkenton, QB
174	Steve Jordan, TE
171	Paul Krause, S
169	Carl Lee, CB
163	Alan Page, DT
160	Matt Blair, LB
160	Bobby Bryant, CB
157	Wally Hilgenberg, LB
157	Fred McNeill, LB
156	Jeff Siemon, LB

ALL-TIME GAMES STARTED
(TOP 20)

270	Jim Marshall, DE
240	Mick Tingelhoff, C
201	Carl Eller, DE
181	Tim Irwin, T
180	Ron Yary, T
178	Grady Alderman, T
171	Fran Tarkenton, QB
160	Alan Page, DT
160	Scott Studwell, LB
160	Roy Winston, LB
150	Paul Krause, S
149	Jeff Siemon, LB
148	Steve Jordan, TE
144	Carl Lee, CB
130	Matt Blair, LB
130	Chris Doleman, DE
128	Bobby Bryant, CB
128	Steve Riley, T
126	Ed Sharockman, CB
121	Fred McNeill, LB

Scoring Statistics – Top 50

		YRS	TDR	TDP	TRt	FGM/ FGA	EPM/ EPA	2pt/ SAF	TOTAL PTS
Fred Cox, K	1963-77	15	—	—	—	282/455	519/539	—	1,365
Fuad Reveiz, K	1990-94	5	0	0	0	107/135	155/157	—	476
Bill Brown, RB	1962-74	13	52	23	1	(1KO)	—	—	456
Chuck Foreman, RB	1973-79	7	52	23	0	—	—	—	450
Rick Danmeier, K	1978-83	6	—	—	—	70/106	154/167	—	364
Anthony Carter, WR	1985-93	9	2	52	0	—	—	—	324
Ted Brown, RB	1979-86	8	40	13	0	—	—	—	318
Sammy White, WR	1976-86	10	0	50	0	—	—	—	300
Chuck Nelson, K	1986-88	3	0	0	0	55/77	128/133	—	293
Tommy Mason, RB	1961-66	6	28	11	0	—	—	—	234
Dave Osborn, RB	1965-75	11	29	7	0	—	—	—	216
Ahmad Rashad, WR	1976-82	7	0	34	0	—	—	—	204
Cris Carter, WR	1990-94	5	0	30	0	—	—	2/0	184
Jan Stenerud, K	1984-85	2	0	0	0	35/49	71/74	—	176
Steve Jordan, TE	1982-94	13	1	28	0	—	—	—	174
John Gilliam, WR	1972-75	4	1	27	0	—	—	—	168
Alfred Anderson, RB	1984-91	8	22	5	0	—	—	—	162
Terry Allen, RB	1990-94	5	23	3	0	—	—	1/0	158
Herschel Walker, RB	1989-91	3	20	5	1	(1KO)	—	—	156
Hassan Jones, WR	1986-92	7	0	24	0	—	—	—	144
Rickey Young, RB	1978-83	6	10	14	0	—	—	—	144
Darrin Nelson, RB 1982-89,91-92		10	18	5	0	—	—	—	138
Gene Washington, WR	1967-72	6	0	23	0	—	—	—	138
Fran Tarkenton, QB 1961-66,72-78		13	22	0	0	—	—	—	132
Clinton Jones, RB	1967-72	6	19	0	1	(1KO)	—	—	120
Rich Karlis, K	1989	1	—	—	—	31/39	27/28	—	120
Jerry Reichow, WR	1961-64	4	0	19	0	—	—	—	114
Allen Rice, RB	1984-90	7	13	6	0	—	—	—	114
Benny Ricardo, K	1983	1	0	0	0	25/33	33/34	—	108
Stu Voigt, TE	1970-80	11	1	17	0	—	—	—	108
Paul Flatley, WR	1963-67	5	0	17	0	—	—	—	102
Leo Lewis, WR	1981-91	11	0	16	1	(1PR)	—	—	102
Joe Senser, TE	1979-84	4	0	16	0	—	—	—	96
John Beasley, TE	1967-73	7	0	12	1	(1FR)	—	—	78
Rick Fenney, RB	1987-91	5	11	2	—	—	—	—	78
Gordon Smith, TE	1961-65	5	0	13	0	—	—	—	78
Jim Lindsey, RB	1966-72	7	6	4	1	(1FR)	—	—	66
Ed Marinaro, RB	1972-75	4	4	7	0	—	—	—	66
Mike Mercer, K	1961-62	2	—	—	—	9/26	39/40	—	66
Oscar Reed, RB	1968-74	7	8	3	0	—	—	—	66
Jim Christopherson, K	1962	1	—	—	—	11/20	28/28	—	61
Donald Igwebuike, K	1990	1	0	0	0	14/16	19/19	—	61
Brent McClanahan, RB	1973-80	7	6	4	0	—	—	—	60
D.J. Dozier, RB	1987-90	4	7	2	0	—	—	—	54
Tony Galbreath, RB	1981-83	3	7	2	0	—	—	—	54
Bob Grim, WR 1967-71, 76-77		7	0	9	0	—	—	—	54
John Henderson, WR	1968-72	5	0	9	0	—	—	—	54
Tommy Kramer, QB	1977-89	13	8	1	0	—	—	—	54
Wade Wilson, QB	1981-91	11	9	0	0	—	—	—	54
Robert Miller, RB	1975-80	6	7	1	0	—	—	—	48
Hal Bedsole, TE	1964-66	3	0	8	0	—	—	—	48

PASSING STATISTCS

	ATT	COMP	PCT	YARDS	TDs	PCT	INT	LG	GAIN	RTG
Fran Tarkenton, 1961-66, 72-78	4569	2635	57.7	33,098	239	5.2	194	89t	7.24	80.2
Sean Salisbury, 1990-94	404	228	56.4	2,772	14	3.5	9	55	6.86	80.2
Warren Moon, 1994	601	371	61.7	4,264	18	3.0	19	65t	7.09	79.9
Jim McMahon, 1993	331	200	60.4	1,968	9	2.7	8	58	5.95	76.2
Rich Gannon, 1987-92	1003	561	55.9	6,457	40	4.0	36	78t	6.44	73.8
Wade Wilson, 1981-91	1665	929	55.8	12,135	66	4.0	75	75t	7.29	73.5
Tommy Kramer, 1977-89	3648	2011	55.1	24,775	159	4.4	157	76t	6.79	73.0
Steve Dils, 1979-83	623	336	53.9	3,867	15	2.4	18	68	6.21	68.8
Brad Johnson, 1992-94	37	22	59.5	150	0	0.0	0	15	4.05	68.5
Bob Lee, 1969-72, 75-78	306	159	52.0	2,153	15	4.9	17	63	7.04	67.8
Archie Manning, 1983-84	94	52	55.3	545	2	2.1	3	56	5.79	66.4
George Shaw, 1961	91	46	50.5	530	4	4.4	4	42t	5.82	64.8
Tony Adams, 1987	89	49	55.0	607	3	3.4	5	63t	6.82	64.3
Gary Cuozzo, 1968-71	556	276	49.6	3,552	18	3.2	23	72t	6.39	63.7
Joe Kapp, 1967-69	669	351	50.2	4,807	37	5.3	47	85t	6.88	62.3
Bob Berry, 1965-67, 73-76	124	63	50.8	708	7	5.6	8	52t	5.71	59.4
Ron VanderKelen, 1963-67	252	107	42.2	1,375	6	2.4	11	53	5.46	49.7
Norm Snead, 1971	75	37	49.3	470	1	1.3	6	55t	6.27	40.3

300-YARD GAMES PASSING

			YDS	COMP	ATT	TD	INT	W-L	W-L
1	Fran Tarkenton vs. Chicago	09/20/64	311	22	34	4	0	0-1	0-1
2	Fran Tarkenton vs. San Francisco	10/24/65	407	21	34	3	0	1-1	1-1
3	Fran Tarkenton vs. Los Angeles	10/16/66	327	21	31	3	1	2-1	2-1
1	Joe Kapp vs. Baltimore	09/28/69	449	28	43	7	0	3-1	1-0
4	Fran Tarkenton vs. Los Angeles	11/19/72	319	14	28	4	0	4-1	3-1
5	Fran Tarkenton vs. New Orleans	12/01/74	317	20	29	3	0	5-1	4-1
6	Fran Tarkenton vs. New Orleans	11/16/75	307	25	39	3	2	6-1	5-1
7	Fran Tarkenton vs. Washington	11/30/75	347	27	37	1	0	6-2	5-2
8	Fran Tarkenton vs. Detroit	11/07/76	347	17	25	2	1	7-2	6-2
9	Fran Tarkenton vs. Oakland	12/17/78	316	23	38	3	5	7-3	6-3
1	Tommy Kramer vs. New England	12/16/79	308	35	61	1	1	7-4	0-1
2	Tommy Kramer vs. Atlanta	09/07/80	395	30	42	3	1	8-4	1-1
3	Tommy Kramer vs. Tampa Bay	11/16/80	324	24	37	2	0	9-4	2-1
4	Tommy Kramer vs. Cleveland	12/14/80	456	38	49	4	0	10-4	3-1
1	Steve Dils vs. Tampa Bay	09/05/81	361	37	62	1	1	10-5	0-1
5	Tommy Kramer vs. Detroit	09/20/81	333	25	42	2	2	11-5	4-1
6	Tommy Kramer vs. San Diego	10/11/81	444	27	43	4	2	12-5	5-1
7	Tommy Kramer vs. St. Louis	10/25/81	343	25	55	2	2	12-6	5-2
8	Tommy Kramer vs. Atlanta	11/23/81	330	24	47	4	4	12-7	5-3
9	Tommy Kramer vs. Green Bay	11/29/81	384	38	55	2	5	12-8	5-4
10	Tommy Kramer vs. Chicago	11/28/82	342	26	35	5	2	13-8	6-4
11	Tommy Kramer vs. N.Y. Jets	12/26/82	328	32	56	2	2	13-9	6-5
2	Steve Dils vs. St. Louis	10/30/83	314	27	38	3	3	13-10	0-2
3	Steve Dils vs. Green Bay	11/13/83	303	21	37	0	1	13-11	0-3
12	Tommy Kramer vs. Tampa Bay	10/07/84	386	27	47	2	2	13-12	6-6
13	Tommy Kramer vs. Chicago	09/19/85	436	28	55	3	3	13-13	6-7
14	Tommy Kramer vs. San Diego	10/20/85	311	31	46	2	2	14-13	7-7
15	Tommy Kramer vs. Tampa Bay	12/08/85	309	21	36	0	2	15-13	8-7
16	Tommy Kramer vs. Atlanta	12/15/85	315	22	43	0	2	15-14	8-8
17	Tommy Kramer vs. Philadelphia	12/22/85	321	21	36	2	1	15-15	8-9
18	Tommy Kramer vs. San Francisco	10/12/86	322	26	41	2	2	16-15	9-9
19	Tommy Kramer vs. Washington	11/02/86	490	20	35	4	1	16-16	9-10
1	Wade Wilson vs. Tampa Bay	11/30/86	339	22	33	3	0	17-16	1-0
2	Wade Wilson vs. New Orleans	12/21/86	361	24	39	3	0	18-16	2-0
3	Wade Wilson vs. Tampa Bay	10/23/88	335	22	30	3	0	19-16	3-0
4	Wade Wilson vs. Detroit	11/06/88	391	28	35	2	1	20-16	4-0
5	Wade Wilson vs. Green Bay	11/26/89	309	23	38	0	2	20-17	4-1
6	Wade Wilson vs. Cincinnati	12/25/89	303	19	35	2	0	21-17	5-1
7	Wade Wilson vs. Tampa Bay	12/16/90	374	39	24	1	4	21-18	5-2
1	Rich Gannon vs. New England	10/20/91	317	63	35	1	0	21-19	0-1
2	Rich Gannon vs. Cincinnati	09/27/92	318	32	25	4	0	22-19	1-1
1	Sean Salisbury vs. San Diego	11/07/93	347	47	29	1	1	22-20	0-1
2	Sean Salisbury vs. Denver	11/14/93	366	37	19	2	1	23-20	1-1
1	Warren Moon vs. Miami	09/25/94	326	37	26	3	0	24-20	1-0
2	Warren Moon vs. Arizona	10/02/94	355	47	29	1	2	24-21	1-1
3	Warren Moon vs. New Orleans	11/06/94	420	57	33	3	1	25-21	2-1
4	Warren Moon vs. New England	11/13/94	349	42	26	1	0	25-22	2-2
5	Warren Moon vs. N.Y. Jets	11/20/94	400	50	33	2	4	25-23	2-3
6	Warren Moon vs. Chicago	12/01/94	306	48	27	2	1	26-23	3-3

RUSHING STATISTICS

		YRS	ATT	YARDS	AVG.	LG	LGt	TD
Chuck Foreman, RB	1973-79	7	1,529	5,879	3.8	51	50t	52
Bill Brown, RB	1962-74	13	1,627	5,757	3.5	48	33t	52
Ted Brown, RB	1979-86	8	1,117	4,546	4.1	60	55t	40
Dave Osborn, RB	1965-75	11	1,172	4,320	3.7	73	58t	29
Darrin Nelson, RB	1982-89,91	10	981	4,231	4.3	72	56t	18
Tommy Mason, RB	1961-66	6	761	3,252	4.3	71	70t	28
Terry Allen, RB	1990-94	4	641	2,795	4.4	45	55t	23
Fran Tarkenton, QB	1961-66,72-78	13	453	2,543	5.6	31	52t	22
Alfred Anderson, RB	1984-91	8	626	2,374	3.8	29	9t	22
Herschel Walker, RB	1989-91	3	551	2,264	4.1	47	71t	20
Clinton Jones, RB	1967-72	6	546	2,008	3.7	43	80t	19
Oscar Reed, RB	1968-74	7	490	1,968	4.0	43	9t	8
Rickey Young, RB	1978-83	6	554	1,744	2.9	26	23t	10
Rick Fenney, RB	1987-91	5	358	1,508	4.2	28	20t	11
Brent McClanahan, RB	1973-80	7	367	1,207	3.3	22	6t	6
Ed Marinaro, RB	1972-75	4	306	1,007	3.3	27	7t	4

100-Yard Games Rushing

			ATT	YDS	AVG	TD	W-L	W-L
1 Ray Hayes vs. Los Angeles	12/03/61		18	123	6.8	1	1-0	1-0
1 Mel Triplett vs. Chicago	12/17/61		15	121	8.1	0	1-1	0-1
1 Tommy Mason vs. Detroit	12/09/62		16	138	8.6	0	1-2	0-1
2 Tommy Mason vs. Baltimore	12/16/62		20	143	7.2	0	1-3	0-2
3 Tommy Mason vs. Baltimore	11/17/63		12	146	12.2	1	1-4	0-3
4 Tommy Mason vs. Baltimore	09/13/64		20	137	6.9	1	2-4	1-3
1 Bill Brown vs. Baltimore	09/13/64		20	103	5.2	0	2-4	1-0
5 Tommy Mason vs. Pittsburgh	10/18/64		14	124	8.9	0	3-4	2-3
2 Bill Brown vs. Baltimore	11/16/64		19	106	5.6	0	3-5	1-1
3 Bill Brown vs. N.Y. Giants	12/06/64		18	103	5.7	0	4-5	2-1
4 Bill Brown vs. Chicago	10/16/65		15	117	7.8	0	4-6	2-2
5 Bill Brown vs. Cleveland	10/31/65		26	138	5.3	0	5-6	3-2
6 Tommy Mason vs. Green Bay	12/05/65		21	101	4.8	0	5-7	2-4
6 Bill Brown vs. Dallas	09/25/66		20	115	5.8	0	5-8	3-3
1 Dave Osborn vs. Chicago	12/18/66		19	118	6.2	0	5-9	0-1
2 Dave Osborn vs. Atlanta	10/29/67		22	103	4.7	0	5-10	0-2
3 Dave Osborn vs. N.Y. Giants	11/05/67		16	115	7.2	0	6-10	1-2
4 Dave Osborn vs. Green Bay	12/03/67		21	155	7.4	1	6-11	1-3
1 Clinton Jones vs. Atlanta	09/14/68		17	101	6.0	0	7-11	1-0
7 Bill Brown vs. Chicago	09/29/68		12	109	9.1	1	7-12	3-4
5 Dave Osborn vs. Chicago	10/12/69		15	106	7.1	1	8-12	2-3
6 Dave Osborn vs. Chicago	12/05/70		29	139	4.8	0	9-12	3-3
2 Clinton Jones vs. Atlanta	11/28/71		22	155	7.0	1	10-12	2-0
1 Oscar Reed vs. Detroit	11/12/72		23	124	5.4	1	11-12	1-0
1 Chuck Foreman vs. Chicago	09/23/73		16	116	7.3	0	12-12	1-0
2 Chuck Foreman vs. Detroit	10/07/73		16	114	7.1	0	13-12	2-0
8 Bill Brown vs. Detroit	11/11/73		19	101	5.3	1	14-12	4-4
3 Chuck Foreman vs. Green Bay	120/8/73		19	100	5.3	1	15-12	3-0
4 Chuck Foreman vs. Detroit	10/19/75		22	107	4.9	0	16-12	4-0
5 Chuck Foreman vs. Chicago	10/27/75		26	102	4.0	1	17-12	5-0
6 Chuck Foreman vs. Atlanta	11/09/75		26	102	4.0	2	18-12	6-0
7 Chuck Foreman vs. New Orleans	11/16/75		24	117	4.9	0	19-12	7-0
8 Chuck Foreman vs. San Diego	11/23/75		33	127	3.8	3	20-12	8-0
9 Chuck Foreman vs. Pittsburgh	10/04/76		27	148	5.5	2	21-12	9-0
10 Chuck Foreman vs. Philadelphia	10/24/76		28	200	7.1	2	22-12	10-0
11 Chuck Foreman vs. Seattle	11/14/76		17	100	5.9	0	23-12	11-0
12 Chuck Foreman vs. Chicago	10/16/77		26	150	5.8	1	24-12	12-0
13 Chuck Foreman vs. Cincinnati	11/13/77		29	133	4.6	2	25-12	13-0
14 Chuck Foreman vs. Green Bay	11/27/77		26	101	3.9	0	26-12	14-0
15 Chuck Foreman vs. Detroit	12/18/77		33	156	4.7	2	27-12	15-0
16 Chuck Foreman vs. New Orleans	09/03/78		18	122	6.8	1	27-13	15-1
17 Chuck Foreman vs. Dallas	10/26/78		22	101	4.6	0	28-13	16-1
1 Ted Brown vs. Chicago	09/21/80		22	113	5.1	2	29-13	1-0
2 Ted Brown vs. Green Bay	09/27/81		21	109	5.2	0	30-13	2-0
3 Ted Brown vs. Tampa Bay	11/08/81		31	129	4.2	1	31-13	3-0
4 Ted Brown vs. Atlanta	11/23/81		16	108	6.8	0	31-14	3-1
5 Ted Brown vs. Dallas	01/03/83		29	100	3.4	1	32-14	4-1
1 Tony Galbreath vs. Chicago	10/09/83		16	104	6.5	1	33-14	1-0

6	Ted Brown vs. Green Bay	10/23/83	29	179	6.1	1	34-14	5-1
1	Darrin Nelson vs. Green Bay	11/13/83	16	119	7.4	0	34-15	0-1
1	Alfred Anderson vs. Philadelphia	09/09/84	20	105	5.3	1	34-16	0-1
2	Alfred Anderson vs. Detroit	09/23/84	19	120	6.3	0	35-16	1-1
2	Darrin Nelson vs. Detroit	11/03/85	25	122	4.8	0	36-16	1-1
3	Darrin Nelson vs. Green Bay	11/10/85	21	146	7.0	1	36-17	1-2
4	Darrin Nelson vs. Cleveland	10/26/86	22	118	5.4	1	36-18	1-3
5	Darrin Nelson vs. Tampa Bay	11/15/87	17	103	6.1	0	37-18	2-3
6	Darrin Nelson vs. Dallas	11/26/87	16	118	7.4	2	38-18	3-3
1	Herschel Walker vs. Green Bay	10/15/89	18	148	8.2	0	39-18	1-0
2	Herschel Walker vs. Atlanta	09/08/91	25	125	5.0	0	40-18	2-0
3	Herschel Walker vs. Denver	09/29/91	12	103	8.6	0	40-19	2-1
1	Terry Allen vs. Tampa Bay	11/03/91	14	127	9.1	2	41-19	1-0
4	Herschel Walker vs. Tampa Bay	12/08/91	16	126	7.9	1	42-19	3-1
2	Terry Allen vs. Green Bay	09/06/92	12	140	11.7	0	43-19	2-0
3	Terry Allen vs. Pittsburgh	12/20/92	33	172	5.2	0	44-19	3-0
4	Terry Allen vs. Green Bay	12/27/92	20	100	5.0	1	45-19	4-0
1	Robert Smith vs. Detroit	10/31/93	23	115	5.0	1	45-20	0-1
1	Scottie Graham vs. Green Bay	12/19/93	30	139	4.6	0	46-20	1-0
2	Scottie Graham vs. Kansas City	12/26/93	33	166	5.0	1	47-20	2-0
5	Terry Allen vs. Chicago	09/18/94	22	159	7.2	2	48-20	5-0
6	Terry Allen vs. Miami	09/25/94	15	113	7.5	1	49-20	6-0
7	Terry Allen vs. Tampa Bay	10/30/94	17	113	6.6	1	50-20	7-0

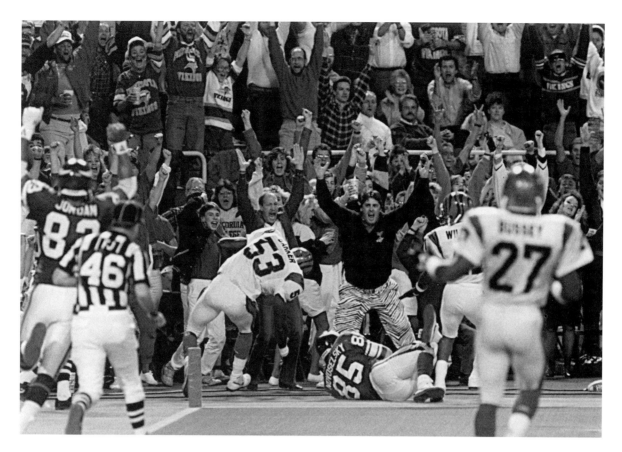

RECEIVING STATISTICS

		YRS	NO	YARDS	AVG	LGt	LG	TD	2pt
Steve Jordan, TE	1982-94	13	498	6,307	12.7	68t	48	26	0
Anthony Carter, WR	1985-93	9	478	7,635	16.0	73t	46	52	0
Ahmad Rashad, WR	1976-82	7	400	5,489	13.7	76t	53	34	0
Sammy White, WR	1976-86	11	393	6,400	16.3	69t	65	50	0
Cris Carter, WR	1990-94	5	360	4,333	12.0	78t	50	30	2
Ted Brown, RB	1979-86	8	339	2,850	8.4	67t	63	13	0
Chuck Foreman, RB	1973-79	7	336	3,057	9.1	66t	46	23	0
Rickey Young, RB	1978-83	6	292	2,255	7.6	25t	48	14	0
Bill Brown, RB	1962-74	13	284	3,177	11.2	76t	57	23	0
Darrin Nelson, RB	1982-89,91-92	10	251	2,202	8.8	25t	68	5	0
Hassan Jones, WR	1986-92	7	222	3,733	16.8	75t	49	24	0
Paul Flatley, WR	1963-67	5	202	3,222	16.0	58t	62	17	0
Leo Lewis, WR	1981-91	10	181	2,924	16.1	76t	56	16	0
Stu Voigt, TE	1970-80	11	177	1,919	10.8	13t	44	17	0
Dave Osborn, RB	1965-75	11	173	1,412	8.2	38t	31	7	0
Gene Washington, WR	1967-72	6	172	3,087	18.0	85t	61	23	0
John Gilliam, WR	1972-75	4	165	3,297	20.0	80t	63	27	0
Joe Senser, TE	1979-84	4	165	1,822	11.0	58t	53	16	0
Tommy Mason, RB	1961-66	6	151	1,689	11.2	74t	41	11	0
Jerry Reichow, WR	1961-64	4	144	2,183	15.2	51t	57	19	0
Ed Marinaro, RB	1972-75	4	125	1,008	8.1	19t	25	7	0
John Beasley, TE	1967-73	7	115	1,242	10.8	13t	40	12	0
Alfred Anderson, RB	1984-91	8	114	1,042	9.1	54t	41	5	0
Brent McClanahan, RB	1973-80	7	107	772	7.2	16t	38	4	0
Allen Rice, RB	1984-90	7	100	1,066	10.6	32t	38	6	0

KICKOFF RETURN STATISTICS

	YRS	NO	YARDS	AVG	LG	LGt	TD
Darrin Nelson, RB	1982-89, 91-92	10	159	3,619	22.8	50	—	0
Eddie Payton, RB	1980-82	3	104	2,353	22.6	59	99t	1
Clinton Jones, RB	1967-72	6	89	2,209	24.8	71	96t	1
Charlie West, S	1968-73	6	78	1,991	25.5	82	—	0
Billy Butler RB	1962-64	3	85	1,898	22.3	35	—	0
Qadry Ismail, WR	1993-94	2	77	1,709	22.2	61	—	0
Buster Rhymes WR	1985-87	3	62	1,558	25.1	88	—	0
Brent McClanahan RB	1973-80	7	66	1,500	22.7	52	—	0
Herschel Walker RB	1989-91	3	62	1,423	23.0	64	93t	1
Jarvis Redwine RB	1981-83	3	50	1,124	22.4	76	—	0
Jimmy Edwards RB	1979	1	44	1,103	25.1	83	—	0
Tommy Mason RB	1961-66	6	45	1,067	23.7	42	—	0

PUNT RETURN STATISTICS

	YRS	NO	FC	YARDS	AVG	LG	LGt	TD
Leo Lewis, WR	1981-91	11	194	91	1,812	9.3	65	78t	1
Charlie West, S	1968-73	6	123	52	820	6.7	55	98t	1
Eddie Payton, RB	1980-82	3	94	22	733	7.8	35	—	0
Billy Butler, RB	1962-64	3	55	10	545	9.9	46	60t	1
Tommy Mason, RB	1961-66	6	46	20	483	10.5	45	—	0
Rufus Bess, CB	1982-87	6	55	23	432	7.9	38	—	0
Anthony Parker, CB	1992-94	3	46	24	431	9.4	42	—	0
Bobby Bryant, CB	1967-80	13	70	75	394	5.6	17	—	0
Kevin Miller, WR	1978-80	3	66	12	324	4.9	47	—	0
Darrin Nelson, RB	1982-89	8	39	12	313	8.0	21	—	0

1,000-Yard Club in a Season
Combined Net Yards

		ATT	RUSH	REC	RETURN	TOTAL
Herschel Walker, RB	1990	263	770	315	966	2,051
Chuck Foreman, RB	1975	354	1,070	691	4	1,765
Ted Brown, RB	1981	357	1,063	694	0	1,757
Chuck Foreman, RB	1976	333	1,155	567	0	1,722
Darrin Nelson, RB	1983	223	642	618	445	1,705
Tommy Mason, RB	1962	221	740	603	353	1,696
Terry Allen, RB	1992	315	1,201	478	0	1,679
Darrin Nelson, RB	1984	169	406	162	1,071	1,639
Bill Brown, RB	1964	279	866	703	68	1,637
Ted Brown, RB	1980	281	912	623	0	1,535
Alfred Anderson, RB	1984	248	773	102	639	1,514
Qadry Ismail, WR	1994	80	0	696	807	1,503
Darrin Nelson, RB	1986	247	793	593	105	1,491
Buster Rhymes, WR	1985	58	0	124	1,345	1,469
Eddie Payton, RB	1980	89	15	0	1,435	1,450
Chuck Foreman, RB	1977	308	1,112	308	0	1,420
John Gilliam, WR	1972	79	14	1,035	369	1,418
Chuck Foreman, RB	1974	253	777	586	30	1,393
Jimmy Edwards, RB	1979	78	0	2	1,289	1,291
Anthony Carter, WR	1988	78	42	1,225	3	1,270
Cris Carter, WR	1994	122	0	1,256	0	1,256
Dave Osborn, RB	1967	249	972	282	0	1,254
Tommy Mason, RB	1963	213	763	365	124	1,252
Darrin Nelson, RB	1985	246	893	301	51	1,245
Rickey Young, RB	1979	260	708	519	0	1,227
Herschel Walker, RB	1989	200	669	162	374	1,205
Bill Brown, RB	1965	201	699	503	0	1,202
Eddie Payton, RB,	1981	77	0	0	1,201	1,201
Bill Brown, RB	1966	288	829	359	0	1,188
Terry Allen, RB	1994	272	1,031	148	0	1,179
Jake Reed, WR	1994	85	0	1,175	0	1,175
Chuck Foreman, RB	1973	219	801	362	0	1,163
Ahmad Rashad, WR	1979	80	0	1,156	0	1,156
John Gilliam, WR	1973	57	71	907	174	1,152
Chuck Foreman, RB	1978	298	749	396	0	1,145
Bill Brown, RB	1968	253	805	329	0	1,134
Kevin Miller, WR	1978	89	0	35	1,095	1,130
Rickey Young, RB	1978	223	417	704	8	1,129
Qadry Ismail, WR	1993	64	14	212	902	1,128
Tommy Mason, RB	1964	207	691	239	186	1,116
Sammy White, WR	1976	68	-10	906	218	1,114
Herschel Walker, RB	1991	236	825	204	83	1,112
Anthony Carter, WR	1989	70	18	1,066	21	1,105
Ahmad Rashad, WR	1980	70	8	1,095	0	1,103
Clinton Jones, RB	1971	201	675	98	329	1,102
Tommy Mason, RB	1961	119	226	122	749	1,097
Cris Carter, WR	1993	86	0	1,071	0	1,071
Hugh McElhenny, RB	1961	167	570	283	214	1,067
Tommy Mason, RB	1965	175	597	321	129	1,047
Darrin Nelson, RB	1991	78	210	142	682	1,034
Anthony Carter, WR	1990	73	16	1,006	0	1,022
Billy Butler, RB	1963	75	48	39	933	1,020
Darryl Harris, RB	1988	79	151	30	833	1,014
Joe Senser, TE	1981	80	2	1,004	0	1,006
Sammy White, WR	1981	69	-1	1,001	0	1,000

KICKING STATISTICS

	YRS	FGA/FGM	PCT	EPA/EPM	PCT	PTS	KO	TB	PCT
Fred Cox, K	1963-77	15	455/282	62.0	539/519	96.3	1,365	1,037	133	12.8
Fuad Reveiz, K	1990-94	5	135/107	79.3	157/155	98.7	476	347	64	18.4
Rick Danmeier, K	1978-83	5	106/70	66.0	167/154	92.2	364	280	10	3.6
Chuck Nelson, K	1986-88	3	77/ 55	71.4	133/128	96.2	293	236	14	5.9
Rich Karlis, K	1989	1	39/31	79.5	28/27	96.4	120	84	7	8.3
Jan Stenerud, K	1984-85	2	49/35	71.4	74/71	96.0	176	140	2	1.4
Benny Ricardo, K	1983	1	33/ 25	75.7	34/33	97.0	108	76	0	0.0
Mike Mercer, K	1961-62	2	26/9	34.6	40/39	97.5	66	68	11	16.2
Jim Christopherson, K	1962	1	20/11	55.0	28/28	100.0	61	26	2	7.7
Donald Igwebuike, K	1990	1	16/14	87.5	19/19	100.0	61	26	2	7.7
Teddy Garcia, K	1989	1	5/1	20.0	8/8	100.0	11	7	0	0.0
Dale Dawson, K	1987	1	5/1	20.0	4/4	100.0	7	8	0	0.0
Mike Wood, P	1978	1	0/ 0	—	0/0	—-	0	32	4	12.5
Erroll Linden, T	1962-65	4	0/ 0	—	0/0	—-	0	24	1	4.2
Jim Gallery, K	1990	1	0/ 0	—	0/0	—-	0	8	1	12.5
Greg Coleman, P	1978-87	10	0/ 0	—	0/0	—-	0	4	0	0.0
Bobby Walden, P	1964-67	4	0/ 0	—	0/0	—-	0	3	0	0.0
Neil Clabo, P	1975-77	3	0/ 0	—	0/0	—-	0	1	0	0.0
Bucky Scribner, P	1987-89	3	0/ 0	—	0/0	—-	0	1	0	0.0

PUNTING STATISTICS

	YRS	PUNTS	YARDS	AVG	LG	TB	IN/ 20	BLK	NET AVG
Harry Newsome, P	1990-93	4	308	13,501	43.8	84	39	80	2	35.3
Bobby Walden, P	1964-67	4	258	11,067	42.9	76	15	61	0	38.2
Mike Saxon, P	1994	1	77	3,301	42.9	67	5	28	0	36.2
King Hill, P	1968	1	33	1,354	41.0	53	1	6	0	37.2
Greg Coleman, P	1978-87	10	721	29,391	40.8	73	82	154	3	34.7
Bucky Scribner, P	1987-89	3	176	7,078	40.2	55	18	43	2	33.6
Mike Mercer, K	1961-62	2	82	3,285	40.1	77	6	22	2	36.0
Neil Clabo, P	1975-77	3	225	8,977	40.0	69	33	43	2	31.6
Bob Lee, QB	1969-72, 75-78	2	156	6,205	39.8	58	9	31	0	34.
Mike Eischeid, P	1972-74	3	201	7,913	39.4	61	18	37	2	32.9
John McCormick, QB	1962	1	46	1,795	39.0	53	2	7	0	34.1
Fred Cox, K	1963-77	1	70	2,707	38.7	57	5	23	0	35.0
Tom McNeill, P	1970	1	61	2,319	38.0	64	3	11	0	31.8
Billy Martin, TE	1968	1	28	1,064	38.0	49	1	7	0	34.0
Wade Wilson, QB	1981-91	11	2	76	38.0	46	0	0	1	36.5
Dave Bruno, P	1987	1	13	464	35.7	53	1	2	0	30.0
Mike Wood, P,	1978	1	31	1,110	35.5	46	2	3	2	26.5
Chuck Nelson, K	1986-88	3	3	72	24.0	31	0	0	0	24.0

TACKLE STATISTICS

		YRS	SOLO	ASST	TOTAL
Scott Studwell, LB	1977-90	14	1,308	673	1,981
Matt Blair, LB	1974-85	12	986	466	1,452
Jeff Siemon, LB	1972-82	11	1,008	374	1,382
Alan Page, DT	1967-78	12	868	252	1,120
Joey Browner, S	1983-91	9	743	355	1,098
Tommy Hannon, S	1977-84	8	728	368	1,096
Fred McNeill, LB	1974-85	12	682	386	1,068
Jim Marshall, DE	1961-79	19	719	269	988
Carl Eller, DE	1964-78	15	766	202	968
Roy Winston, LB	1962-76	15	689	205	894
Carl Lee, CB	1983-93	11	566	189	755
Wally Hilgenberg, LB	1968-79	12	565	183	748
Chris Doleman, DE	1985-93	9	489	207	696
Paul Krause, S	1968-79	12	447	219	666
Henry Thomas, DT	1987-94	8	471	193	664
Gary Larsen, DT	1965-74	10	443	164	607
Mark Mullaney, DE	1975-87	13	374	223	597
John Turner, S	1978-83, 85, 87	8	406	152	558
Mike Merriweather, LB	1989-92	4	348	194	542
Lonnie Warwick, LB	1965-72	8	433	104	537
Rip Hawkins, LB	1961-65	5	401	122	523
Bobby Bryant, CB	1967-80	14	420	98	518
Jack Del Rio, LB	1992-94	3	339	168	507

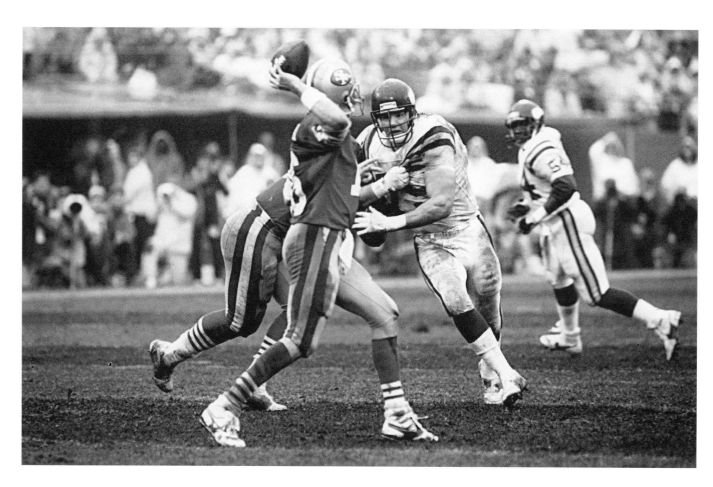

Quarterback Sack Statistics

		YRS	NO	YARDS	AVG./SACK
Carl Eller, DE	1964-78	15	130	1,015	7.8
Jim Marshall, DE	1961-79	19	127	1,030	8.1
Alan Page, DT	1967-78	12	108	797	7.6
Chris Doleman, DE	1985-93	9	88.5	691	7.8
Doug Martin, DT	1980-89	10	60.5	475	7.8
Henry Thomas, DT	1987-94	8	56	374	6.7
Keith Millard, DT	1985-91	7	53	339	6.4
John Randle, DT	1990-94	5	47	281	6.0
Mark Mullaney, DE	1975-87	13	41.5	308	7.4
Gary Larsen, DT	1965-74	10	37	284	7.4
Al Noga, DE	1988-92	5	29.5	184	6.2
Randy Holloway, DE	1978-84	7	28.5	196	6.9
Doug Sutherland, DT	1971-81	11	28	244	8.7
Paul Dickson, DT	1961-70	10	28	244	8.7
James White, DT	1976-83	8	25	184	7.4
Matt Blair, LB	1974-85	12	23	195	8.5
Neil Elshire, DE	1981-86	6	18.5	120	6.5
Jim Prestel, DT	1961-65	5	18	150	8.3
Fred McNeill, LB	1974-85	12	16.5	118	7.2
Roy Winston, LB	1962-76	15	11	91	8.2
Bob Lurtsema, DE	1972-76	5	11	84	7.6
Don Hultz, DE	1963	1	10.5	84	8.0
Mike Merriweather, LB	1989-92	4	10	49	4.9

INTERCEPTION STATISTICS

		YRS	NO	YARDS	AVG	LG	LGt	TD
Paul Krause, S	1968-79	12	53	852	16.1	81	77t	2
Bobby Bryant, CB	1967-80	13	51	749	14.7	46	46t	3
Ed Sharockman, CB	1962-72	11	40	804	20.1	40	47t	3
Joey Browner, S	1983-91	9	37	465	12.6	45	39t	3
Nate Wright, CB	1971-80	10	31	272	8.8	44	—	0
Carl Lee, CB	1983-93	1	29	350	12.1	36	58t	2
John Turner, CB	1978-83, 85	7	22	227	10.3	36	33t	1
Audray McMillian, CB	1989-93	5	19	227	11.9	25	51t	3
Karl Kassulke, S	1963-72	10	19	187	9.8	27	—	0
Matt Blair, LB	1974-85	12	16	119	7.4	20	—	0
Earsell Mackbee, CB	1965-69	5	15	280	18.7	40	32t	1
Tommy Hannon, S	1977-84	8	15	202	13.5	52	41t	1
Willie Teal, CB	1980-86	7	15	123	8.2	15	53t	1
Vencie Glenn, S	1992-94	3	14	169	12.1	39	—	0
Issiac Holt, CB	1985-89	5	14	166	11.9	27	90t	1
Rip Hawkins, LB	1961-65	5	12	232	19.3	34	56t	3
Lonnie Warwick, LB	1965-72	8	12	145	12.1	23	—	0
Roy Winston, LB	1962-76	15	12	138	11.5	23	29t	1
Jeff Wright, S	1971-78	7	12	130	10.8	31	—	0
John Swain, CB	1981-84	4	12	70	5.8	18	—	0
Charlie West, S	1968-73	6	11	243	22.1	89	—	0
Jeff Siemon, LB	1972-82	11	11	104	9.5	23	—	0
Scott Studwell, LB	1977-90	14	11	97	8.8	20	—	0
Reggie Rutland, CB	1987-92	6	10	188	18.8	36	97t	1

MISCELLANEOUS STATISTICS

YEARS OF SERVICE:

Most seasons: 19 Jim Marshall 1961-79

Most games played: 270 Jim Marshall 1961-79

Most consecutive games played: 270 Jim Marshall (282 Jim Marshall career)
9/17/61 - 12/16/79 NFL Record

Most seasons, Coach: 18 Bud Grant, 1967-1983, 85

SCORING:

Most consecutive seasons leading team: 11 Fred Cox, 1963-73

Most seasons leading team: 12 Fred Cox, 1963-73, 1976

Most seasons 100 or more points: 4 Fred Cox, 1964-65, 1969-70

Most points rookie season: 60 Sammy White, 1976

Most consecutive games scoring: 151 Fred Cox, 9/15/63 - 12/1/73

TOUCHDOWNS:

Most consecutive seasons leading team: 4 Chuck Foreman, 1974-77

Most seasons leading team: 5 Bill Brown, 1964, 66-68, 72

Most touchdowns rookie season: 10 Sammy White, 1976 (10p)

Most consecutive games scoring: 7 Chuck Foreman, 9/15/74 - 10/27/74

POINTS AFTER TOUCHDOWNS:

Most consecutive seasons leading team: 15 Fred Cox, 1963-77

Most seasons leading team: 15 Fred Cox, 1963-77

Most consecutive PAT's: 199 Fred Cox, 9/15/68 - 9/15/74

FIELD GOALS:

Most consecutive seasons leading team: 15 Fred Cox, 1963-77

Most seasons leading team: 15 Fred Cox, 1963-77

Most consecutive games with FGs: 31 Fred Cox, 11/17/68 - 12/2/70 NFL Record

Most consecutive field goals: *28 Fuad Reveiz, 10/10/94 -

SAFETIES:

Most safeties career: 2.5 Chris Doleman, 1985-92

Most safeties season: 2 Alan Page, 1971 Ties NFL Record

RUSHING:

Most consecutive seasons leading team: 6 Chuck Foreman, 1973-78

Most seasons leading team: 6 Chuck Foreman, 1973-78

Most seasons 1,000 or more yards: 3 Chuck Foreman, 1975-77

Most games 100 or more yards: Career - 17 Chuck Foreman, 1973-79
Season - 5 Chuck Foreman, 1975

Most consecutive 100 yard games: 3 Chuck Foreman, 11/9/75 - 11/23/75

Most consecutive games TD's: 6 Bill Brown, 9/14/68 - 10/20/68

Most attempts rookie season: 201 Alfred Anderson, 1984

Most yards rookie season: 801 Chuck Foreman, 1973

Most TDs rookie season: 5 Fran Tarkenton, 1961

Most games 20 att. minimum: Career: 31 Chuck Foreman
Season: 8 Chuck Foreman, 1975
Consec: 8 Chuck Foreman 10/12/75 - 11/30/75

Most Attempts Rookie Game: 24 Robert Smith vs. N.O., 11/28/93

Most Yards Rookie Game: 123 Raymond Hayes vs. L.A., 12/3/61

RECEIVING:

Most consecutive seasons leading team: 4 Anthony Carter, 1987-90,4 Cris Carter 91-94

Most seasons leading team: 4 Anthony Carter, 1987-90, 4 Cris Carter, 1991-94

Most consecutive games receptions: 80 Anthony Carter, 10/27/85 - 12/30/90

Most seasons 50 or more receptions: 6 Ahmad Rashad, 1976-81

Most players with 50 or more receptions in a season:

    4 in 1978 - (Rickey Young, 88; Ahmad Rashad, 66; Chuck Foreman, 61; Sammy White 53)

    4 in 1980 - (Rashad, 69; Young, 64; Ted Brown, 62; White, 53)

    4 in 1981 - (Brown, 83; Joe Senser, 79; White, 66; Rashad, 58)

Most players with 500 or more receiving yards in a season: 5 in 1986 -

    (Steve Jordan, 859; Anthony Carter, 686; Leo Lewis, 600; Darrin

    Nelson, 593; Hassan Jones, 570)

First player to catch 100 passes (2 seasons): Rickey Young 160 (1978-79)

    Joe Senser 121 (1980-81)

    Ahmad Rashad 104 (1976-77)

Most seasons 1,000 or more yards: 3 Anthony Carter, 1988-90

Most 200 yard games: Career - 1 Sammy White, Paul Flatley

Most 100 yard games: Career - 18 Anthony Carter

    Season - 5 Gilliam, 1972; Anthony Carter, 1985

Most seasons leading team in TD's: 6 Anthony Carter, 1985-90

Most Consecutive games TD reception: 4 Sammy White, 11/27/77 - 12/19/77

    4 Sammy White, 9/25/78 - 10/15/78

    4 Qadry Ismail, 11/6/94 - 11/27/94

Most games in a season with a TD reception: 8 Jerry Reichow, 1961

    8 Bill Brown, 1964

    8 Sammy White, 1977

    8 Anthony Carter, 1990

Most receptions rookie season: 51 Sammy White, 1976, 51 Paul Flatley, 1963

Most yards rookie season: 906 Sammy White, 1976

Most touchdowns rookie season: 10 Sammy White, 1976

COMBINED NET YARDS:

Most consecutive seasons leading team: 6 Chuck Foreman, 1973-78

Most seasons leading team: 6 Chuck Foreman, 1973-78

TOTAL TACKLES:

Most consecutive seasons leading team: 6 Scott Studwell, 1980-85

Most seasons leading team: 8 Scott Studwell, 1980-85; 88-89

SOLO TACKLES:

Most consecutive seasons leading team: 6 Scott Studwell, 1980-85

Most seasons leading team: 7 Scott Studwell, 1980-85; 89

ASSISTED TACKLES:

Most consecutive seasons leading team: 3 Scott Studwell, 1983-85

    3 Jack Del Rio, 1992-94

Most seasons leading team: 6 Scott Studwell, 1981; 1983-85; 88-89

SACKS:

Most consecutive seasons leading team: 6 Jim Marshall, 1961-66

Most seasons leading team: 7 Jim Marshall, 1961-66;68

    6 Alan Page, 1967-68; 71; 74-76

PASSES DEFENSED:

Most consecutive seasons leading team: 3 Carl Lee, 1987-88; 90
Most seasons leading team: 4 Bobby Bryant, 1970; 73; 75; 79

FORCED FUMBLES:

Most consecutive seasons leading team: 4 Alan Page, 1974-77
Most seasons leading team: 6 Alan Page, 1971-72; 74-77

INTERCEPTIONS:

Most consecutive seasons leading team: 2 Ed Sharockman, 1962-63
    2 Bobby Bryant, 1977-78
    2 Willie Teal, 1981-82
    2 Vencie Glenn, 1993-94
Most seasons leading team: 4 Ed Sharockman, 1962-63, 65, 70
    4 Bobby Bryant, 1969, 73, 77-78
Most consecutive games with an interception: 6 Paul Krause, 1968
Most touchdowns career: 3 Rip Hawkins, 1961-65
    3 Ed Sharockman, 1962-72
    3 Bobby Bryant, 1967-80
    3 Joey Browner, 1983-90
Most Interceptions rookie season: 6 Ed Sharockman, 1962

OWN FUMBLES RECOVERED:

Most consecutive seasons leading team: 5 Chuck Foreman, 1973-77
Most seasons leading team: 6 Fran Tarkenton, 1965-66; 73; 76-78
Most fumbles recovered: Career - 31 Fran Tarkenton, 1961-66, 72-78
    Season - 8 Billy Butler, 1963 Ties NFL Record

OPPONENT FUMBLES RECOVERED:

Most consecutive seasons leading team: 3 Jeff Siemon, 1972-74;
    3 Joey Browner, 1984-86
Most seasons leading team: 6 Jim Marshall, 1961-62; 65; 69; 73;75
Most fumbles recovered - Career: 29 Jim Marshall 1961-79 NFL Record
    Season: 9 Don Hultz, 1963 NFL Record
Most touchdowns from recoveries: 2 Paul Krause, 1968-79

PUNTING:

Most seasons leading team: 10 Greg Coleman, 1978-86
Most punts inside 20: Career - 154 Greg Coleman, 1978-87
    Season - 28 Greg Coleman, 1983
    Game - 5 Fred Cox vs. L.A. Rams, 11/3/63
    5 Mike Saxon vs. New Orleans, 11/6/94

PUNT RETURNS:

Most consecutive seasons leading team: 5 Charlie West, 1968-72; Leo Lewis, 1987-91
Most seasons leading team: 5 Charlie West, 1968-72; Leo Lewis, 1987-91
Most touchdowns: Career - 1 Hugh McElhenny, 1961
    1 Billy Butler, 1963
    1 Charlie West, 1968
    1 Leo Lewis, 1987
Most returns rookie season: 48 Kevin Miller, 1978
Most return yards rookie season: 239 Kevin Miller, 1978
Highest return average rookie season: 10.4 Tommy Mason, 1961

KICKOFF RETURNS:

Most consecutive seasons leading team: 3 Billy Butler, 1962-64

        3 Brent McClanahan, 1973-75

Most seasons leading team: 4 Clinton Jones, 1967,69,71-72;

        Darrin Nelson 1983-84,89,91

Most touchdowns: Career - 1 Bill Brown, 1963

        1 Lance Rentzel, 1965

        1 Clinton Jones, 1967

        1 Keith Nord, 1980

        1 Eddie Payton, 1981

        1 Herschel Walker, 1989

Most returns rookie season: 53 Buster Rhymes, 1985

Most return yards rookie season: 1,345 Buster Rhymes, 1985 (NFL Record)

Highest return average rookie season: 26.2 Lance Rentzel, 1965

BLOCKED KICKS:

Most seasons leading team: 7 Alan Page, 1969;71-72;74-76;78

Most consecutive seasons leading team: 4 Matt Blair, 1979-82

Most blocked kicks - Career: 20 Matt Blair, 1974-83 (16 PAT, 3FG, 1 punt)

    Season: 5 Matt Blair, 1979 (5 PAT)

        5 Alan Page, 1976 (3 PAT, 2FG)

      Game: 2 Alan Page, (1 PAT, 1 FG) vs. Pitts., 10/4/76

        2 Matt Blair, (2 PAT) vs. Dallas, 10/7/79

        2 Matt Blair, (2 PAT) vs. Green Bay, 11/11/79

        2 Tim Irwin, (2 FG) vs. Atlanta, 12/15/85

        2 Neil Elshire, (2 PAT) vs. Washington, 11/2/86

PASSING:

Most seasons leading team: 13 Fran Tarkenton, 1961-66, 72-78

Most consecutive seasons leading team: 7 Fran Tarkenton, 1972-78

Most consecutive passes completed: 16 Tommy Kramer vs. Green Bay, 11/11/79

Most seasons 4,000 yards passing: 1 Warren Moon, 1994

Most seasons 3,000 yards passing: 5 Tommy Kramer, 1979-81, 85-86

Most seasons 2,000 yards passing: 11 Fran Tarkenton, 1962-66, 72-76, 78

Most seasons 1,000 yards passing: 13 Fran Tarkenton, 1961-66, 72-78

Average gain qualifiers:

    Career - 7.33 Wade Wilson, 1981-90, (11,310 yards on 1,543 attempts)

    Season - 8.27 Wade Wilson, 1988, (2,746 yards on 332 attempts)

    Game - 14.00 Tommy Kramer vs. Washington, 11/2/86 (490 yards on 35 attempts)

Most 400 yard games passing: 4 Tommy Kramer, 1977-88

Most 300 yard games passing: 18 Tommy Kramer, 1977-88

        9 Fran Tarkenton, 1961-66, 72-78

Most 200 yard games passing: 76 Fran Tarkenton, 1961-66, 72-78

Most 100 yard games passing: 156 Fran Tarkenton, 1961-66, 72-78

Most consecutive games TD pass: 15 Fran Tarkenton, 11/3/74 - 12/14/75

Fewest passes had intercepted qualifiers:

    Season - 2 Sean Salisbury, 1992 (175 attempts)

Most consecutive passes without being intercepted:

    156 Rich Gannon, 12/30/90 - 10/27/91

Lowest percentage of interceptions (qualifiers)

    Career: 2.9 Steve Dils, 1979-83 (623 attempts)

    Season: 1.1 Sean Salisbury, 1992 (175 attempts)

    Game: 0.0 Rich Gannon vs. New England, 10/20/91 (63 attempts) (NFL Record)

Most 300 yard games passing in a season: 6 Warren Moon, 1994

Most games without an interception (20 att. min.): Fran Tarkenton, 39

FIRST-ROUND DRAFT CHOICES

Number following name designates order of selection overall

1961	Tommy Mason, RB, Tulane (1)
1962	Traded to the New York Giants for George Shaw (2)
1963	Jim Dunaway, DT, Mississippi State (3)*
1964	Carl Eller, DE, Minnesota (6)
1965	Jack Snow, WR, Notre Dame (8)*
1966	Jerry Shay, DT, Purdue (7)
1967	a. Clinton Jones, RB, Michigan State (choice from NY Giants) (2)
	b. Gene Washington, WR, Michigan State (8)
	c. Alan Page, DT, Notre Dame (choice from Los Angeles) (15)
1968	a. Ron Yary, T, USC (choice from NY Giants) (1)
	b. Traded to the New Orleans Saints for Gary Cuozzo (7)
1969	Traded to the New Orleans Saints for Gary Cuozzo (17)
1970	John Ward, T, Oklahoma State (25)
1971	Leo Hayden, RB, Ohio State (24)
1972	a. Jeff Siemon, LB, Stanford (choice from New England) (10)
	b. Traded to the NY Giants for Fran Tarkenton (24)
1973	Chuck Foreman, RB, Miami (Fla.) (12)
1974	Fred McNeill, LB, UCLA (choice from Atlanta) (17)
	b. Steve Riley, T, USC (25)
1975	Mark Mullaney, DE, Colorado State (25)
1976	James White, DT, Oklahoma State (25)
1977	Tommy Kramer, QB, Rice (27)
1978	Randy Holloway, DE, Pittsburgh (21)
1979	Ted Brown, RB, North Carolina State (16)
1980	Doug Martin, DT, Washington (9)
1981	Traded to the Baltimore Colts for two 2nds and a 5th in 1981 (18)
1982	Darrin Nelson, RB, Stanford (7)
1983	Joey Browner, DB, USC (19)
1984	Keith Millard, DE, Washington (13)#
1985	Chris Doleman, LB, Pittsburgh (4)
1986	Gerald Robinson, DE, Auburn (14)
1987	D.J. Dozier, RB, Penn State (14)
1988	Randall McDaniel, G, Arizona State (19)
1989	Traded to the Pittsburgh Steelers for rights to LB Mike Merriweather
1990	Traded to the Dallas Cowboys as part of the Herschel Walker trade (1989)
1991	Traded to the Dallas Cowboys as part of the Herschel Walker trade (1989)
1992	Traded to the Dallas Cowboys as part of the Herschel Walker trade (1989)
1993	Robert Smith, RB, Ohio State (21)
1994	Dewayne Washington, CB, North carolina State (18) (choice from Atlanta)
	Todd Steussie, T, California (19)
1995	Derrick Alexander, DE, Florida State (11)
	Korey Stringer, T, Ohio State (24) (choice from Denver through Atlanta)

*Did not Sign
#Did not sign until 1985

PURPLE HEARTS AND GOLDEN MEMORIES